Secret Faith
in the
Public Square

An Argument for the Concealment
of Christian Identity

Jonathan Malesic

BrazosPress
a division of Baker Publishing Group
Grand Rapids, Michigan

Published by Brazos Press
a division of Baker Publishing Group
P.O. Box 6287, Grand Rapids, MI 49516-6287
www.brazospress.com

Printed in the United States of America

Library of Congress Cataloging-in-Publication Data
Malesic, Jonathan, 1975–
    Secret faith in the public square : an argument for the concealment of Christian
identity / Jonathan Malesic.
        p.   cm.
    Includes bibliographical references and index.
    ISBN 978-1-58743-226-2 (pbk.)
    1. Identification (Religion) 2. Christian life—United States. 3. United States—Religious life and customs. 4. Identification (Religion)—History of doctrines. 5. Secrecy—Religious aspects—Christianity—History of doctrine. I. Title.
BV4509.5.M2563 2009
248.40973—dc22   2009013061

Secret Faith
in the
Public Square

To the memory of

Msgr. Stephen P. Happel

1944–2003

"Beware of practicing your piety before others in order to be seen by them. . . . But whenever you pray, go into your room and shut the door and pray to your Father who is in secret; and your Father who sees in secret will reward you."

Matt. 6:1, 6

Contents

Acknowledgments

This book was conceived in a parking lot.

I had written a dissertation on secrecy in Christianity, but it took a fortunate chance encounter with Charles Marsh in the Corner Parking Lot across the street from the University of Virginia in Charlottesville—he the customer who had just parked his car, I the PhD-holding attendant sitting in the booth at the exit to the lot—for my outlook on that research to shift decisively. Until then, I hadn't thought that I was advocating secrecy about Christian identity at all, but Charles convinced me that this was just what American Christianity needed at a time when its identity was so often abused in public life.

I was lucky to have also been at that time a Visiting Fellow at the Center on Religion and Democracy, a part of the Institute for Advanced Studies in Culture at the University of Virginia, where conversation with scholars from many disciplines helped make me aware of the range of ways to think about this project. James Hunter and Joe Davis kindly opened the doors of the center to me, and Chuck Mathewes, Slavica Jakelić, Justin Holcomb, Jennifer Geddes, Josh Yates, Murray Milner, and Pete Slade were superb conversation partners.

Prior to that, the religious studies department at the University of Virginia was my institutional home. I began this research under the judicious and generous guidance of Jamie Ferreira, whose academic virtues themselves provided me countless lessons. Additionally, Gene

Rogers, Walter Jost, Larry Bouchard, Peter Ochs, Robert Wilken, and Cindy Hoehler-Fatton shaped my thinking and offered helpful criticism and advice early on.

Many friends from U.Va. read parts of the manuscript, suggested different angles for the argument, and listened to me think about the project aloud: Jason Danner, Jacquie Bussie, Brian Sholl, Jenny McBride, Trent Pomplun, Willie Young, Troy Dahlke, Craig Danielson, and Greg Hite. Likewise, the participants in a Mellon Foundation dissertation seminar led by Herbert Tucker brought needed commentary from several other disciplines.

Recently, King's College has done much to support the completion of this book. The college provided me with a generous summer research grant and the flexibility in scheduling to afford me time to write. Thanks to Rev. Tom Looney, CSC, Rev. Tony Grasso, CSC, and Nick Holodick. I am grateful to my insightful, supportive, and patient colleagues in the Theology Department at King's: Joel Shuman, Janice Thompson, Phil Muntzel, Anna Minore, and Rev. Dan Issing, CSC. Beth Admiraal, Regan Reitsma, Garrett Barr, and Anne Bramblett gave their time and moral support in many conversations about this project.

Thanks also to colleagues at other institutions who read, heard, and commented on the work in progress: Chris Denny, Michael Raposa, and Alexis Doval. The comments of four anonymous reviewers commissioned by Brazos Press greatly helped strengthen the argument once it neared completion.

The staff at Brazos Press provided outstanding support and guidance through the publishing process. Rodney Clapp believed in the project's merit early on and gave wise editorial counsel throughout. Special thanks are due to Steve Ayers for bringing the project to Rodney's attention. Thanks also to Lisa Ann Cockrel, Jeremy Wells, and Julie Noordhoek for their efforts in bringing the project to its audience.

Parts of chapter 7 appeared in my article, "A Secret both Sinister and Salvific: Secrecy and Normativity in Light of Kierkegaard's *Fear and Trembling*," *Journal of the American Academy of Religion* 74 (2006): 446–68.

Thanks to my family for tremendous trust and love. My parents and my sister Nicole have always supported my career and writing endeavors, no matter how improbable their success might have seemed.

My wife, Ashley, always seemed to know just what I and the book needed at every step of the way: to be listened to, to be criticized, to be propped up. She did these and many other works, great and small, always with love and patience. She deserves many thanks.

Finally, I wish that my teacher, mentor, and friend Msgr. Stephen P. Happel could have seen this work completed. In gratitude for everything he taught me, I dedicate this book to his memory.

Introduction

Secrecy and Christian Faith in Contemporary America

On two separate occasions when my parents-in-law were taking bids on some work they wanted done on their house, the contractor made sure to point out that he was a member of the First Baptist Church in a nearby town. In that context, such a confession could only have been intended as a selling point—evidence, perhaps, that the contractors were hard-working, honest men, not of the sort who break contracts or run off with the money. These contractors echoed nearly exactly a typical statement of religious identity that Max Weber heard during his visit to the United States at the turn of the twentieth century: when a physician in Cincinnati asked his patient how he was feeling, the patient said, "I am from the Second Baptist Church in X Street." Weber reasoned that the statement was a way of telling the doctor, "Don't worry about your *fee!*" Weber concludes that in America, "The question concerning church affiliation, officially frowned upon, but privately still highly significant, is on par with the Homeric question regarding place of birth and parentage."[1]

Religious identity has long been a form of currency in American society. Even though it is unconstitutional to require public offi-

---

1. Max Weber, "'Churches' and 'Sects' in North America: An Ecclesiastical and Sociopolitical Sketch," in *The Protestant Ethic and the "Spirit" of Capitalism and Other Writings*, ed. and trans. Peter Baehr and Gordon C. Wells (New York: Penguin, 2002), 205.

cials to pass a religious test or to inquire about religion on census forms—and thus "officially" a particularistic religious identity and American public life have nothing to do with each other—it is often said that an atheist couldn't get elected dog-catcher in this country. As a whole, we Americans do expect our public officials to exhibit a religious identity. In pockets of American society, we expect them to exhibit a religious identity that is quite particularistic. In my city in 2006, for instance, a candidate for a seat in the state legislature felt compelled, after the questions asked in an opinion poll seemed to insinuate that he was a Scientologist, to affirm publicly that he is a committed Catholic. According to a newspaper report, the candidate "belongs to St. Therese's Church in Wilkes-Barre and attends Mass every Sunday with his family." That the reporter also noted that the candidate "receives Communion" weekly suggests that in my district, simply claiming belief in God or allegiance to a Christian church is not enough.[2] It is clear that displaying a Christian identity is thought to win politicians votes. It also can help someone advance a career in business. Corporations now routinely build chapels and meditation rooms in their offices and hire chaplains to minister to employees during work hours.[3] Is it hard to imagine a supervisor in such an office taking note of who visits the chapel regularly, and making promotion decisions accordingly? Is it hard to imagine an employee visiting the chapel in the hopes of being noticed by a Christian supervisor? This trend mirrors one in which many evangelical Christian corporate managers are making their religious identities more visible and drawing upon networks of well-placed coreligionists to attain and fill positions.[4]

Such practices presume that religion, and Christianity in particular, has much to contribute to political, economic, and social life. They are so widespread in the culture of American elites that this presumption is never examined to see what damage it has done to Christianity itself. The rules of a highly competitive American pub-

2. Jennifer Learn-Andes, "Scientology Question Surfaces in 121st Poll: Candidate Brian O'Donnell, who Studied the Religion, Calls Tactic 'A Whisper Campaign,'" *Times Leader* (Wilkes-Barre, PA), March 24, 2006.

3. "Praying for Gain," *The Economist*, August 25, 2007, 60.

4. D. Michael Lindsay, *Faith in the Halls of Power: How Evangelicals Joined the American Elite* (New York: Oxford University Press, 2007). See especially Part IV.

lic life (encompassing not only politics, but the market, the media, and the workplace as well) and the rules of being a Christian are very different. Contemporary American society is ordered in large part by competition, with the imperative to exploit any advantage, including any personal identities, available to the person. When rules like this bleed into Christians' self-understanding, Christianity stands to lose its distinctive self-conception and, ultimately, the force of its message. Can Christians be witnesses to the hard truths of the gospel in a land where being Christian is a form of political or social capital? What is the theological cost of the church becoming a constituency, a network, a market? What about when Christian identity has become a brand? How can Christian identity be saved from American public life, which so easily distorts and converts it into something meant to benefit individuals in that public life?

This book is a theological answer to questions like these. The answer begins by my showing that secrecy about the most distinctive aspects of Christian identity—including prayer and liturgy and explicitly Christian justifications for public actions—is a real though underemphasized theme in Christian theological, liturgical, and spiritual tradition. I will thus lift this theme into relief, relying principally on three major voices from the tradition. In so doing, I show that secrecy of this kind has historically been employed to resist Christians' tendencies to overidentify with the secular and to use their Christian identity for gain in the public sphere. These tendencies pose problems insofar as they break down the distinction between Christian identity and a person's many other secular social identities, such as citizen or employee. Such a breakdown results in the loss of Christian identity's distinctiveness and the gospel's hard edges. These dangers are present once again in significant pockets of American public life—especially in the public lives of the American bourgeoisie. I therefore recommend that these American Christians conceal the distinctive aspects of their Christian identity in their public lives as citizens, workers, and consumers. If American Christians want to continue to seek status in public life, then this is the only way they can prevent the continued degradation of their religious identity.

Although there are very good reasons to claim that this secrecy is a sound general strategy for Christians in the public life of any historical context, I see it as a therapy needed by the church—in particular, the privileged church—in America right now. In large patches of American society we remain in what Charles Taylor calls a "neo-Durkheimian" relation between religion and public life. That is, in many jurisdictions, corporations, and institutions, Christian denominations collectively function as unofficial civic religions.[5] (This is not the case across the board, of course; Colorado Springs is not Berkeley.) A "post-Durkheimian" future, in which religion is fully disembedded from public life, has not materialized despite the increasingly vocal impatience of many nonreligious Americans toward religious speech and symbolism in the public square. Perhaps a post-Durkheimian situation would result from this therapy. Like any therapy, especially one that has not been tested on similar patients, there is no telling how long it will be necessary. Perhaps for a generation or two. Perhaps for as long as there is a United States of America. My hope is that if American Christians took this therapy seriously, they would find one day that their religious language was no longer tainted by the materialistic self-interest that helped to melt down and mint their Christian identity into a coin of the realm.

Secrecy and Christian Theology

The sense of the word "secrecy" that I will use most often in this book is intentional concealment of knowledge from another person. The word's etymology—it derives from the Latin verb *sēcernēre*, "to sort out"—hints toward the inherently social character of secret-keeping, as a secret separates people into (at least) two sorts: those who do know the secret and those who do not. Significant social exchanges happen between these two sorts of people, as the concealed knowledge is protected, betrayed, sold, earned, stolen, publicized, or forgotten and then sought again. Our public life is paradoxically already shot through with secrets, although secrecy is often viewed with suspicion because of its associations with shadowy or inegalitarian activity.

Other senses of secrecy will appear in this book from time to time. For instance, because secret-keeping entails a number of skills that can be honed over time (recognizing others who know the secret, the

5. Charles Taylor, *A Secular Age* (Cambridge, MA: Belknap Press, 2007), 455, 487.

ability to talk around the secret with people looking to find it out, good judgment in discerning when to let someone in on the secret), secret-keeping can eventually become largely unconscious, thereby mitigating the intentionality the definition requires.

Religions also sort people and things out—the sacred and the profane, the church and the world, the elect and the nations—and these divisions and the transactions that occur across them often enough follow logic similar to that of keeping and telling secrets. Because these divisions are often permeable, secrecy can be an attempt—surely quixotic at times—at shoring up blurred religious distinctions. It is thus not surprising to find that there is a growing scholarly literature on secrecy in religions, produced primarily by scholars taking historical or social scientific approaches to religion.[6] Although their insights are generally not theological or normative, these can be put to good use by scholars trying to understand culture theologically. Secrecy's theological significance lies in part in the historical and sociological fact that Christianity has used secrecy to sort people out, and these groupings have been justified theologically. For example, sociological questions concerning who could know about the sacraments, and from whom they should be concealed, mattered to bishops in the first five centuries of the church because the questions touched upon the purpose of the sacraments, the membership of the church, and the nature of acquiring Christian faith.

The tension between concealment and disclosure in Christianity begins in the gospels, as Jesus repeatedly tells his disciples to keep his identity as the Messiah a secret from the general public (Mark 3:12), only later declaring his identity openly (Mark 8:31–33). Jesus also admonishes the disciples not to "throw your pearls before swine" (Matt. 7:6), keeping the precious truth of his message from those who are unwilling to receive it. After his resurrection, however, he commissions them to "make disciples of all nations" (Matt. 28:19). This tension mirrors Christianity's tension between the universalism of the call and the particularism of election. The literary critic Frank Kermode explores this tension in Jesus' parables, arguing that "Par-

6. Two good introductions to this area of research are *Secrecy in Religions*, ed. Kees W. Bolle (Leiden: E. J. Brill, 1987) and the more recent special issue of the *Journal of the American Academy of Religion* 74 (2006): 273–482, devoted to the theme "Religion and Secrecy."

able . . . may proclaim a truth as a herald does, and at the same time conceal truth like an oracle,"[7] depending on whether the interpreter has been initiated into the "spiritual sense" necessary to interpret the parable correctly. Indeed, Kermode argues that the parables may be obscure specifically in order to sort people out, keeping the un-initiated at a distance from their true meaning.[8] Furthermore, Jesus explicitly states in Matthew 6 that his followers should give visible expression of their piety only behind closed doors, precisely so that they do not try to parlay their religious identity into acclaim in public life, as the hypocrites do.

Although secrecy in Christianity is related to the theological idea of mystery, the terms are not equivalent. A mystery does share with a secret the character of being knowable, but not being known to all. A mystery is in principle knowable, but it exceeds the finite grasp of the unaided human intellect. Rather, mysteries "are accessible through revelation."[9] The mystery underlying all mysteries is God's grace, which enables humans to gain access to any and all mysteries.[10] As I will show later, the church in its responsibility to mediate grace can surround divine mysteries with a fence of secrecy by limiting access to the sacraments, for instance. Here again the theological is overlaid with a sociological category, and understanding one gives an insight into the other.

Despite the theological import of secrecy, Christian theologians have given little attention to secrecy recently.[11] This book attempts to fill that gap. It also attempts to articulate a position that the contemporary theologians generally do not even consider, much less advocate. Many theologians have written on Christianity and American public life in recent decades, and nearly all of them argue

7. Frank Kermode, *The Genesis of Secrecy: On the Interpretation of Narrative* (Cambridge, MA: Harvard University Press, 1979), 47.

8. Ibid., 33.

9. Karl Rahner, "Mystery," in *Sacramentum Mundi: An Encyclopedia of Theology*, vol. 4, ed. Karl Rahner, SJ, et al. (New York: Herder and Herder, 1969), 133.

10. Ibid., 135.

11. One exception is Charles Marsh, who recommends that American evangelicals "join the keepers of the mystery in a season of silence and together pray for deliverance and renewal" in the wake of their having co-opted Christianity for social and political gain. Marsh, *Wayward Christian Soldiers: Freeing the Gospel from Political Activity* (New York: Oxford University Press, 2007), 154.

in one way or another that specifically Christian identity and language should be ever more salient in that life. (Remarkably, even
some prominent secular thinkers have joined this chorus.[12]) Many
do not even consider reticence about expressing that identity as a
remote possibility. Charles Mathewes, for instance, claims, "Vigorous
Christian belief entails a serious commitment to expressing the faith.
Conversely, a lack of expressing the faith leads to pallid believing.
Christians cannot hide their lamp under a bushel; real Christians
will not do so, and are not doing so."[13] A glance around the world
would seem to bear this observation out, as in many places world-
wide, contrary to the previous orthodoxy of secularization theory,
Christian movements have become more prominent and publicly
influential.[14] But in fact Mathewes's remark gives voice to a considerable blind spot in contemporary theology. Mathewes lumps a great
many exemplary Christians in with lily-livered churchgoers who are
afraid of upsetting their polite company by making unapologetically
theological claims.

The trouble is not that Christians might bother others with the
light from their lamp and so they should keep that light hidden; the
problem is that too often in American public life, the light is used
to illumine the Christians themselves, bringing glory to precisely the
wrong person. Too often, the light is made to lie. I call for Christians
to conceal their religious identity because Christians—humans—are
self-interested and sinful.

This book therefore presupposes an attitude of suspicion. The
nineteenth century's "masters of suspicion" suspected that many of
our highest ideals were in fact masks for base projects—including
projects we were not fully aware of undertaking. Although these
masters and their disciples so often tried to unmask Christianity, thus
earning the epithet "enemies of Christendom," Christian theologians

12. See, for instance, Jeffrey Stout, *Democracy and Tradition* (Princeton, NJ: Princeton
University Press, 2004). Richard Rorty was even convinced by Nicholas Wolterstorff to
back away from his opposition to the idea of religious reasoning being brought to bear on
public debates. See Rorty, "Religion in the Public Square: A Reconsideration," *Journal of
Religious Ethics* 31 (2003): 141–49.

13. Charles Mathewes, *A Theology of Public Life* (Cambridge: Cambridge University
Press, 2007), 25.

14. José Casanova, *Public Religions in the Modern World* (Chicago: University of Chicago Press, 1994).

today need to practice a hermeneutic of suspicion in recognition of how human actions are so often tainted by sin.[15] The human project of Christendom *deserves* suspicion. Theologians know how easy it is to deceive oneself about one's true motivations for any apparently good action. The hermeneutic of suspicion recognizes that the distance between one's overt and covert motivations is often great, and so this interpretive strategy seeks to uncover unflattering reasons for actions in the public sphere. The suspicious interpreter acknowledges that layers of rationalization and repression often allow us to convince ourselves and others that we are perfectly virtuous.

The masters of suspicion always looked to see what interests were at stake in cultural orthodoxies. How does an alienating belief in God grease the gears of *das Kapital*? Who benefits from the beatitudes? What neuroses does believing spare a person from having to confront? A suspicious theologian in America today might want to interrogate the orthodoxy claiming that both the church and democracy need Christians to make a highly public witness to the faith in their public lives.

Politicians are the most obvious potential beneficiaries of presenting oneself as a Christian in public, but only because politicians' public lives are so widely visible and because the potential payoffs associated with selling their various identities are so great. I suspect that politicians are simply one segment of a much larger trend. In fact, I suspect that many American Christians' true motivations for displaying their religious identities issue not from an uncontrollably effervescent faith but rather from the desire to exploit every possible advantage in their public lives. Jesus warned his disciples to be suspicious and look out for wolves in sheep's clothing (Matt. 7:15). For as long as Christian identity has been acceptable in public life, people have used it to get ahead. The trend is not new. The question some Christian thinkers asked in the early years of Christianity's public acceptability must be raised again now: how can this trend finally be stopped?

Although this book presupposes suspicion, it does not terminate there. The point is not merely to uncover American Christian hy-

15. See Merold Westphal, "Nietzsche as a Theological Resource," *Modern Theology* 13 (1997): 213–26.

pocrisy and self-deception, but rather to suggest a way to mitigate them. Granting that American Christians often give into the temptation to score points in their public lives by making a show of their Christianity, I hope to show how American Christians can save their religious identity from their own opportunistic impulses.

Secrecy, Identity, and Public Life

Public life in the modern West encompasses our participation in the economy, the sphere of public debate, and the nation, legitimated by popular sovereignty. These elements comprise a major aspect of what Charles Taylor terms the "modern social imaginary."[16] That is, the popular mind imagines our society as a set of spaces in which we play out our social lives. The arenas of the economy, the state, and discourse are all public arenas: in these spaces, statuses are arbitrated and goods are apportioned based on what can be seen by other participants. But of course, not everything about ourselves can be seen by any others who care to look. Some aspects of our selves (mental states, for example) are inherently inaccessible to others, and we furthermore keep secrets, intentionally withdrawing aspects of ourselves from others. In this respect, secrecy runs counter to the idea of public order. If I am to argue that Christian identity can and should be concealed in the modern public order, then I need first to explain what kind of thing Christian identity is that it can be made secret in public life, and what consequences that secrecy would hold for one's identity and standing in public life.

Most often, "public" is set in opposition to "private." Thus secrecy can appear to be a rough cognate of privacy. In fact, this is not the case. As the sociologist Alan Wolfe has argued, the "grand dichotomy" between public and private has been useful in negotiating a number of moral, social, and political issues, but it has also outworn its usefulness, as evidenced by the seeming inconsistency with which the distinction is applied today. What one theorist counts as public, another counts as private. Moreover, many aspects of social life do not fit into either category. The distinction has furthermore been discredited by a host of critics—feminists, queer

---

16. Taylor, *A Secular Age*, 171–76.

theorists, and Marxists in particular. It is thus an inadequate tool for resolving issues related to identity politics, religious liberty, and sexual morality today.

Wolfe is right to suggest that we speak instead of a trichotomy: the public realm of government, the private realm of individual rights and property, and a range of "publics"—like families, ethnic groups, sexual minorities, and religious groups—that serve both individual and common goods.[17] One thing that distinguishes these publics from *the* public is their relative exclusiveness; they have internal lives of their own that do not always bear overtly on nonmembers, and thus nonmembers need not always be concerned with the inner workings of these publics with the intensity they bring to observing the government. But someone can hardly avoid publics altogether. Any one person will be a member of and interact with a range of publics of varying scope and size. These publics also lend corresponding identities to their members. For example, my family is a public that I joined at birth. My birth and upbringing in the Malesic family constitute the ground for my familial identity. That I identify myself to others as a member of the family makes my being a Malesic a part of my public identity.

But a person's membership in publics can be taken out of circulation in other corners of society. People can, and do, keep secrets about their identities as members of different publics, and they do so without wholly sacrificing those publics' influence over the other areas of their lives.

I could decide not to identify myself outside the family as a member of my family. If being a Malesic carried some strong connotation in the wider culture (rich, powerful, despicable, etc.), I might change my last name in order to be evaluated by others on my own merits. And yet, I might nonetheless consider myself still to be a member of the family and continue to have great affection for my relatives when we were together and out of the sight of non-Malesics. I might still do what I could to support the family's causes in the wider world and adhere to long-standing family codes of conduct, and so my

17. Alan Wolfe, "Public and Private in Theory and Practice: Some Implications of an Uncertain Boundary," in Jeff Weintraub and Krishan Kumar, eds., *Public and Private in Thought and Practice: Perspectives on a Grand Dichotomy* (Chicago: University of Chicago Press, 1997), 182–203.

family membership would still be significant to my life outside the family. My relatives might even understand my reasons for changing my name. They might even have encouraged it. Changing my name would be a public act in the sense of the public as a realm encompassing the law, my job, and even other "publics" in which I participated, like a religious or ethnic group (for example, I might change my name to Lucic). By keeping this aspect of my identity secret, then, I foreswear any benefit or penalty it could bring me in another social sphere without thereby consigning that identity to the private. And I can always reveal my true familial identity—opportunistically, defiantly—sometime later.

If we accept Wolfe's trichotomy, then from the perspective of American society, the Christian church is a public. Or rather, it is an enormous number of publics that overlap in large and small ways.

I am concerned in this book with secrecy about membership in the public of the church. My proposal is an answer to the question of what individual Christians should do when non-Christian publics, especially the overarching and competitive public spheres of government, work, and the market pose danger to the integrity of the Christian public. I maintain that when Christian identity is thought to be useful largely to confer status on someone in one of these spheres, then the true purpose of being a member of the public known as the church has been lost. Being Christian is meant to serve ends beyond public and private and anything in between.

I will not, for obvious reasons, continue to refer throughout the book to the distinction between *the* public and *a* public. Hereafter, unless otherwise and very clearly noted, terms like "American public life" or "the public square" are meant to signify the fairly large realm of social, political, and economic interactions characteristic of Taylor's modern social imaginary and modern moral order together with the collective range of publics other than the church.

Before I turn to an overview of the chapters, I should say briefly what readers will not find in this book. This is not a book about governmental secrecy. I make no normative claims about the stances Christians should take toward a secretive government. Neither does my contention here that secrecy is imperative for Christians in public life mean that secrecy is likewise imperative for government. In fact, I would argue exactly the opposite, as chapters 3, 4, and 7 should make clear. I am also in no way arguing that Christians should *ignore* their religious identity in their public lives; that identity absolutely should inform Christians' decisions about what work to do, what products to buy, for whom to vote, and so forth. I am only arguing that Christians should not make that identity publicly known when acting on those decisions. Thus I do not think that Christian convictions are private in the sense of having no concrete bearing on public matters. And as far as I am concerned here, I have no opinion about whether Jewish or Muslim or Buddhist or indigenous American religious convictions should be put forward in American public life. In addition, the book neither presupposes nor defends political liberalism. The theological course I take to arrive at my conclusion signals how much my argument is unlike that of secular liberals who advocate removing the markers of Christian identity from public life. They argue that visible Christian identity is bad for American democracy; I argue that it is bad for Christianity. Furthermore, this book's thesis is addressed more to individuals than to institutions. Christian universities or hospitals have more complex public lives than I can account for here. Institutions, unlike individuals, are always on public display, which alters the character of how they can care for the Christian tradition and Christian identity in contemporary America. I leave the task of exploring this issue to those with greater competence in this area. And finally, because this book is meant as a corrective to both theological and popular thinking, it may come across as unbalanced, ignoring the command for the disciples not to hide their lamps. In my view, the theology of public life has been unbalanced for decades and has thus abetted the central social problem I address here. Theology and the privileged church need a weight added on the opposite side of the scale, and not at the fulcrum, in order to be truly balanced now.

Overview of the Chapters

Part 1 explores the warrant for my position in the Christian theological tradition. These chapters show how three major Christian intellectuals called for Christians to protect their distinctive identity against a public sphere that tends to collapse the distinction between

24

Christian identity and identity as a citizen or a consumer. In these chapters, I examine texts from periods when Christianity's position in public life was fiercely contested—Cyril of Jerusalem's catechetical and mystagogical homilies, from the late fourth century; Søren Kierkegaard's *Works of Love*, from the mid-nineteenth; and Dietrich Bonhoeffer's lectures, his book *Discipleship*, and his prison letters, from the mid-twentieth. Our times are like the times these authors addressed in surprising ways. Thus their proposals for preventing Christianity and worldliness from collapsing together into a fat and happy Christendom still obtain. Equally surprising is how, despite these authors' apparent differences, their thought in the texts under investigation echo each other. The authors were chosen not only for ecumenical appeal but also for the way Cyril's liturgical practice and Kierkegaard's moral outlook converge in the work of Bonhoeffer, who studied both thinkers.

Cyril, in his practice of the so-called *disciplina arcani*, or "discipline of the secret," in his rite of initiation, is very open about the fact that he is keeping secrets from the unbaptized, frequently tantalizing them with hints about the sacramental rites they will receive when they are initiated. In chapters 1 and 2, I argue that Cyril promoted the reputation of secrecy in part to draw catechumens to the water of baptism—and, thereby, to the church's moral authority—by promising to reveal secrets to them, specifically the creed, baptism, and the Eucharist. Cyril recognized that, in an era when the life of the church and the life of the empire were fusing and when being nominally Christian could win someone public benefits, many wanted to enroll as catechumens and become nominal Christians for opportunistic reasons. Few, however, desired baptism, which would demand an unappealing moral purity. The reputation of secrecy lures catechumens to baptism, and then, after they have become stakeholders in the faith, Cyril charges them with the responsibilities to remain sinless and to protect the faith against pagans and heretics by holding it in reserve. Cyril thus identifies a basic problem this book addresses: Christian identity being exploited to benefit the public life of the (nominal) Christian. This problem persists today in the practices of "cosmopolitan evangelicals" who use an occasionally tenuous relationship to the church to gain the benefit of an elite social network. Cyril also identifies a basic solution: establishing secrecy around the sacraments and promoting the reputation of secrecy in order to manage prospective Christians' motivations and thereby keep public life from co-opting Christian identity.

Kierkegaard's authorship opposed bourgeois European culture as much as it did European philosophy. The cultural parallel to the Hegelian collapse of the distinction between the inner and the outer is the collapse of the distinction between Christianity and public life. I argue in chapters 3 and 4 that Kierkegaard saw the consumer capitalist mentality as a threat to the distinctiveness of Christian love. His answer to this threat was to affirm the need to conceal Christian faith and love. For Kierkegaard in *Works of Love*, secrecy protects the integrity of Christian identity in two ways: (1) it protects the faith from being corrupted through accommodation to worldly ideas; and, in particular, (2) it protects the integrity of Christian altruism by keeping the works from becoming part of a *quid pro quo*. Two theological positions promote this protective strategy. First, although true faith is so radically individual as to be incommunicable to another person, faith must nevertheless be protected like a secret, as if it could be told. Second, when performing good works (the fruits of which are necessarily observable), the agent must conceal his or her agency, in order both to protect the works' origin in genuine faith and to render reciprocation impossible. Kierkegaard's response to the perceived threat to Christianity is not to mount a noisy, triumphalist counteroffensive against the world, nor to withdraw entirely from the world, but to withdraw the specific marks of Christian identity from the world, lest Christians allow the world to compromise them.

In chapters 5 and 6, I show how Bonhoeffer builds on both the ancient liturgical traditions and on an ethical doctrine with Kierkegaardian affinities in his idea of a Christian *Arkandisziplin* that will protect Christian identity from a public sphere that wants to distort or destroy it. Although Bonhoeffer's context presents an extreme case and appears not to bear much upon ours, his very last thoughts about what the church should be after the collapse of the Third Reich show that he did not simply advocate a return to the *status quo ante*. The "world come of age" requires a different conception of the church. It is clear from his *Letters* that Bonhoeffer believes that the world that gave rise to Hitler cannot hear the gospel, and Christians will only disfigure the gospel by trying to accommodate it to that world's ears. Given that Bonhoeffer explicitly links the secret discipline to the distinction between the penultimate and the ultimate, we must conclude that he thought that secrecy might obtain until the Eschaton. So Bonhoeffer contended that Christians must confess their Christian identity in secret, waiting and praying and celebrating the sacraments behind closed doors—perhaps until the end of time. This does not mean, however, that Christians have no work to do in the world. This hidden religious life goes in tandem with a public "religionless" life of self-interpreting deeds performed unselfconsciously, in imitation of Christ but not in his name.

After showing in Part 1 that there are important figures in the Christian intellectual tradition who advocated the concealment of Christian identity in public life, I argue in the three chapters that make up Part 2 that secrecy is the approach that individual Christians should take in their public lives in contemporary America. Much of the constructive work here depends very heavily on concepts that came out of my investigation of Cyril, Kierkegaard, and Bonhoeffer. I hope that what I argue in Part 2 will seem a natural outgrowth of the discussion in Part 1.

In chapter 7, I address the links that lead from the interiority of selfhood presupposed by the experience of secret-keeping, to the self-scrutinizing self of the Western monotheistic traditions, to a radical responsibility for the self's neighbor. At the center of this chapter is Abraham, the model disciple in both Kierkegaard's and Bonhoeffer's accounts. The secret about the sacrifice God has commanded Abraham to undertake, which Abraham keeps from Isaac in Genesis 22, amounts to Abraham's concealing his religious identity from his (limited) public life. In doing so, Abraham does indeed break from the communicative norms of public life, but he recovers a form of responsibility for Isaac that would not be accessible through public means and that is compatible with the responsibility incumbent on Christian disciples in any historical context. We see, then, a strong relation between secrecy and responsibility: not only does responsibility make you secretive, but secrecy makes you responsible for something.

Christian disciples exist together in the church, a body that has an inner communal life of preaching, prayer, and sacraments, but that also must engage the world in some way. Chapter 8 explains how the hiddenness of discipleship that I call for in chapter 7 is compatible with the church's mission to spread the gospel more widely. The church, as a community of hidden disciples, evangelizes by silently drawing others into the church's life of love. This reserve about Christian identity is ultimately ordered toward handing that identity on in a sacramental context, however, as both Cyril and Bonhoeffer acknowledged. Those who are brought within that life of love may in time be drawn to the sacramental life, at which point they become like Cyril's catechumens, subject to the *disciplina arcani* until such time as they can be told everything openly.

In chapter 9, then, I show how keeping a secret responsibility for the tradition and the neighbor better preserves the distinctiveness of Christian identity than does the highly influential proposal for the relation between Christians and the public sphere put forth over the last several decades by Stanley Hauerwas. Hauerwas offers a great challenge to American Christians: to stand as a visible social and political alternative to the violent ways of the world, bearing witness to the gospel in works of love and mercy. In his focus on Christians' responsibility to care for their own tradition, Hauerwas's position is close to mine, although his advocacy for a visibility of that witness that excludes any form of secrecy or invisibility places our proposals in opposition. Yet the visibility Hauerwas calls for is on inadequate footing. It rests in part on the assumptions that the church is solely a visible reality, that any call for Christian identity to be concealed is a capitulation to liberalism, and that secrecy about one's identity is untruthful in an unacceptable way for Christians. I show in this chapter that these assumptions are unsound. The problems in Hauerwas's position play out in his inaccurate reading of Bonhoeffer. As Bonhoeffer teaches us, secrecy about Christian identity can be the realization, not the abandonment, of Christianity's distinctiveness with respect to the world. Like leaven in the dough, the Christian church invisibly acts upon the world and transforms it.

In a brief epilogue, I liken the secrecy incumbent upon American Christians today to the ambiguous religious identity exhibited by two characters from mid-twentieth-century American novels: Hazel Motes from Flannery O'Connor's *Wise Blood*, and the black man visiting the Catholic church at the end of Walker Percy's *Moviegoer*. Because what might be the signs of faith—the sharp stones in

Haze's shoes, ashes on the man's dark forehead—are hidden, "it is impossible to say" if they are true Christians, to borrow the words of Percy's narrator, Binx Bolling. Their observers' curiosity about these men, however, betrays their own distance from genuine Christian faith and their sharing in a cynicism typical of our time that sees piety as pointless unless it results in benefits in public life.

Some readers may find it ironic, or even hypocritical, that I use distinctively Christian language to call for Christians to keep the marks of Christian identity out of public circulation in a published book that anyone can read. There are two main practical reasons why I do not think my publishing this argument thereby refutes it.

First, it is easy to imagine situations in which a noisy group of people needs to be quieted down. Someone mindful of the need for quiet will only be able to get the group to be quiet by briefly and forcefully contributing to the noise. It's true that someone shouting, "Let's all be quiet!" is not adhering to his or her own stated standard, but only a cynic would take that as a sufficient reason to dismiss the demand. As Kierkegaard taught, communicating knowledge to people is very often a paradoxical business, as much knowledge must often first be taken away. I side with him in claiming that the needs of the learner must come before the strictest demands of consistency, particularly when the truths being communicated themselves contain paradoxes. My argument might also appear self-refuting partly because the more prevalent argument is so self-reinforcing. There is nothing inconsistent about someone proclaiming the need for more proclaiming; such an argument in fact fulfills its own demand. But it is a trivial argument, and it might not actually fulfill the needs of the recipients of the proclamation. Practically speaking, making my argument in a public forum is the only way it could be made effectively.

Second, it is significant that this book is published by an explicitly Christian press that aims principally at an audience of theologians and other highly educated and committed Christians. Like any author, I welcome any and all serious readers, no matter their religious commitment, but I have tried to craft the argument to convince mainly other theologians. (Many other people in America need no convincing; they already think that Christian identity should be invisible in American public life, even if they think so for reasons quite different from those I present here.) As a theological argument, then, my argument is in an important sense a part of the internal conversation of the Christian church in the United States. As later chapters will show, this conversation should not cease, for it is essential to the maintenance of Christian identity. Its participants should nonetheless always remember that they are contributing to an internal debate.

Theological publishing is one of many places where the "public" of the church overlaps another public. These overlaps may ultimately mean that what I call for in this book can never be implemented perfectly. But theologians and other American Christians can certainly be much more vigilant than they have been about finding and preserving the boundaries between their public and religious identities. The gains for the church even in a modest heightening of vigilance could be great. Such vigilance will also have to be accompanied by a shift in expectations among Christians and non-Christians in the United States. The reduction of Christian identity to a consumer identity will continue for as long as American Christians allow pandering to work as a marketing strategy. If Christians ceased to expect that Christian identity can and should be a highly visible element in a Christian's public life, then perhaps Christians who have or seek political or economic power would cease exploiting the Christian tradition for worldly gain.

As Karl Barth wrote in *The Epistle to the Romans*, "just as genuine coins are open to suspicion so long as false coins are in circulation, so the perception which proceeds outwards from God cannot have free course until the arrogance of religion be done away."[18] To Barth and to Bonhoeffer, "religion" is a human invention, instituted to meet particular human needs: comforting us, dazzling us, answering our "ultimate questions," making the public life of our societies run smoothly. For "religion" in the Barth quote, we could easily substitute "Christendom," a term that captures the Durkheimian synthesis of Christianity and public life. Christendom is arrogant, equating the

18. Karl Barth, *The Epistle to the Romans*, 6th ed., trans. Edwyn C. Hoskyns (London: Oxford University Press, 1968), 37.

purposes of public life with God's purposes. I hope this book will help convince American Christians to replace the falsehood and arrogance of Christendom with a truer, humbler, and more vigilant discipleship, beginning by concealing their Christian identity for the sake of Christianity itself.

Concealment of Christian Identity in the Theological Tradition

1

Promoting Secrecy in a Christian Empire

Cyril of Jerusalem's Discipline of the Secret

A paradox of the ancient Christian church is that it did not give up on secrecy when it left the catacombs. In fact, the really interesting story of Christian secrecy did not begin until the fourth century, when Christians no longer needed to fear persecution and the church became a fixture in public life.

Modern theologians and historians have given the name *disciplina arcani*, or "discipline of the secret," to the Christian liturgical practice of withholding all knowledge of the sacraments from catechumens until their baptism.[1] In ancient practice, this meant that any unbaptized in the congregation would be dismissed before the celebration of the Eucharist. This discipline persists today; Catholic and Orthodox

1. The term arose in the seventeenth century in a treatise by the Protestant theologian Jean Daillé, in the context of polemics traded by Protestant and Catholic theologians and historians in the seventeenth and eighteenth centuries. See G. Ferrari, "Discipline of the Secret," in *New Catholic Encyclopedia*, vol. 13 (New York: McGraw-Hill, 1967), 26–27. For a thorough discussion of the modern debate, see Christoph Jacob, *"Arkandisziplin," Allegorese, Mystagogie: Ein neuer Zugang zur Theologie des Ambrosius von Mailand*, Theophaneia 32 (Frankfurt am Main: Verlag Anton Hahn, 1990), 43–117.

catechumens—adults seeking to be baptized—are dismissed at the end of the Catholic Liturgy of the Word and the Orthodox Liturgy of the Catechumens. In principle, the discipline also provides grounds for not teaching catechumens about the sacraments at all until after catechumens receive them. In practice, however, catechumens today receive extensive instruction on the sacraments as part of their pre-baptismal catechesis.

Rudimentary elements of the discipline of the secret appeared in the second and third centuries, but the practice was far from universal at that time. Whereas Justin Martyr spoke "freely to a pagan audience concerning the Eucharist,"[2] Hippolytus separated catechumens from the faithful and gave mystagogical homilies to neophytes, explaining the sacramental mysteries to them after their baptism.[3] The discipline of the secret became widespread late in the fourth century and into the fifth, employed by such leading catechists as Ambrose, Augustine, John Chrysostom, and the subject of this chapter, Cyril, who served as bishop of Jerusalem, with interruptions, from about 350 to 387 CE. After the fifth century, however, the discipline all but disappeared, along with the adult catechumenate itself.[4]

The reasons for the discipline's demise are not hard to imagine. Once the Roman Empire became largely Christian and infant baptism became standard practice, there was little need for a catechumenate. Without anyone around who does not have access to the sacraments but wants access, there is no point in having a liturgical rite for the purpose of holding those people at arm's length from the sacraments. It is also possible that the discipline's liturgical esotericism did not disappear so much as become transformed into Christian mysticism, owing in large part to the "interiorization"

---

2. Edward Yarnold, "The Awe-Inspiring Rites," in *The Awe-Inspiring Rites of Initiation*, 2nd ed. (Collegeville, MN: Liturgical Press, 1994), 55.

3. "Mystagogy" literally means "teaching the mysteries." The practice involves teaching newly baptized Christians about the sacraments they recently received and acquainting them with Christian living. It is in a sense the counterpart to pre-baptismal catechesis, which in the ancient church typically did not involve instruction on the sacraments. Michel Dujarier, *A History of the Catechumenate: The First Six Centuries*, trans. Edward J. Haasl (New York: Sadlier, 1979), 51–52; William Harmless, SJ, *Augustine and the Catechumenate* (Collegeville, MN: Liturgical Press, 1995), 45.

4. Dujarier, *History of the Catechumenate*, 135.

of Christian selfhood exemplified by the work of Augustine and Gregory the Great.[5]

Though we can easily find reasons for the decline of the discipline of the secret, the same is not true of its rise. Especially obscure are the reasons why it arose only *after* Constantine legalized Christianity and the empire began to Christianize. Although it would be a mistake to posit a sharp distinction between a secretive and oppressed pre-Constantinian Christianity and a highly public post-Constantinian Christianity—Christians were increasingly visible in the third century, a period of on-again, off-again persecution—there can be no doubt that Christianity in Cyril's time was much more visible than it had been before. In earlier centuries, pagan critics saw Christians as overly concerned with the reform of the individual and in private gatherings and not concerned enough with "public piety."[6] The third-century critic Celsus, for instance, characterized Christianity as insular, an "obscure and secret association" that did not partake of public life.[7] Such criticism could not be leveled against Christians in the second half of the fourth century.

The fact that the discipline became widespread only later in the fourth century rules out two explanations for its rise. First, there was no need to protect Christians against persecution, so the discipline could not have served as a kind of ecclesial witness protection program. Second, the physical actions performed in the liturgy were not entirely secret even to non-Christians in the fourth century, and so the discipline of the secret could not have been part of an all-out effort at jealously guarding any and all knowledge about the sacraments. In our day, Christian liturgies are broadcast on television. In the fourth century, Christians literally paraded the liturgy through the streets of cities like Jerusalem.

Even fourth-century city-dwellers who avoided going into the churches could not entirely avoid seeing Christian worship performed, as the liturgy would come to them as a procession down

---

5. Guy G. Stroumsa, "From Esotericism to Mysticism in Early Christianity," in *Secrecy and Concealment: Studies in the History of Mediterranean and Near Eastern Religions*, ed. Hans G. Kippenberg and Guy G. Stroumsa (Leiden: E. J. Brill, 1995), 289–309.

6. Robert Louis Wilken, *The Christians as the Romans Saw Them* (New Haven and London: Yale University Press, 1984), 202.

7. Origen, *Contra Celsum* 8.17, quoted in Wilken, 45.

city streets. Cyril was a major figure in the rise of the form of outdoor and processional worship known as stational liturgy. Described by one historian as "*the* urban liturgical celebration of the day," stational liturgy was led by the local bishop and moved from one site to another throughout the city according to a calendar of holy days.[8] Stational liturgy arose in the post-Constantinian period, becoming a part of the campaign to put Christianity and its holy sites on triumphant display. Although most of the stations in the Jerusalem liturgy had churches built at the sites as part of Constantine's building campaign, even toward the end of Cyril's episcopate the liturgy was celebrated at open-air shrines.[9] The processions between sites may have been meant to attract people to liturgy, as some bishops at the time complained about sparse attendance on Sundays.[10] That this fourth-century urban liturgy was preeminently public means that bishops could not have maintained the discipline in order to prevent knowledge of the liturgy and sacraments from spreading.

For these reasons, the discipline of the secret has been a conundrum for some scholars of Christian antiquity. To John Baldovin, the discipline is "awkward" and stands "in tension" with the public nature of Christian worship at the time.[11] Jan Willem Drijvers, author of a book on Cyril's political life, surmises that it "may have been a fiction since the creed and the liturgical mysteries as well were probably already public knowledge by the fourth century."[12]

But there are too many good reasons for keeping Christian liturgy secret in that context to dismiss the practice as aberrant or fictional. For one, keeping the sacraments secret from catechumens will help to instill awe in them. The dramatic play of concealment and disclosure in Cyril's liturgy of initiation might have been meant to transform the catechumens' curiosity about the unknown into wonder at the sacramental mysteries. Furthermore, ancient bishops favored a pedagogy in which someone should have an experience before

8. John F. Baldovin, SJ, *The Urban Character of Christian Worship: The Origins, Development, and Meaning of Stational Liturgy* (Rome: Pont. Institutum Studiorum Orientalum, 1987), 36–37.

9. Ibid., 52.

10. Ibid., 261.

11. Ibid., 85 fn.

12. Jan Willem Drijvers, *Cyril of Jerusalem: Bishop and City* (Boston and Leiden: E. J. Brill, 2004), 89 fn.

learning what it means—the opposite of how we moderns tend to teach.[13] While these bishops were developing liturgies of initiation, they were simultaneously developing a theory of the physical and spiritual senses. According to that emerging theory, catechumens lacked the spiritual senses needed to understand that what someone sees in the Eucharist is the body and blood of Christ. To spare the catechumens the pain of seeing wrongly, then, their catechists kept them from seeing the eucharistic rite at all. Baptism would grant the spiritual senses to the catechumens, allowing them to see the Eucharist properly.[14]

Fourth-century bishops' recognition of these psychological and theological factors helps explain the spread of the discipline of the secret in the fourth century, but I believe that historical factors made the decisive contribution. In saying this, I am edging away from theology's comfort zone. We theologians are all Hegelians in our hearts; we suppose that historical events are shaped largely by theological ideas. This is why we do things like blame the ills of twenty-first-century society on fourteenth-century Franciscans who gave up on the *analogia entis*.[15] Historians know, however, that religious orthodoxy and orthopraxy are to some extent the products of specific historical conditions. In the fourth century, the bishops, having assumed the authority of both the martyrs and the apologists,[16] were by far the most important arbiters of right belief and right action. As the leaders of religious communities, the bishops were subject to the pressures of politics and management: on the one hand, dealing with their superiors and equals; and on the other, organizing their subordinates. By keeping this in mind, we can see that the reasons the discipline of the secret reached its apex in the second half of the fourth century might be as much political and managerial as they are theological.

I explore in this chapter and the next an explanation for the rise of secrecy in Christian initiation in the second half of the fourth

13. Edward Yarnold, "Introduction," in *Cyril of Jerusalem*, (London and New York: Routledge, 2000), 50.

14. Georgia Frank, "'Taste and See': The Eucharist and the Eyes of Faith in the Fourth Century," *Church History* 70 (2004): 619–43.

15. See, e.g., Catherine Pickstock, *After Writing: On the Liturgical Consummation of Philosophy* (Oxford: Blackwell, 1998).

16. H. A. Drake, *Constantine and the Bishops: the Politics of Intolerance* (Baltimore: Johns Hopkins University Press, 2000), 110.

century that takes into account how secrecy and claims to secrecy are often the means religions use to negotiate their positions in public life. I argue that Cyril of Jerusalem developed the discipline of the secret as a response to the massive wave of Christianization sweeping Jerusalem during his episcopacy. For Cyril, the claim that the church held secrets, despite the fact that Christianity was becoming a fixture in public life, was an act of resistance against both the empire and a crowd of opportunists eager to be baptized into the church and thereby to improve their social standing. In this respect, secrecy helped Cyril assert the primacy of the worshipping community, rather than the purportedly "Christian" public sphere, in forming the person's Christian identity. Again, I am not arguing that political and managerial expediency by themselves account for Cyril's use of secrecy; theology and pedagogy played significant roles as well. Indeed, I hope to show that Cyril's genius was in his ability to use the discipline of the secret to accomplish theological, pedagogical, political, and managerial purposes.

The Rumor of Secrecy

When underground religions become public and popular, they do not give up on secrecy right away. Why should they? Secrecy is a powerful social force, capable of ordering social relationships by establishing a boundary between insiders and outsiders.[17] A secret can thus protect a group or its knowledge. It can establish trust among those who hold the secret. It can force the members of a tightly knit secret society to depend wholly on the society as their source of knowledge. It can train initiates in silence and moral discipline. Secret societies are often hierarchized, such that holding more important secrets lends one a higher status in a secret society. Secrecy is often highly ritualized—and rituals are often secret, even in societies that otherwise place little value on secrecy. In addition to providing a basis for group identity, a secret can also be an invitation for transactions between groups to

17. This observation was first made a century ago by the sociologist Georg Simmel. See Simmel, "The Secret and the Secret Society," in *The Sociology of Georg Simmel*, ed. and trans. Kurt H. Wolff (New York: Free Press, 1950), 305–76. The original essay was published in 1906.

the extent that betraying the secret is an enticing prospect. Secrecy's sociological power means that the content of secrets is not nearly as important as the way secrets order relationships within and between groups. Indeed, it's possible for me to order the relation between you and me simply by saying, "I know something you don't know," even if I do not really have a secret at all.

The ethnographer Paul Christopher Johnson calls such public advertising of an alleged secret "secretism." While we typically think of secrets as hidden, "Secretism is freely and generously shared. . . . It is through secretism, the circulation of a secret's inaccessibility, the words and actions that throw that absence into relief, that a secret's power grows, quite independently of whether or not it exists."[18] Although secrecy and secretism are distinct categories, they are "not . . . mutually exclusive."[19] They can indeed overlap while working toward contrary purposes in a religion: to draw attention to it, and to keep outsiders at a distance from it.

Merely having a secret does not necessarily give you power, and thus does not necessarily do any work to organize social relationships. For that to happen, other people need to know that you have a secret, and they need to want to learn the secret from you. Thus, you have to advertise the fact that you hold a secret of some importance.

What this means for the study of the discipline of the secret is that we need to see it not only as a liturgical, pedagogical, or theological issue, but a social and political one, too. By taking this approach, we sidestep the tricky historical issue of the extent to which the eucharistic liturgy was public knowledge in the middle and late fourth century. Whether or not the creed, the Lord's Prayer, baptism, or the Eucharist were genuine secrets, unknown except to the faithful, is only of secondary importance. Of primary importance is the fact that Cyril and other bishops at the time openly claimed to an audience of the unbaptized that baptism was the entryway to a trove of secrets.

For Johnson, secrecy is not a universal structure of religions, but a strategy that appears in religions seeking to defend their integrity against "an outside Third's penetration," particularly in times of

18. Paul Christopher Johnson, *Secrets, Gossip, and Gods: The Transformation of Brazilian Candomblé* (New York: Oxford University Press, 2002), 3.
19. Ibid., 184.

41

transition, either when a religion is on its way to being publicly prominent or losing its prominent position and being resigned to the margins.[20] Secretism is a means for religions newly synthesized into public life to assert that there is more to them than meets the eye—that denizens of the dominant public sphere might not know quite as much as they think they do. Claiming to hold deeper secrets helps religious leaders themselves maintain control over their religions even as the state claims an interest in them. Public legitimacy is an ambiguous blessing for a religion; it is rightly met with the ambiguous measures of secrecy and secretism.

Though Johnson hesitates to say that his theory "will explain secrecy in religion" in general,[21] the dynamic he describes is a plausible explanation for why the discipline of the secret reached its height only late in the fourth century, decades after Christianity was legalized and became a means for uniting a culturally diverse empire. To see to what extent this theory accounts for the development of the discipline of the secret in fourth-century Jerusalem, we need first to see how Cyril promoted the reputation of secrecy in his liturgy of initiation.

Cyril's Use of Secretism in Pre-baptismal Catechesis

Cyril was quite open about the fact that he was keeping secrets. In several places in his pre-baptismal homilies, delivered in 351,[22] Cyril directly refers to the fact that he was intentionally withholding intellectual or experiential knowledge from his baptismal candidates. Cyril delivered these homilies in a court that stood between the Holy Sepulchre complex's major church, the Martyrium, and the Anastasis, the chapel centered on the cave of the Resurrection. The candidates,

20. Ibid., 5. The religion Johnson studies in *Secrets, Gossip, and Gods*, Candomblé, is historically analogous to fourth-century Christianity. Candomblé gained state approval in the 1940s and quickly became the subject of scholarly and journalistic writing, a theme in popular films (including American films like *Woman on Top*), and a tool for advertising the Brazilian airline Varig. By the 1960s and 70s, its quasi-sacramental rituals became public knowledge, and in response, practitioners of Candomblé began to employ secretism, claiming to hold deep secrets that the wider public still did not know. See Johnson, *Secrets, Gossip, and Gods*, 17.

21. Ibid., 179.

22. Alexis Doval, "The Date of Cyril of Jerusalem's Catecheses," *Journal of Theological Studies* 48 (1997): 129–32.

then, received instruction in a place that highlighted their transitional status within the Catholic Church. They were physically separated from the more public Martyrium, which was close to the street and which catechumens could enter, and the more secret Anastasis, a site they would not visit until after they were baptized. From this position, their bishop could use physical space to promote the reputation that he and his church held secrets, reminding the candidates about secrets they had already learned and offering hints about secrets that still remained ahead of them.

In the *Procatechesis*, delivered on the day at the beginning of Lent when the catechumens gave their names as candidates for baptism (and thereby become *phōtizomenoi*, "candidates for enlightenment"), Cyril tells his hearers that they are being entrusted with secrets, warning them not to betray these secrets:

> When an instruction is given, if one of the catechumens asks you what the teachers have said, say nothing to the outsider. We are entrusting you with a mystery and the hope of life to come. Keep the mystery safe for the One who will reward you. Be warned in case someone says to you: "What harm does it do if I get to know as well?" The sick are like that when they ask for wine. If it is given when it is bad for them, it makes them delirious and has two harmful results: the patient dies and the doctor is blamed. It is like that with the catechumen if he learns from one of the Faithful. The catechumen is delirious because he doesn't understand what he is told; while the Faithful is condemned for betraying the secret. You are standing between two frontiers. Make sure that you don't talk carelessly, not because what you are told isn't fit to talk about, but because your listener isn't fit to hear it. You used to be a catechumen yourself, and I didn't explain to you then what the future had in store. When you learn from experience [i.e., through baptism] how sublime the teaching is, then you will understand that catechumens are not fit to hear it. (P 12)[23]

One of the ways secretism causes authority to accrete to the person advertising the secret is by forcing the inquirer to trust that person.

23. Unless otherwise noted, all translations are from Edward Yarnold, *Cyril of Jerusalem* (London: Routledge, 2000). All subsequent references to Cyril's works will be parenthetical, with the following abbreviations used: *P, Procatechesis*; *C, Catecheses*; *MC, Mystagogic Catecheses*; *LC, Letter to Constantius*; *HPP, Homily on the Paralytic by the Pool*.

In this passage, Cyril is asking the candidates to trust him doubly: first, to trust that he will explain all the doctrines they need to know as they need to know them, and second, to trust that when he does explain the doctrines, the candidates will realize that any impatience they had with their teacher was unwarranted. It's a strong assertion of authority, akin to the authority that parents hold over their children and college professors hold over our students. So we say things like, "You'll thank me when you're older," or, "You'll understand when you're out in the 'real world.'"

In this passage, we also see Cyril's first attempt at charging the candidates with a responsibility to act as caretakers of the tradition by having them keep aspects of the tradition secret from the catechumens, the group the candidates have just left behind. While Cyril is making the candidates submit to secretism, he wants the candidates to do the same for the catechumens, denying any catechumen's request for knowledge about the doctrines the candidates receive and the rites they undergo. If any catechumens did badger candidates in this manner, the consequences of the candidates' new status level were probably not lost on the catechumens: people who had been curious about what the faithful did behind closed doors were now unwilling to speak about it. Cyril likely hoped that the candidates' reticence would fan the catechumens' curiosity, so that they would be motivated to give their names for baptism the following year. If the catechumens wanted to learn the secret, then they themselves would have to make that step up in status and responsibility.

A few homilies later, Cyril tells his candidates just how little they know about the baptism they have promised to undergo. In *Catechesis 3*, after discussing how some martyrs, even without being baptized with water, still are saved because "during persecutions" they were baptized "in their own blood," Cyril assures the candidates that "you too will make your profession," just as the martyrs did. But immediately after suggesting that the candidates are about to undergo a rite that is, in the eyes of the church, equivalent to being put to death, Cyril stops himself, saying, "But it is not yet the time for you to learn about these things" (C 3.10).

Even if the candidates had been told about baptism, Cyril is banking on their not having been told that baptism is a baptism into death (Romans 6:3 is the reading corresponding to this homily). Although

44

we might imagine that Cyril is trying to inspire the fear of death in his listeners, the prospect of martyrdom might have appealed to many candidates as "the epitome of all the aspirations of fourth-century Christians."[24] Whether martyrdom was an object of hope or fear, it was certainly an object of wonder and fascination. By alluding to martyrdom and then suddenly retreating from it, Cyril is tantalizing his catechumens. He is claiming that a boundary between them and the faithful exists, promising them that something dreadful and fascinating awaits them on the other side of that boundary. But he is also telling them that they will have to wait.

Cyril likewise makes a show of surrounding the creed—the central statement of what defines the worshipping community of the church—with an air of secrecy. In the homily Cyril gave immediately prior to presenting the creed to the candidates, a homily on Hebrews 11:1, "Faith is the assurance of things hoped for, the conviction of things not seen," Cyril rightly contends that the creed is a concise summary of the faith, easily learned even by the illiterate. Its accessibility makes it easy to protect but also easy to exploit. For this reason, Cyril warns his candidates to be very cautious with its formula:

> I want you to memorize it word for word, and to recite it very carefully among yourselves. Do not write it down on paper, but inscribe it in your memories and in your hearts. But when you repeat it, make sure that none of the catechumens overhears the words that have been handed on to you . . . So see to it, brethren, and "hold fast to the traditions" which will now be entrusted to you; and engrave them "on the tablet of your heart" (2 Thess. 2:15; Prov. 7:3).

> Guard them religiously, in case the Enemy should try to rob any of you who grow slack. Do not let any heretic pervert any of the traditions (C 5.12–13).

Cyril believed that the creed was highly valuable. In the next paragraph he even compares the faith contained in the creed to "money entrusted to a banker; God requires you to submit accounts of deposit. . . . The treasure of life has now been entrusted to you; the

---

24. R.A. Markus, *The End of Ancient Christianity* (Cambridge: Cambridge University Press, 1990), 72.

Master will demand his deposit at his appearing" (C 5.13). All of this is because faith is the saving grace; any perversion of the faith will spoil it and the individual's hope for salvation.

After hearing this homily, the candidates will have taken an important step up in their status in the church. They will be given an important Christian formula, the profession of which signals that one is a Christian, and in the remaining Lenten catecheses (C 6–18), they will receive point-by-point instruction on the articles of the creed, in accordance with Cyril's promise that "in due time you will be taught the proof from the holy Scriptures for each point it contains" (C 5.12). Thus, while the candidates have been let in on an important secret, they have also been reminded by their superior that they still do not fully understand; more secrets lay ahead, and their disclosure must be deferred.

Even after delivering the creed and beginning to explain its contents point by point to the candidates, Cyril continues to remind them that they are receiving secret knowledge. After giving a lengthy refutation of Manichean and other heretical doctrines about God, Cyril explicitly claims that learning these doctrines is a privilege:

> These mysteries, which the Church now explains to thee who art passing out of the class of Catechumens, it is not the custom to explain to heathen. For to a heathen we do not explain the mysteries concerning the Father, Son, and Holy Ghost, nor before Catechumens do we speak plainly of the mysteries: but many things we often speak of in a veiled way, that the believers who know may understand, and they who know not may get no hurt. (C 6.29; trans. Gifford[25])

Cyril supports his policy with appeal to Bishop Archelaus, who argued in a disputation with Mani that God conceals his truth from unbelievers (C 6.28; trans. Gifford). In the quotation Cyril cites, Archelaus refers to several passages from the New Testament in support of his claim: "And even if our gospel is veiled, it is veiled to those who are perishing" (2 Cor. 4:3); "Do not give what is holy to

---

25. Cyril of Jerusalem, *Catechetical Lectures*, trans. Edward Hamilton Gifford, in *Nicene and Post-Nicene Fathers*, ed. Philip Schaff and Henry Wace, second series, vol. 7 (Peabody, MA: Hendrickson, 1994).

dogs" (Matt. 7:6); "The reason I speak to them in parables is that 'seeing they do not perceive'" (Matt. 13:13); and "to those who have, more will be given; and from those who do not have, even what they seem to have will be taken away" (Luke 8:18). As the reference to these texts indicates, Cyril thinks that in keeping some things secret, he is keeping them from people who are rightfully excluded: the unregenerate, the infidels, the obtuse. In fact, the act of keeping secrets and sharing them only with select others is indistinguishable from sorting or separating people into the worthy and the unworthy, the living and the dead, humans and animals. Although they have not yet been baptized (and hence, Cyril's promise in *Catechesis* 3 that he has more secrets in store), Cyril promotes the reputation of secrecy here by applauding the candidates for at least having come over to the right side of the fence—they are now in a position to understand things that catechumens are not.

Baptism and the creed are elements in the life of the worshipping community that make someone a full member of the community (baptism) and allow those members to articulate the beliefs they share (the creed). Performed within the worship practice characteristic of this worshipping community, they form and formulate, better than anything else does, the particular identity shared by members of this body. For both baptism and the creed, as well as for various related points of doctrine, Cyril establishes secrecy, casting the boundary between the faithful and the unbaptized in terms of knowing a secret or remaining ignorant of it. In each case there is also secretism, the active promotion of "the reputation of secrecy."

According to Egeria, a religious woman from the Iberian Peninsula who visited Cyril's church near the end of his episcopate,[26] the bishop continued this strategy of secretism right up to the days just prior to the candidates' baptism. At the beginning of Holy Week, the congregation gathers in the Martyrium, and the bishop calls the candidates forward with their sponsors and asks them to recite the creed to him—a rite known in Latin as *redditio symboli*. After that, Egeria reports that the bishop had these words for his candidates:

---

26. Paul Devos, "La date du voyage d'Égérie," *Analecta Bollandiana* 85 (1967): 165–94, as cited in Yarnold, *Cyril of Jerusalem*, 191.

During these seven weeks you have received instruction in the whole biblical Law. You have heard about the faith, and the resurrection of the body. You have also learned all you can as catechumens of the content of the creed. But the teaching about baptism itself is a deeper mystery, and you have not the right to hear it while you remain catechumens.[27] Do not think it will never be explained; you will hear it all during the eight days of Easter after you have been baptized. But so long as you are catechumens you cannot be told God's deep mysteries.[28]

This passage independently confirms many of the themes Cyril employs in the *Procatechesis* and *Catecheses*. Indeed, the words Egeria attributes to the bishop are remarkably similar to those Cyril uses in the *Procatechesis*. We see also in Egeria's account confirmation of the bishop's practice of the discipline of the secret and active advertising of the secret.

The Creed as Password and Pact

In addition to being advertised as a secret itself, the creed served in Cyril's liturgy as a valuable secret password that granted access to the deeper secret of baptism. For this reason the role of the creed in Cyril's catechesis deserves additional attention. As I noted above, in the homily he delivered on the day he gives the creed to the candidates (the rite of *traditio symboli*) Cyril compares the catechumens' being entrusted with the creed to their being lent money to hold in a trust fund (C 5.13).[29] This is a warning against taking the creed lightly; because this "deposit" must be redeemed to God, it must not be given away to anyone else. Not only must the catechumens return the creed to God when he asks for it, but they must also recite

27. A disagreement with the *Procatechesis*, in which they are told, "you used to be a catechumen yourself" (P 12). The *Procatechesis*, delivered at the beginning of Lent, was the first time Cyril addressed his audience as "candidates." The homily Egeria refers to was delivered later in Lent, when the appropriate term for the candidates for baptism would still be "candidates."

28. *Egeria's Travels* 46.6, trans. John Wilkinson (London: SPCK, 1971), 145.

29. Cyril repeats this analogy in the next homily: "Be an approved banker" (C 6.36; trans. Gifford, 43).

it to their bishop when he asks for it in the *redditio symboli* prior to their baptism.

Cyril was not the only bishop of the time for whom keeping the creed as a secret was a necessary condition for his candidates to be baptized. A generation after Cyril, Augustine explained the creed in business terms, though his analogy is slightly different from Cyril's. For Augustine, the creed is like a compact, something on which to base a "spirited partnership," like a business partnership. According to William Harmless, it "was a *symbolum*, a secret 'password' that marked one off as an orthodox Christian."[30] Indeed, the creed was used by Cyril and Augustine as something quite like a password, in their practices of the *redditio symboli*.[31]

The link between Cyril and Augustine here may be Ambrose. Ambrose, whose initiation practices in Milan were likely directly influenced by Cyril's,[32] believed both that the creed must be protected by secrecy, and that the creed itself serves as a secret that binds Christians together. In *Explanatio symboli* 2, Ambrose plays on the Latin word for creed, *symbolum*, claiming that in Greek it means "contribution," as to a business collective.[33] Ambrose explains that someone's "contribution" to the Christian collective makes it incumbent upon him or her to keep the creed "whole and inviolable," lest he or she be "tossed out as a cheat."[34] William Harmless explains that Ambrose's "analogy may rely on a suspicious confusion of Greek terms—*symbolum* ('password,' 'token') with *symbola*

30. Harmless, *Augustine and the Catechumenate*, 278–79; for a summary of arguments about why the creed came to be called a *symbolum*, see J. N. D. Kelly, *Early Christian Creeds*, 3rd ed. (London: Longman, 1972), 52–61.

31. See *Egeria's Travels* 46.5, Wilkinson, 145; and Augustine, *De Symbolo ad Catechumenos* 1, trans. C. L. Cornish, in *A Select Library of the Nicene and Post-Nicene Fathers*, ed. Philip Schaff, first series, vol. 3 (Buffalo: The Christian Literature Company, 1887), 369. In *De Symbolo ad Catechumenos* 1, Augustine also tells his hearers that "The Creed no man writes so as it may be able to be read," exhorting them to learn it by heart.

32. Edward Yarnold, "Did St. Ambrose Know the Mystagogic Catecheses of St. Cyril of Jerusalem?" *Studia Patristica* 12 (1975): 184–89.

33. In *C* 5.12, Cyril uses *Pistis* to refer to the creed. W. C. Reischl and J. Rupp, *Cyrilli Hierosolymarum archiepiscopi opera quae supersunt omnia*, vol. 1 (Munich: Libraria Lentneriana, 1848; reprint, Hildesheim, Germany: Georg Olms Verlagsbuchhandlung, 1967), 150 (page references are to reprint edition).

34. Ambrose, *Explanatio symboli* 2, trans. R. H. Connolly (Cambridge: Cambridge University Press, 1952; reprint, Nendeln, Liechtenstein: Kraus Reprint, 1967), 19–20 (page references are to reprint edition).

('contribution'), but it is a fine pedagogical device. . . . Ambrose's accent [is] ominous: to warn the *competentes* [candidates for baptism] that credal fraud resulted in expulsion from the community."[35] The implication seems to be that the creed stands as the basis for the candidates to form their collective identity; it is a pact that they enter into and mutually agree to uphold. It is unclear what Ambrose would imagine as "committing fraud" against the creed and the community surrounding it, but the business analogy suggests that he meant to warn the candidates against seeking some kind of personal gain from the compact by "selling off" this collective property (akin to a mutual fund[36]) to someone outside the circle of the faithful. Although Ambrose's analogy is contractual, rather than bodily, it is also true that mistreating the creed, itself an element in the liturgy, violates the worshipping body's integrity and in so doing, violates the body of Christ itself.

We cannot be completely certain that Ambrose employed the creed as a password. Although "Ambrose makes no explicit mention of the *redditio symboli*," he tells the candidates in one Lenten prebaptismal homily that they "'have yet to deliver' the Creed."[37] Still, both Augustine's and Ambrose's treatment of the creed as the basis for a compact sheds some light on Cyril's use of the business analogy in *Catechesis* 5.13. These Latin bishops taught that the creed was the "token" of the candidates' status as stakeholders in the faith. Like a partnership based on secrecy, the partnership based on the creed can be betrayed; as stakeholders, then, the candidates have a responsibility to protect the faith by not speaking casually about it. Whether the creed is valuable as a secret that can only be told to the bishop or to God (as it is for Cyril and Augustine), or whether it is valuable as the basis for a "spirited partnership" among those who hold it (as it is for Ambrose and Augustine), the creed is valuable enough that giving it away to the wrong person is a grave offense, punishable even by excommunication.

While in one sense, "giving away" the creed to another person does not cause one to lose it (in the way that giving away a coin would),

---

35. Harmless, *Augustine and the Catechumenate*, 97.

36. Craig Allan Satterlee, *Ambrose of Milan's Method of Mystagogical Preaching* (Collegeville, MN: Pueblo, 2002), 154.

37. Ibid., 155.

both Cyril and Ambrose suggest that someone who is careless with the creed *will* lose it, because to do so is to demonstrate that one does not understand its value. In this respect, giving away the creed is like giving away a secret: if I tell you a secret, I still have the knowledge I gave you, but that knowledge takes on a very different character, because it is no longer a secret to you. Knowledge that once separated us now might bind us together—or it might separate me from the rest of the group as a traitor. In the latter case, what had been a secret has become perverted, just as Cyril and Ambrose thought that the one who hands over the creed shows himself or herself not to be worthy of it.

The creed, like a secret, sifts or sorts people out. It demarcates the Christian community from the non-Christian; it is thus a source of the Christian's identity, for without a real or imagined "them" to set one's own group in opposition to, there can be no "us," no collective identity. For Cyril, "them" included "a hostile angel," "the Enemy," and the "heretic" (C 5.12–13). In Ambrose's account, the creed binds together a circle of trust, protecting their common possession against outsiders, for the Christian community is one that is identified by its members sharing a secret "token."

We will see in chapters 3 and 4 that Søren Kierkegaard (whose knowledge of patristic authors was quite limited) in *Works of Love* presents the faith as a secret that must not be betrayed. This notion, recognized equally by a fourth-century bishop dealing with rapid Christianization and a nineteenth century Protestant layperson who perceived the faith as being for sale, is central to my overall argument that Christians today, as caretakers of a tradition, have an obligation to keep their faith hidden when they live out their public lives. For now, though, we still need to see how the discipline of the secret helped Cyril to negotiate Christians' relationship to public life in Jerusalem under Roman rule.

Conclusion

So far, I have tried to show that in continually reminding his baptismal candidates of the boundary separating them from the faithful, and in promising to reveal to them what they do not know, Cyril was practicing what Paul Johnson calls secretism, the active promotion of the reputation of secrecy. This alone, however, does not answer the question I brought up at the beginning of this chapter; namely, why the sort of secretism Cyril practiced flourished when it did.

Recall that Johnson aimed in part to historicize religious secrecy, showing how it is "a transitional structure" taken up "in the face of the perceived cultural threat of an outside Third's penetration," appearing as a "self-conscious defense" when a religion makes a transition from the cultural margins to the center, or vice versa.[38] Without question, Christianity in Cyril's era was undergoing just such a change, as the Roman Empire threatened to intervene in the relationship between the faithful and the catechumens, or, more broadly, between Christians and non-Christians.

In the next chapter, I will explore two motivations for Cyril's deployment of secretism in the context of a rapidly Christianizing empire. I mentioned earlier the need to remember that as a bishop, Cyril bore political and managerial responsibilities. I suggest that it was these responsibilities that led him to pursue a strategy of secretism in his liturgy of initiation.

---

38. Johnson, *Secrets, Gossip, and Gods*, 5.

2

Liturgical Secrecy as Cyril's Defense against Opportunism and Imperial Authority

Secrecy means power. Very often secrecy surrounds political power, especially in more authoritarian political forms. Indeed, secrecy may be the most reliable indicator of authoritarian strains in government. Furthermore, to the extent that knowledge is power, a state's denial of knowledge to its citizens and to other states by means of keeping secrets will enhance or protect the state's authority.[1] But as historian of religions Hugh Urban points out, "the practice of secrecy is a highly malleable and double-edged kind of strategy,"[2] because it can also be a means for a weaker person or group to take power from those higher up on the power spectrum by claiming to have secrets that the superiors do not have.

I noted another aspect of secrecy's ambivalence in the last chapter: secrecy's power both to attract and to repel, paradoxically drawing

1. For one historical example of how secrecy and secretism can underwrite the power of an authoritarian state, see Paul Christopher Johnson, "Secretism and the Apotheosis of Duvalier," *Journal of the American Academy of Religion* 74 (2006): 420–45.

2. Hugh B. Urban, "The Torment of Secrecy: Ethical and Epistemological Problems in the Study of Esoteric Traditions," *History of Religions* 37 (February 1998): 247.

outsiders closer and holding them at a distance at the same time. In religious secrecy the outsider is often the state, an entity whose proximity could benefit a religion tremendously, but which could compromise a religion's independence and authenticity if brought in too far. Secrecy, then, is a particularly expedient strategy for negotiating a religion's position in public life. The state might perceive a secretive religion as powerful, either a threat or a potential tool for extending state authority, and thereby as an organization that should be either investigated or granted special privileges. The religion, on the other hand, can assert the secrecy of its sacred doctrines or practices to prevent state interference.[3]

Cyril the Politician

During the fourth century the relationship between the church and the state was hotly contested. Or rather, a major point of contestation was over whether there could even *be* a relationship between ecclesiastical and temporal power, because in the pre-Constantinian Roman Empire, there was no perceived difference between religious and political power.[4] During and after Constantine's reign, bishops' authority grew in both scope and weight; by the end of the fourth century, the bishops had replaced the senate and the armies as the source of the emperor's legitimacy.[5] In getting to that point, it is reasonable to suppose that the bishop in a major see would use a variety of means—his preaching, his liturgy, his direct dealings with other bishops and with state authorities themselves—to negotiate an advantageous relationship with the empire.

The record of Cyril's political life is limited to a letter he wrote to the emperor Constantius in 351, scattered remarks about imperial influence on Jerusalem in the *Catecheses*, and the accounts of church historians like Jerome, Theodoret, and Sozomen. Still, Jerusalem's rapid rise in status during the fourth century and Cyril's three exiles

3. See Michael Barkun, "Religion and Secrecy After September 11," *Journal of the American Academy of Religion* 74 (2006): 275–301.

4. Drake, *Constantine and the Bishops*, 127–28; Hugo Rahner, SJ, *Church and State in Early Christianity*, trans. Leo Donald Davis, SJ (San Francisco: Ignatius, 1992), 39–79.

5. Drake, *Constantine and the Bishops*, 440.

from his see suggest that Cyril was more engaged with public life than his record immediately indicates. Theology certainly was a major factor in Jerusalem's rise and Cyril's exiles—I will touch on Cyril's relationship to Arianism below—but recent scholars have looked for explanations of them in what we would today call politics, even if theology and politics were not clearly separate categories in the fourth century. These studies reveal what kind of public figure Cyril was: how he, like his brother bishops, wittingly or unwittingly defined the church's position in public life.

Given this context, and given the close relationship between secrecy and power, can we read Cyril's employment of the discipline of the secret as a means to gain political power for himself or his see? To answer this question, I will take a brief look at Cyril's relationship with the two offices that most clearly held power over him: the bishop of neighboring Caesarea and the emperor.

Jerusalem and Caesarea competed for imperial and ecclesial favor throughout the fourth century and the first half of the fifth. Jerusalem was, in the two centuries leading up to Constantine's time, Palestine's second city both politically and ecclesially. Caesarea, where Constantine's biographer Eusebius had been bishop, was the metropolitan see. Through Constantine's patronage, however, Jerusalem gained in prominence; by the time Cyril was bishop, Jerusalem was recognized by the church at large as ranking below only Rome, Antioch, and Alexandria in importance. In spite of this, the bishop of Caesarea still held sway in the ecclesial province of Palestine. Adding to this tension was the Caesarean bishop Acacius's Arianism. Acacius ordained Cyril bishop—likely leading Jerome to classify Cyril among the Arians—but tension between the two developed quickly. Cyril was deposed twice by Acacius (having regained the bishop's chair following a successful appeal to Constantius in 359) and once during the reign of the Arianizing emperor Valens.[6]

Cyril appears to have been no passive political victim, however: after Acacius' death in 365, Cyril gained the authority to nominate and consecrate the bishop of Caesarea, and, after his first nominee

6. Drijvers, *Cyril of Jerusalem*, 35–44; Alexis James Doval, *Cyril of Jerusalem, Mystagogue: The Authorship of the Mystagogic Catecheses* (Washington, DC: The Catholic University of America Press, 2001), 19–20.

was deposed by loyalists to Acacius, Cyril nominated his own nephew, Gelasius. Gelasius was deposed, too, though later he was reinstated. Gelasius may indeed have been Cyril's puppet.[7] In general, Jan Willem Drijvers describes Cyril as "an ambitious politician who wanted to establish the primacy of his see in Palestine and who desired that Jerusalem be recognized as an apostolic see and become the most holy city in the Christian world."[8]

Informed by Johnson's theory of secretism, we should not be surprised that competition of the sort that obtained between Jerusalem and Caesarea would eventually involve claims to secrecy. The same logic of attracting and controlling people through secretism that works for a religion as a whole also works for individual leaders or locales within the religion; a leader can try to attract more followers or prestige than his or her rivals by claiming to hold deeper secrets than other leaders within the same religion do.[9] While Cyril was not competing with the Caesarean bishop for adherents, he certainly seems to have been competing with him for prestige. Promoting the cult of the cross was one element in Cyril's campaign to demonstrate Jerusalem's status as a holy city and therefore by rights a politically important city.[10] Even if theology was the primary cause of the conflict with Caesarea's bishop,[11] sticking resolutely to Nicene orthodoxy was not the only possible solution for Cyril. Because in this period theology and politics were inextricably linked, it is reasonable to suppose that Cyril addressed Jerusalem's rivalry with Caesarea with measures other than theology. Cyril's promoting the reputation of secrecy reinforces his greater project of gaining status for Jerusalem. The cross was something that pilgrims could see; the secrets were things that catechumens, at any rate, could not. And the reputation of secrecy spread as far abroad as the reputation of the holy sites did, as Egeria's account of the Jerusalem initiation rite indicates. We must remember that Cyril need not actually have had

7. Ibid., 43–45.
8. Ibid., xiv. Although Doval does not see Cyril's actions in the political terms that Drijvers does, he does affirm Cyril's "independent character," which led him to seek the preservation of his and Jerusalem's autonomy. Doval, *Cyril of Jerusalem, Mystagogue*, 23.
9. Johnson *Secrets, Gossip, and Gods*, 182.
10. Drijvers, *Cyril of Jerusalem*, 156–59.
11. Alexis James Doval, review of *Cyril of Jerusalem: Bishop and City* by Jan Willem Drijvers, *Journal of Early Christian Studies* 14 (2006): 124–25.

any secrets that the Caesarean bishop lacked (like the sacraments) in order to convince people that he did. But if the bishop of Caesarea did not practice secretism, then his power would wane relative to Cyril's, simply because secrecy and the rumor of secrecy are such effective means for getting and maintaining power.

Cyril also saw his brand of orthodox Christianity as competing with other religious groups for converts.[12] His *Catecheses* display a fear that his catechumens might fall in with heretical sects. For instance, he warns the candidates against walking into just any "house of the Lord," for it may in fact be the church of the Manicheans or Marcionites and not the Catholic Church (C 18.26; trans. Gifford). Furthermore, former Manichees had evidently enrolled for baptism (C 15.3; trans. Gifford). Circulating a reputation of holding great secrets would have drawn the attention of any residents of Jerusalem who were testing the religious marketplace. Such interreligious competition led Cyril (and Hippolytus a century and a half before, for that matter) to model parts of the initiation liturgy on Greco-Roman mystery cults.[13]

The influence of the former pagan Constantine left deep marks on the church over which Cyril presided. The sites of Golgotha and the tomb were discovered by an archaeological expedition sponsored by Constantine, and the emperor ordered the construction of a magnificent church over the site. Architecturally, however, the tomb, the site of the resurrection, was enclosed in a magnificent rotunda, thereby enjoying pride of place. Golgotha, on the other hand, stood in a corner of the court separating the Anastasis from the Martyrium, off the main axis of the church complex. As Dayna Kalleres argues, Cyril saw Constantine's preference for the tomb as self-serving, equating the emperor with *Christus Victor*. According to Kalleres, Cyril emphasized Golgotha and the humanity of Christ over the tomb and Christ's divinity in his homilies in order to undo the work Constantine and Eusebius had done to link the resurrected Christ to the emperor: "Eusebius promoted an enduring homology: just as Christ rose from the tomb, Constantine resurrected Jeru-

---

12. See Drijvers, *Cyril of Jerusalem*, 97–125, for a thorough summary and analysis of Cyril's attitude towards heretical Christian groups, Judaism, and paganism.

13. Yarnold, *Cyril of Jerusalem*, 52–55.

salem to its former glory."[14] Cyril's use of secrecy and secretism, too, aimed at actively determining the shape of Christianity in Jerusalem, rather than allowing it to be determined by outsiders, either from Constantinople or Caesarea, Eusebius's see a generation earlier. For this reason we must read Cyril's 351 letter to the Arianizing emperor Constantius (whom Hugo Rahner describes as "the personification of state control of the Church"[15]) as insincere in its praise for the emperor's piety and its favorable comparison of Constantius to Constantine.

Cyril the Manager

Although Cyril was a clever politician and propagandist, he was also a sincere catechist who genuinely hoped that his catechumens and candidates would develop an abiding Christian faith and live a moral life. Politicians today certainly want to get and maintain power, but the best among them want to use that power to accomplish something positive. For them, power is not an end in itself. The power that secrecy causes to accrue to the secret-keeper likewise must be dissipated eventually as the keeper accomplishes his or her aims. In this sense, "spending the secret [is] built into the secret itself."[16]

Cyril used the power that secretism granted him to manage the motivations of his catechumens and candidates—he wanted to throw stumbling blocks in the way of any opportunists seeking to improve their standing in the public sphere through becoming one of those who worshipped the emperor's God. Because much more evidence exists of Cyril's dealings with his congregation than of his dealings with imperial or ecclesiastical authorities, I will explore this reason in greater depth.

Because being a Christian in the fourth century afforded a range of privileges—including easier access to funds, tax exemptions, the right to make legal appeals to bishops, and preferential treatment in

14. Dayna S. Kalleres, "Cultivating True Sight at the Center of the World: Cyril of Jerusalem and the Lenten Catechumenate," *Church History* 74 (2005): 439.

15. Hugo Rahner, *Church and State*, 49.

16. Michael Taussig, *Defacement: Public Secrecy and the Labor of the Negative* (Stanford: Stanford University Press, 1999), 82.

seeking public office—while pagan cults became increasingly circum-scribed by law,[17] waves of converts sought to be numbered among the Christians. In offering such privileges, Constantine inaugurated a period of opportunism, lax standards for baptism, and reduced religious fervor.[18] Large numbers of people entered the catechumenate but then delayed baptism for years—content, perhaps, to stand at the entryway to Christianity and reluctant to submit to Christian morality.[19] Many elite converts simply ignored the moral requirements entirely.[20] Even leading bishops like "Chrysostom, Basil, Ambrose, and Gregory of Nazianzus . . . delayed their baptisms."[21]

This situation called out for reforms of the catechumenate, both in its structure (linking baptism to Easter and making Lent a period of catechesis[22]) and in catechetical methods. If it is true that Christi-anity's cultural normalization is inversely related to religious fervor and moral strictness, then the discipline of the secret was a clever tool in reversing this trend and getting catechumens to realize that Christianity is about much more than cultural status. The discipline drew catechumens to baptism, and thereby under the wing of the church's moral authority, by first exploiting their curiosity with the promise of secrets.

Evidence from Cyril's *Procatechesis* supports this hypothesis. There, Cyril admits that not everyone seeking baptism in Jerusalem had sincere motivations. In this homily, preached to those who had just announced their intention to be baptized at Easter, Cyril piques the candidates' curiosity by advertising the fact that he and the church hold secrets, while at the same time repeatedly warning those who may have been led to his church by "idle curiosity" that while they

17. Harmless, *Augustine and the Catechumenate*, 53; A. H. M. Jones, *The Later Roman Empire, 284–602: A Social, Economic, and Administrative Survey*, vol. 1 (Norman: University of Oklahoma Press, 1964; reprint, Baltimore: Johns Hopkins University Press, 1986; reprint of Norman: University of Oklahoma Press, 1964), 91 (pages references are to reprint edi-tion); Ramsay MacMullen, *Christianizing the Roman Empire (A.D. 100–400)* (New Haven and London: Yale University Press, 1984), 52–58, 96–99.

18. Markus, *End of Ancient Christianity*, 32; Dujarier, *History of the Catechumenate*, 79.

19. Drijvers, *Cyril of Jerusalem*, 87. See also Harmless, *Augustine and the Catechume-nate*, 58–61.

20. MacMullen, *Christianizing*, 57.

21. Doval, *Cyril of Jerusalem, Mystagogue*, 32.

22. Ibid.

will receive the water of baptism, they will not receive the grace of the Spirit (*P 5*). Still, Cyril is confident that even if the merely curious will not be genuinely converted, the opportunistic will. Addressing these, Cyril says,

> Perhaps some man among you has come because he wants to win the approval of his girl-friend; the same can apply to women, too. Perhaps a slave has wanted to please his master or someone has wanted to please a friend. I accept this as bait for my hook and let you in. You may have had the wrong reason for coming, but I have good hope that you will be saved. You have swum into the Church's net. Allow yourself to be caught; don't try to escape. (*P 5*)

Cyril's promise to give the candidates secrets makes them a captive audience; from there he has a measure of power over them that he can use to form their faith and morals, giving them the "right" reasons to convert. He likewise warns them against "hypocrisy" in seeking baptism in a later *Catechesis*, reminding them that the Holy Spirit does not "cast pearls before swine" (*C* 17.35–36). For Cyril, undergoing the bodily rite of baptism is meaningless if the candidate does not reform morally. As we will see, his revelation of the sacramental secrets in his post-baptismal instructions has, ultimately, a moral purpose.

The Revelation of Doctrine in the *Mystagogic Catecheses*

It is possible to defer the revelation of a secret endlessly, continually promising the revelation for a later time. In religious initiations, the superior can justify continually withholding the secret as a means of giving the postulants the discipline that religious life requires. Urban observed as much in the initiation practices of the Kartābhajās, a Bengali esoteric sect. In that case and in others, "The true meaning of a real secret is always reserved for the next meeting, the next stage of spiritual attainment."[23]

In deferring revelation of secrets, though, a religious superior runs the risk that his or her postulants will call the perceived bluff.

23. Urban, "The Torment of Secrecy," 236.

If the postulants are in the market for secrets, submitting themselves to the authority of someone who always demands their trust, but they are not receiving any secrets, they might give up on initiation or seek to join a different religious group that promises access to deeper or more authentic secrets or that gives a clearer timetable for the revelation of secrets. A religion can gain status or authority by claiming to possess secrets, but it will lose that status if it never gives those secrets away.

Several times in the pre-baptismal *Catecheses* Cyril promises his candidates that he would reveal a number of secrets to them after they were baptized. In making these promises, Cyril invites the candidates to trust him. By trusting Cyril, the candidates allow the bishop to transform their curiosity, their desire to learn secrets, into a desire for moral reform. In his final instruction before his candidates' baptism, Cyril makes one last promise: "After the holy and saving day of Easter, starting on Monday every day of the following week, after the assembly you will enter the holy place of the resurrection, where, God willing, you will hear further catechetical instructions. You will receive further teaching about the reasons for everything that is done," including a full explanation of how to receive the Eucharist (C 18.33).[24]

On the night before Easter, the candidates would finally be initiated fully into the church. The highly dramatic initiation rite itself exhibited similarities with initiation into pagan mystery cults. The candidates would be ushered, in the dark, from room to room in the baptistery next to the church, ordered to renounce Satan and pledge their allegiance to Christ, told to strip naked, anointed with oil, and then brought into the baptismal font, immersed, taken out of the font, anointed again with oil, dressed in a white garment, and finally taken into the Anastasis, the site of the Resurrection, a part of the church complex they had not been allowed to enter until that moment.[25] The exorcisms that the candidates had undergone during Lent had

---

24. Yarnold argues that this paragraph was a later addition to C 18. If so, then it stands as evidence that Cyril did intend, especially late in his career, to promise to reveal secrets, and then make good on his promise. See Yarnold, *Cyril of Jerusalem*, 201–202; Yarnold, "The Authorship of the *Mystagogic Catecheses* Attributed to Cyril of Jerusalem," *Heythrop Journal* 19 (1978): 159–61.

25. Yarnold, *Cyril of Jerusalem*, 53–54; see also Yarnold, "Baptism and the Pagan Mysteries in the Fourth Century," *Heythrop Journal* 13 (1972): 247–67.

similarly exploited the play of denying the intellect and the sense of sight in favor of the senses of hearing and touch, as during those rites, the candidates' faces were veiled and they were blown upon, to blow away demons with the breath of the Holy Spirit (P 9).

In Cyril's sacramental theology, the anointing that followed the baptismal water bath "sealed" the neophytes ("newly enlightened," as the candidates would be called after their baptism), making them, in a sense, watertight vessels for preserving the sacramental grace within them (P 16, C 3.3–4, C 17.35, MC 3). The final step to becoming a Christian, then—after first learning that there were secrets, after then learning a few of the secrets, and after undergoing a rite one knew little about going into it—is to become something of a secret oneself.[26] This happens through the ritual action of cleansing Christian initiates and sealing them with oil. The action separates the welcome from the unwelcome and makes the initiates into symbolic containers for the Holy Spirit, sealed off from Satan and the temptations to sin.

The day after the neophytes' baptism, Cyril fulfills his promise to explain everything to them in his five *Mystagogic Catecheses*.[27]

26. Johnson saw this as the final step in initiation into Candomblé as well: there, the initiate's body becomes a secret in the rite of "making the head." See Johnson, *Secrets, Gossip, and the Gods*, 123–24.

27. Scholarly controversy has followed the *Mystagogic Catecheses* for centuries. The major points of contention have included the date of the Mystagogia and their authorship—many scholars have thought that they are the work of Cyril's successor, John II. Alexis Doval has answered these questions to most other scholars' satisfaction in his exhaustive study, *Cyril of Jerusalem, Mystagogue*, in which he argues in favor of Cyrilline authorship of the *Mystagogic Catecheses*, which date from 383–86, the last four years of Cyril's episcopate (Doval, *Cyril of Jerusalem, Mystagogue*, 79).

There are only five lectures in the *Mystagogic Catecheses*, even though Cyril seems to promise seven (C 18.33), a promise corroborated by Egeria (46.6). Doval maintains that the *Mystagogic Catecheses* were preached only in the Anastasis (see C 18.33, 167; MC 2.1, 173; and Egeria 47.1), and neither Cyril nor Egeria counted the two days of Easter week when stational liturgies were held elsewhere in the city (Doval, *Cyril of Jerusalem, Mystagogue*, 77–78).

For my purposes, the question of the relation between the *Catecheses* and the *Mystagogic Catecheses* is paramount. Doval (*Cyril of Jerusalem, Mystagogue*, 83–205) notes dozens of similarities and parallels in theology, liturgy, and rhetoric between the two texts. Although the temporal distance between the two sets of homilies means that some liturgical and homiletical development occurred, the vast number of parallels makes it reasonable to suppose that the Lenten instruction Cyril gave late in his career, when he delivered the *Mystagogic Catecheses*, closely resembled the *Catecheses*. Thus, I will treat the two texts

Whereas he had cast the candidates as seekers after secrets in the pre-baptismal *Catecheses*, Cyril casts the neophytes as new recipients of secrets. In a manner parallel to how he had used a bait-and-switch strategy in the *Catecheses*, hoping to get the candidates to submit to the Church's moral authority by promising them secrets, Cyril moralizes the neophytes' new secret knowledge in the *Mystagogic Catecheses*, explaining that keeping the secrets entails keeping oneself morally pure in order to remain worthy of the secrets.

Cyril delivered these lectures in the Anastasis, the site of the resurrection, noting how the neophytes' faith permits them to see where "Christ was taken from the cross to the tomb which stands before you" (*MC* 2.4). As he had so often done in the *Catecheses*—where he refers thirteen times to Golgotha, the site of the *Catecheses*[28]—Cyril makes frequent reference in the *Mystagogic Catecheses* to the site of these post-baptismal lectures. These references likely reinforce the change that has occurred in the neophytes: that they now have access to experiences, truths, and even places they did not have before. Indeed, references to the tomb are occasionally conspicuous in their absence from the *Catecheses*. In one *Catechesis*, Cyril mentions the cross when explaining the doctrine of the crucifixion, stating that Christ "was truly crucified for our sins. For even if you would like to deny it, the place visibly refutes you, this blessed place of Golgotha where we are now congregated because of the one who was crucified here" (*C* 4.10). But when he turns to the topics of the burial and resurrection, Cyril makes no mention of the site of the resurrection in the very next room. As he did in discussing the crucifixion, Cyril emphasizes that the burial and resurrection really happened—"He was truly placed in the rock tomb as man" (*C* 4.11) and "on the third day the buried Jesus truly rose again"—but here his proof is not the site itself, but the testimony of the apostles in scripture (*C* 4.12). Cyril may have thought that discussion of the tomb was inappropriate for the unbaptized to hear.[29] Surely the candidates knew

---

as being in close relation, assuming that someone who received pre-baptismal instruction similar to the *Catecheses* received post-baptismal instruction similar to the *Mystagogic Catecheses*, and vice versa.

28. Drijvers, *Cyril of Jerusalem*, 156.

29. In one *Catechesis*, however, Cyril mentions "Holy Golgotha, which rises above us here" and "The Holy Sepulchre and the stone still lying there" in consecutive sentences (*C* 10.19).

that the tomb was there, but Cyril does not mention it here, where it would make sense to mention it—perhaps because the candidates are not yet worthy to see it, but perhaps also because he wants to heighten their anticipation.

After baptism, their anticipation would be fulfilled. The very first instruction Cyril's neophytes heard after their baptism concerned how they were suddenly worthy to be told the secrets that had been kept from them during Lent. Cyril welcomes them warmly, claiming that his anticipation of this moment of disclosure had grown as acute as theirs: "True-born and longed for children of the Church, for some time I have been looking forward to the day when I would explain to you these spiritual and heavenly mysteries" (MC 1.1). Then he explains why he had not instructed them about the sacraments sooner:

> Since I saw clearly that seeing is much more convincing than hearing, I waited until the present moment, until this night had made you more receptive to what I was going to say, so that I could lead you into the brighter and more fragrant meadow here in Paradise. Besides, you are now able to understand the more divine mysteries concerning baptism, the divine source of life. (MC 1.1)

Although this lecture was delivered more than thirty years later than the *Procatechesis*, the explanation given here is remarkably consistent with the promise he had given there, that "When you learn from experience how sublime the teaching is, then you will understand that catechumens are not fit to hear it" (P 12). In both cases the key to understanding a sensory experience is provided by the experience itself. The *Mystagogic Catecheses*, then, give intellectual depth to the latent, bodily understanding of baptism that the neophytes received with the sacrament itself. Indeed, according to Cyril, the full truth can be given to the neophytes because they have shared analogically in the experience of Christ's death and resurrection (MC 2.4–5). They evidently welcomed the mystagogy as warmly as Cyril welcomed them into the church, as Egeria's testimony indicates:

> During the eight days from Easter Day to the eighth day, after the dismissal has taken place in the church and they have come singing into the Anastasis, . . . the bishop stands leaning against the inner

screen in the cave of the Anastasis, and interprets all that takes place in Baptism. The newly-baptized come into the Anastasis, and any of the faithful who wish to hear the Mysteries; but, while the bishop is teaching, no catechumen comes in, and the doors are kept shut in case any try to enter. The bishop relates what has been done, and interprets it, and, as he does so, the applause is so loud that it can be heard outside the church. Indeed the way he expounds the mysteries and interprets them cannot fail to move his hearers.[30]

Cyril's neophytes, then, exhibited just the sort of fervor that historians claim was lacking in the fourth-century Christians.

Just as many of the *Catecheses* do, each of the five *Mystagogic Catecheses* concludes with an exhortation. Four of them are moral, urging the neophytes to remain free from sin. One of them (the second) enjoins the neophytes to maintain secrecy about the sacraments. In the context of the other four, the instruction to keep their knowledge about baptism secret stands as a parallel to Cyril's "bait" in the *Catecheses*, with which he claimed to be luring his candidates to him by promising them secrets and then using their presence in the church and interest in these secrets to stimulate moral reform in them.

The first *Mystagogic Catechesis* explains the renunciation of Satan the neophytes made just before they entered the baptismal font. At the end of this instruction, Cyril tells the neophytes to guard against Satan's continued temptation, to "be strengthened by these words, and be sober. For our enemy the devil, as we have just heard in the reading, is prowling round like a lion seeking someone to devour" (*MC* 1.10).

In *Mystagogic Catechesis* 2, Cyril links baptism with secrecy as he had done in the *Catecheses*. Here, he explains that even the neophytes' physical movement in the baptismal rite a few days before reinforced this idea that to be baptized was to gain access to something previously hidden. The neophytes' "pass[ing] from the old state to the new" (*MC* 2.1) is reflected in their moving from the "outer room," in which they renounced Satan (*MC* 1.11) to the "inner room" of the baptistery (*MC* 2.1).

At the end of *Mystagogic Catechesis* 2, Cyril echoes what he had said about the creed in *Catechesis* 5.12, reminding the neophytes of

---

30. *Egeria's Travels* 47.1–2, trans, John Wilkinson (London: SPCK, 1971).

the need to safeguard what the bishop hands on to them: "Now that you have been given a full explanation of these truths, I urge you to keep them in your memory, so that I can say of you, unworthy though I am: 'I love you, because you always remember me and have kept the traditions which I passed on to you' [1 Cor. 11:2, adjusted]" (*MC* 2.8). In becoming followers of Christ like the disciples and like Cyril their teacher, the neophytes take on the same responsibility incumbent upon Cyril and the rest of the faithful to act as caretakers of the most privileged Christian knowledge.

The final three *Mystagogic Catecheses* conclude with exhortations to preserve the condition of the neophytes' souls, so that they could remain worthy to continue to receive the sacramental mysteries. In the third lecture, Cyril explains the anointing with chrism the neophytes received after they emerged from the baptismal pool, telling them that chrismation has made the neophytes "christs" (*MC* 3.1), so they must remain worthy of the title by practicing Christlike works:

> Preserve this anointing unstained, for it will teach you everything if it remains in you. . . .
> Now that you have been anointed with holy *muron*, keep it pure and spotless within yourselves by making progress in good works and becoming pleasing to the 'pioneer of your salvation' (Heb. 2:10), Christ Jesus. (*MC* 3.7)

The exhortation in the fourth *Mystagogic Catechesis* is similar, though here the emphasis is on the need to remain worthy of receiving the Eucharist:

> So strengthen your heart by partaking of this bread in the knowledge that it is spiritual, and make the face of your soul joyful. So with a 'pure conscience' (1 Tim. 3:9, 2 Tim. 1:3), 'with face unveiled', 'and reflecting the glory of God', may you go forward 'from glory to glory' (2 Cor. 3:18) in Christ Jesus our Lord. (*MC* 4.9)

Likewise, the way to maintain access to the sacramental mysteries is to "keep yourselves free from offence," avoiding "the stain of sin" (*MC* 5.23). Although the intellectual knowledge of the sacraments will not disappear, the experience of receiving the sacraments is a privilege. Access is not granted to all. Indeed, access to baptism is granted only to those who can recite the creed from memory and thereby pass the bishop's examination at the rite of *redditio symboli.* Baptism itself, then, is a secret rite that, once undergone, grants someone access to the deeper secret of the Eucharist; maintaining that access, however, entails great moral responsibility. As was the case in the *Catecheses,* secrecy here leads ultimately to morality.

All along, Cyril's practice of the discipline of the secret, with the many promises and deferrals of revelation, has been done with an eye toward the eventual revelation of all the secrets after Easter. The final marks of the neophytes' arrival as Christians are their access to the site of the resurrection and the communion table, and their responsibility to participate in accomplishing the aims of the discipline of the secret themselves. Now that they are numbered among the faithful, Cyril thinks that the task of protecting Christian practice and doctrine is incumbent on them. This is not the terminus of their responsibility, though. They also must protect their access to the sacraments through continual moral vigilance. To "Preserve these traditions inviolate" (*MC* 5.23; cf. *C* 5.12), then, connotes both retaining them behind a veil of secrecy so that heretics and pagans do not "pervert" them (*C* 5.13), and protecting one's own moral purity, so that sin does not pervert one's soul. The duty to keep the secret, then, gives way to the duty to lead a sinless life.

Living a Christian life also requires concealing the good works that one does. In his *Homily on the Paralytic by the Pool,* probably delivered while he was still a presbyter and not yet bishop, Cyril instructs the congregation to be secretive about their moral goodness in order not to fall into hypocrisy. Secrecy in this case is not meant to protect Christian doctrine or practice, but to be a good disciple of Christ:

> The man who was healed did not know who his Healer was. We can see how far our Saviour was from vainglory. Having worked the cure, he slipped away, not wanting to receive credit for the cure. We do just the opposite. If we ever experience dreams, or perform works of healing with our hands, or drive away demons by an invocation, we are so far from hiding our success that we boast of it even before we are questioned. Jesus teaches us by his own example not to speak about ourselves. Once the cure was provided, he slipped away so as not to receive the credit. He withdrew at the right time, and came back at the right time. In order to set healing of the soul alongside

the physical cure, he came once the crowd had dispersed, and said: 'See, you are cured. Do not sin any more.' (*HPP*, 16).

Søren Kierkegaard, too, teaches the necessity for Christians to keep their good works secret—even works that bear fruits as visible as the healing of the paralytic. As I will show later in this book, Kierkegaard's advice to conceal one's agency when performing works of love, so as not to receive credit in exchange, is a means for Christians to ensure the purity and distinctiveness of their ethical approach in the face of the broader culture's economic paradigm of beneficial exchange. For the purposes of this chapter, though, it is enough to note that for Cyril a discipline of secrecy incumbent upon baptized Christians extends well beyond the creed and the sacraments and into the moral life. In fact, given how many layers of secrecy Cyril's catechumens had to go through to learn about the need for remaining sinless, it seems that Christian morality was the ultimate secret all along.

The Awesome Mysteries

Secrecy is not the only tactic religions use to get people to submit to a moral authority. Instilling awe or dread in people is a similar tactic. Rudolf Otto, in his classic study *The Idea of the Holy*, argues that the fear and awe people feel when confronted by the numinous is rarely an end in itself. The encounter with *mysterium tremendum et fascinans* paradigmatically leads to a moral imperative—feeling small and insignificant in the face of the mystery will make you seek moral conversion.[31]

Cyril recognized that people are awed by the unknown. If Otto is right about how awe leads to a felt need for moral conversion, then a Christian catechist like Cyril can exploit his hearers' ignorance and curiosity to prod them toward moral reform. Cyril claims to be trying to instill awe in his candidates right from the start of their Lenten catechesis. In the *Procatechesis*, shortly after quoting

31. Rudolf Otto, *The Idea of the Holy: An Inquiry into the Non-Rational Factor in the Idea of the Divine and its Relation to the Rational*, trans. John W. Harvey (London: Oxford University Press, 1931), 52–60.

Psalm 45:10, "Be still and know that I am God," Cyril tells the candidates to "Try to experience a reverent awe [*phobon*]," shunning more trivial thoughts when in church (*P* 13). Secrecy and secretism contributed to inspiring awe and fear in Cyril's candidates as they approached baptism. The entire rite of initiation at the Easter vigil appears to have been orchestrated to evoke awe. Indeed, Cyril calls the renunciation of Satan—performed just prior to baptism—"an awe-inspiring [*phrikōdestatēn*] moment" (*MC* 1.5). Edward Yarnold remarks that "This defiance cast in Satan's face in the darkness of the baptistery must have been a particularly spine-chilling experience. In fact all the initiation-rites must have had a cumulative effect of this kind."[32] There is no evidence that Cyril ever gave his candidates an advance warning about this dramatic renunciation. To be sure, having such a warning would seriously compromise the dread felt at such a moment, a moment at which one must declare in an instant one's rejection of a powerful and fearsome enemy. Cyril keeps such an explanation secret from the candidates so that their experience can be all the more awe-inspiring and their faith can be rooted in the emotion felt at a particular place and time.[33] The succession of events at the Easter vigil "seems to be calculated explicitly to stir up emotions of spiritual exhilaration and awe, which will help to make of baptism a lifelong and profound conversion," and certainly for the candidate who, after being compelled in the darkness to renounce Satan, "finds himself stripped, anointed, pushed down into the water, . . . greeted with joy, dressed in white, led into the Church, shown for the first time the secret rites of the Mass; receives the sacred meal of bread and wine—often without a word of explanation."[34] The

32. Yarnold, "Introduction," *Cyril of Jerusalem*, 51. On the renunciation as a means of incorporating the candidates into the drama of salvation history, see Hugh M. Riley, *Christian Initiation: A Comparative Study of the Interpretation of the Baptismal Liturgy in the Mystagogical Writings of Cyril of Jerusalem, John Chrysostom, Theodore of Mopsuestia and Ambrose of Milan* (Washington, DC: Catholic University Press, 1999), 44–48.

33. Cyril's appreciation for the awe-inspiring character of the sacraments is not limited to baptism. In explaining the Eucharistic prayer, he calls the instant following the call to "lift up your hearts," "this most awesome hour" (*MC* 5.4). Doval supports the thesis linking the *disciplina arcani* to the aim of inspiring awe in the candidates, claiming that "This belief in the awesome nature of the sacraments is . . . evidenced in the practice of the *disciplina arcani*." Doval, *Cyril of Jerusalem, Mystagogue*, 186.

34. Yarnold, "The Awe-Inspiring Rites," *The Awe-Inspiring Rites of Initiation*, 59–60.

candidate will most likely feel fear, wonder, joy, and confusion—and will perhaps above all else want to know what it all meant.

The notion that someone can be led toward illumination through the experience of awe was an old one even in Cyril's time. The Greco-Roman mystery religions, which were becoming extinct in the fourth century, employed such a strategy. So does Socrates in Plato's *Theaetetus*. According to Socrates, a "sense of wonder is the mark of the philosopher. Philosophy indeed has no other origin."[35] Socrates promises to tell the young man Theaetetus about philosophical secrets, but first Theaetetus must "just take a look round and make sure that none of the uninitiate overhears us," drawing a distinction between the "remarkably crude" materialists and the "more refined and subtle" philosophers.[36] Theaetetus's wonder at a philosophical puzzle shows him to be worthy of being under the authority of Socrates, who promises to tell Theaetetus secrets that will place him intellectually above thinkers who do not know the secrets.

We must remember that, unlike Socrates's work of initiating Theaetetus into philosophical knowledge, the initiatory experience Cyril choreographed to inspire fear, dread, and awe was a collective experience. This is likely what Ambrose hoped to emphasize when he explained the etymology of the word *symbolum* to his candidates. There are indications that Cyril hoped the experience would encourage the baptismal candidates to form a group bond among themselves. Following the admonition that becoming a Christian requires keeping the tenets of the faith secret, Cyril advises the candidates of their responsibility for one another, suggesting that the place of the candidates in the interstices of a boundary established by secrecy requires them to act as each other's caretakers:

> Now that you have been enrolled you have become sons and daughters of the same mother. . . . If one of you is missing, go to look for him. If you had been invited to a dinner-party, wouldn't you wait for your fellow-guest? If you had a brother, wouldn't you look for what was good for him? (*P* 13)

35. Plato, *Theaetetus*, trans. F.M. Cornford, in *The Collected Dialogues of Plato*, ed. Edith Hamilton and Huntington Cairns, Bollingen Series LXXI (Princeton: Princeton University Press, 1961), 155d, 860.
36. Ibid., 155e-156a, 860–61.

The common plight of these candidates is unique; they can no longer look for support among those who remain catechumens, but neither can they yet be counted among the faithful, and so they must become responsible for each other, forming a small and temporary community among themselves. Cyril later (*P* 14) encourages the candidates to study together, without a catechist leading them, again, reflecting the comradeship he expects of those who will be baptized together at Easter.

Such social and moral bonding among the candidates is precisely what the anthropologist Victor Turner would have predicted to happen to an initiatory group that stands, as Cyril describes them, "between two frontiers" (*P* 12). Because of the close association between liminality and the spontaneous social bonding Turner calls "communitas," the social relations of the candidates, who for eight weeks are a small community on the margins of the larger ecclesial structure, come to resemble "an unstructured or rudimentarily structured and relatively undifferentiated *comitatus*, community, or even communion of equal individuals who submit together to the general authority of the ritual elders." They exhibit "lowliness [with respect to the faithful] and sacredness, . . . homogeneity and comradeship."[37] Because the candidates cannot seek moral support from those either above or below them in the church structure (both in terms of social structure and physical structure), they are expected to develop a special bond, not with those either higher or lower than them, but rather with one another. The liminal stage of Lent, then, is for Cyril's candidates a trial that induces them to seek moral support from others in the same stage, a stage defined by Cyril's intentionally withholding select knowledge from the candidates.

Conclusion

Last chapter I said that scholars have little trouble explaining the decline of the discipline of the secret in the fifth century but cannot account for its prominence in the middle and late fourth century. Perhaps we have an easier time coming up with reasons for the dis-

37. Victor W. Turner, *The Ritual Process: Structure and Anti-Structure* (Chicago: Aldane, 1969), 96.

cipline of the secret's disappearance than we do for its appearance because scholars of Christianity have so far not fully understood secrecy or appreciated how Christianity has been a religion that, in part, keeps and tells secrets. Unlike secret societies or indigenous religions, Christianity is generally thought to be public, open, and universalistic. Christianity is also evangelistic, as witness has always been paramount. What's more, trigger-happy heresy hunters are always ready to level a charge of Gnosticism against anyone who suggests that Christians could or should trade in secrets.

In the transitional period of the fourth century, when Christians were negotiating the role their religion could take in public life, one leading bishop—though he was certainly not the only one—actively promoted the reputation of secrecy in his liturgy and catechesis in order to exercise independent control over his see and to transform the moral lives of any opportunists seeking baptism for wordly reasons. The need for the discipline of the secret was less acute both before and after this period. In the pre-Constantinian period, being a Christian offered no increase in social standing because Christianity was still persecuted. Although there were elements of secrecy in this period, attested to by Hippolytus, Tertullian, and Origen, among others, there were not the efforts at secretism we find in the fourth century. Once Christianization became complete, being a Christian once again did not offer a person a social advantage relative to most other people, and secretism subsided in Christendom.

The standard story of ancient Christianity's employment of secrecy—that Christians had to hide to avoid persecution, and then after the religion gained imperial approval, they no longer had any reason to hide anything—is thus well off the mark.[38] It is, however, a convenient story if a scholar wants to maintain that Christian identity must always be highly visible. By overlooking the century of transition, when some forms of secrecy persisted and even thrived as they never did before or since, we overlook most of what is interesting about how secrecy figured in Christianity's forging its place in public life. In this period when the church became a powerful force in public life, being a nominal Christian—as a catechumen who

38. This is exactly the story told by Georg Simmel, the sociologist who set the standard for the study of secrecy. See Simmel, "The Secret and the Secret Society," 347.

never really intends to enroll for baptism, for instance—could offer
a person advantages in that public life. But for Cyril, what made
someone truly a Christian was not something public; indeed, the
way to become a Christian was to submit to a variety of secret doctrines and rites. That conversion in turn makes a secret responsibility
incumbent on the neophyte.

The point of Cyril's discipline of the secret was to get the neophytes to take on responsibility in two ways. First, by becoming stakeholders in the Christian tradition, the neophytes have a responsibility
to "hold fast to the traditions" of liturgy and doctrine, even to the
point of ensuring that the unbaptized do not learn about them and
heretics do not get a chance to twist them around. Cyril took this
threat so seriously that he warned the candidates not to take up a
different creed, even if the church itself decided to teach a different
one. This was bold advice in a period of constant doctrinal reformula-
tion, but advice that Cyril was able to back up through his efforts at
the Council of Constantinople, which adopted a creed remarkably
similar to the one Cyril taught in his *Catecheses* (C 5.12).

The second form of responsibility that learning the secrets of the
tradition made incumbent on the neophytes was a moral responsibility to preserve their souls in a state of grace by avoiding sin. In
encouraging this latter responsibility, Cyril attempted to solve the
problem of catechumens delaying their baptisms so that they could
avoid Christians' rigorous moral discipline. Here we see Cyril at his
most innovative, exploiting the lure of secrecy to accomplish a moral
aim. As far as his writings indicate, Cyril was not a great theologian
like Athanasius, Gregory of Nyssa, or Augustine. Because no writings addressed to Cyril's fellow bishops have survived, we cannot
conclude that he possessed a talent for speculation; he even seems
averse to speculative theology because it can lead to error (C 11.12;
trans. Gifford). Instead, Cyril's homilies show that his genius lay in
his ability to weave together the theological, the political, and the
pastoral in his liturgy of initiation. Even more specifically, he did so
in the use of the discipline of the secret.

Secrecy, then, holds much promise as a means to preserve Christian identity in periods of transition. But what about periods when
Christianity has become utterly *de rigueur*, when a Christian could
assume that every person he or she encountered in public life would

be just as Christian as himself or herself? How might the expansion of the middle class, in which a Christian can be safe not only from persecution but from any form of material deprivation, affect Christian identity? These questions, which lead us closer to our own cultural situation in twenty-first-century United States of America, take us first to the Christian ethics of nineteenth-century Denmark's prophet of inwardness, Søren Kierkegaard. In the next two chapters, we will see how being Christian in an age that assumes itself to be Christian requires that one act in secret. That secrecy is in turn a sign of deep responsibility—in this case, responsibility for the neighbor.

3

The Secret of Faith
in Kierkegaard's *Works of Love*

Except for a few months when he taught Latin to the teenage sons of Copenhagen's upper class so that he could pay off a debt to his father, Søren Kierkegaard never worked a day in his life. He didn't have to; his father—a hosier who tried to instill in young Søren the idea that "God does not listen to the prayers of do-nothings"[1]—was one of the wealthiest men in Denmark and bequeathed a small fortune to his two surviving children. Kierkegaard lived lavishly off of his inheritance, ravenously consuming not only books and theater tickets but hats, coats, boots, wine, coffee, tobacco, and walking sticks.[2] He died shortly before the money ran out, collapsing in the street at age forty-two. For the last decade of his life, his writing was largely polemical, aimed at a materialistic Danish society that he claimed had sold off authentic Christian faith. Kierkegaard wrote his book on Christian ethics, *Works of Love*, in 1847 in an apartment in the

1. M. Nielsen, "School Testimony" for Søren Aabye Kierkegaard, in *Encounters with Kierkegaard: A Life as Seen by His Contemporaries,* trans. Bruce H. Kirmmse and Virginia R. Laursen, ed. Bruce H. Kirmmse (Princeton: Princeton University Press, 1996), 17.

2. Joakim Garff, *Søren Kierkegaard: A Biography*, trans. Bruce H. Kirmmse (Princeton: Princeton University Press, 2005), 516–19.

family home overlooking Nytorv, one of Copenhagen's major civic and commercial squares. That building is gone, demolished to make space for a bank, but Nytorv and the adjacent Gammeltorv anchor the west end of a busy commercial district, where shoppers dart into large department stores whose window displays show off the latest in Scandinavian design, from furniture to eyewear. Kierkegaard no doubt darted into the same buildings; during breaks in his busy writing schedule, he walked the bustling streets of the city, and he was well acquainted with its cafés, markets, and shops, particularly the more expensive ones.

Because he was rich, Kierkegaard never had to write for money.[3] Free from the need to play to the crowd, he denounced the crowd and its "chatter," and in *Works of Love* he disparaged how the crowd borrowed its ethical paradigms from the commercial realm. And because the interest on his trust fund (had he not squandered it) could have earned him much more than a professor's salary, Kierkegaard never had to teach for money. Without the need to prove himself as a scholar, he parodied the scholarly establishment, pointing out the tedious banality of their pursuits. In *Philosophical Fragments*, for instance, Kierkegaard writes that if God had become incarnate in the nineteenth century, "the wise and learned" would "no doubt first submit sophistic questions to him, invite him to colloquia or put him through an examination, and after that guarantee him a tenured position and a living."[4]

Being rich and practicing the conspicuous consumption Thorstein Veblen would name half a century later, yet being staunchly critical of capitalism's and bourgeois morality's degrading effects on modern Christians, Kierkegaard is himself a paradox as knotty as those that suffuse his work. Indeed, just as Kierkegaardian faith requires the believer not to attempt to resolve the paradox of faith, but maintain it through the passionate exercise of the imagination,[5] so Kierkegaard may have seen the impulse to reconcile his own material wealth with

---

3. He nevertheless complained, as writers do, about never making enough in royalties from his book sales. Ibid., 513–15.

4. Kierkegaard, *Philosophical Fragments* and *Johannes Climacus*, ed. and trans. Howard V. Hong and Edna H. Hong (Princeton: Princeton University Press, 1985), 57.

5. M. Jamie Ferreira, *Transforming Vision: Imagination and Will in Kierkegaardian Faith* (Oxford: Clarendon, 1991), 5, 57.

his critique of the pursuit of wealth as a weak-kneed capitulation to Hegelianism. The scholar, then, who attempts to reconcile apparent contradictions in Kierkegaard's life does little more than betray a severe lack of imagination.

Works of Love is a major piece in Kierkegaard's attempt to subvert "Christendom," the threefold alliance among the church, the crown, and the marketplace characteristic of Protestant countries at the time. For Kierkegaard, this alliance endangered the distinctiveness of Christian identity by equating being a good Christian with being a good citizen and a good participant in the economy—two of the major roles offered to persons by the modern social imaginary. *Works of Love*'s strong argument against reciprocity in ethical dealings suggests that the capitalist economy's success cheapens Christian belief and ethics, making the market model of exchange the predominant model for all activity, including ethical activity. *Works of Love*, then, aims to reacquaint Christians with the ethic of selfless neighbor love that springs from the individual Christian's relationship of faith in God.

Works of Love also is a book about secrecy. One of the book's messages is that Christian love will simply suffocate to death if Christians do not keep certain secrets. In its attention to secrecy, *Works of Love* is not all that different from a number of Kierkegaard's other works. Secrecy indeed permeates Kierkegaard's entire authorship, even where it receives no explicit discussion. As George Steiner points out in a comment on Kierkegaard's aesthetic literature, "That the spell of secrecy and of the silence which is the voice of secrecy lay heavily on Kierkegaard is obvious. . . . There is a genuine sense in which the prolixity of Kierkegaard's published discourse is, in effect, an attempt to keep inviolate a central zone of unspeakable secrecy."[6] The overriding question for Kierkegaard and many of his Romantic contemporaries was how to be an individual "in the face of a clamorous mass culture. . . . One answer lies in the custody of a secret, a secret grave and spacious enough to guard the soul against dispersal."[7]

6. George Steiner, *Antigones: How the Antigone Legend Has Endured in Western Literature, Art, and Thought* (Oxford: Clarendon, 1984; reprint, New Haven and London: Yale University Press, 1996), 64 (page references are to reprint edition).

7. Ibid., 65.

For Kierkegaard in *Works of Love*, the only way to save Christianity from mass culture's uncritical embrace of consumer capitalism is for Christians to conceal their religious identity from public view when acting in the world. Such secrecy aims to safeguard the integrity of authentic Christian identity in two ways: (1) it protects the faith from being corrupted through accommodation to worldly ideas and, in particular, (2) it protects the altruistic character of works of love against becoming an element in reciprocal exchange. Kierkegaard establishes two theological positions that promote this protective strategy. First, although faith is so radically individual as to be incommunicable to another person, faith must nevertheless be protected like a secret, as if it could be told. I address this position in the present chapter. In the next chapter, I explore the second line of theological defense against the exchange paradigm: when performing good works (which are necessarily observable), the agent must conceal his or her agency in order both to protect the works' origin in genuine faith and to render reciprocation impossible. Kierkegaard's response, then, to the threat to Christianity he perceives is not to mount a noisy, triumphalist counteroffensive against the world, nor is it to withdraw entirely from the world; instead, he advocates withdrawing the specific things that make one a Christian from the world, lest Christians allow them to be corrupted.

The focus of these chapters is slightly different from the focus of the last two. There, the major issue was what secrecy and secretism could do to negotiate a mass religious movement's relationship to the public sphere. Although I addressed Cyril's strategy for eliciting a genuine conversion in the individual, my primary interest was in understanding the stance that Christian faith and practice would take in the Christianizing public sphere of the fourth-century Mediterranean. I showed there how secrecy was a tool for Cyril to ensure that Christianization did not become merely a pious veneer over mores that remained essentially unchanged after the empire's conversion. The issue in this chapter is also determining how Christianity can be distinctive in a culture that is, at least nominally, overwhelmingly Christian. My emphasis, however, will shift to the individual Christian's role in public and moral life, for the commodification of Christianity is accomplished or forestalled by individuals negotiating the relation between their religious and economic lives.

Accordingly, these chapters on Kierkegaard also feature a different, but complementary, sort of secrecy than was discussed in the previous two chapters.

Cyril's and Kierkegaard's different historical situations contribute to the difference in the types of secrecy they advocate. Cyril concealed the sacraments and promoted the reputation of their secrecy in large part to get his baptismal candidates to locate the source of their religious identity in the community gathered explicitly to worship the one who raised Jesus from the dead, rather than in the public life in which they could gain status by being nominally Christian. Kierkegaard lived on the far side of the shift that began under Constantine. The question for Kierkegaard is no longer one of people's motives to convert, but rather one of their becoming reacquainted with the essentially Christian. Kierkegaard hopes to get Christians to locate their religious identity in their faith in God (even if he places less emphasis on the worshipping community than Cyril does), but first he needs to get them to acknowledge a difference between being Christian and being a participant in the public life of Christendom. Secrecy in this case helps to ensure that the paradigms of public life do not intrude upon distinctively Christian paradigms of thought and action.

These two types of secrecy are complementary, as should become clear by the end of chapter 6. Secrecy about the distinctively Christian life of the church, and secrecy about those things that would give away the distinctively Christian identity of the individual when he or she acts in the world outside the church, both help maintain the distinction between Christianity and public life. Both help convince people to locate their religious identity only in distinctively Christian sites: the worshipping community and one's faith in God and love of neighbor.

Consumption and Its Antidote

Kierkegaard's writings from the years prior to the publication of *Works of Love* display his concern that bourgeois society, particularly in its economic aspects, was corroding the European individual, as images of consumption and trade appear at important points in works from his highly prolific "first authorship," which concluded in 1846. Kierkegaard's concern arises from his insistence on maintaining the distinction between the inner and the outer, keeping worldly notions out of the inward sphere of religiousness. Although scholars have given much attention to Kierkegaard's critique of the assertion he attributes to Hegelianism, that "the outer is the inner and the inner is the outer,"[8] Kierkegaard does not see speculative philosophy as the only threat to the Christian's inner life. The cultural parallel to the Hegelian collapse of the distinction between the inner and the outer is the collapse of the distinction between Christianity and public life, particularly the public life of the marketplace. Indeed, while bourgeois Danes in Kierkegaard's time might have encountered a Hegelian pastor's sermon once a week, if at all, they would have had daily experience in buying, selling, and seeking profits in an economy shifting from mercantilism to capitalism. If anything, the ideals drawn from the marketplace posed a greater, though subtler, threat to the integrity of Christians' inner lives than the lessons taught in the ivory tower did.

Images evoked at the opening and closing of *Fear and Trembling*, published in 1843, illustrate Kierkegaard's concern with the encroachment of the market onto the inner life. At the outset, the pseudonymous Johannes de Silentio laments the cheapening of faith in his remark that "Not only in the business world but also in the world of ideas, our age stages *ein wirklicher Auskauf* [a real sale]. Everything can be had at such a bargain price that it becomes a question whether there is finally anyone who will make a bid."[9] He concludes the book with an anecdote expressing the same idea: "Once when the price of spices in Holland fell, the merchants had a few cargoes sunk in the sea in order to jack up the price. This was an excusable, perhaps even necessary, deception. Do we need something similar in the world of the spirit?"[10] The pursuit of profit leads to efficiency and lower prices, eventually to the point that products such as spices cease to be luxury items. In an age that sees

8. Kierkegaard, *Either/Or*, part I, ed. and trans. Howard V. Hong and Edna H. Hong (Princeton: Princeton University Press, 1987), 3.

9. Kierkegaard, *Fear and Trembling* and *Repetition*, ed. and trans. Howard V. Hong and Edna H. Hong (Princeton: Princeton University Press, 1983), 5.

10. Ibid., 121.

no difference between the inner and the outer, Silentio seems to be saying, it stands to reason that we should improve efficiency in the production of intellectual and spiritual goods, too, so that everyone can easily have them. To the extent that rationalist philosophical systems, liberalizing preachers, and the establishment of the state church has done this, faith has become so easy to acquire that it is no longer a sign of distinction. Silentio implies, then, that faith must be made more difficult to obtain. Christian leaders must "jack up the price" of faith by emphasizing how Christianity is necessarily an offense to reason and a cause for suffering in the individual's worldly affairs.

Silentio's paragon of faith, Abraham, has a faith so far from being a commodity that it cannot even be communicated. "Speak he cannot," Silentio says of Abraham, for "he speaks no human language. And even if he understood all the languages of the world, even if those he loved also understood them, he still could not speak—he speaks in a divine language, he speaks in tongues."[11] The radical particularity of Abraham's faith means that he cannot even answer the simple and direct question asked by his son as the two of them ascend Mount Moriah. The unique covenant Abraham has struck makes him keep the plan to sacrifice Isaac secret.

Similar themes appear also in the 1846 *Concluding Unscientific Postscript to* Philosophical Fragments, in which the project of reclaiming inwardness so that Christendom can become Christian again is partly an anti-consumerist project. As always, Kierkegaard's method for this project is indirect communication, the array of literary and rhetorical techniques Kierkegaard used to "*deceive into the truth*."[12] Because Kierkegaard believes that the truth is not merely a proposition one can give assent to, but is also *how* one assents to it (i.e., with the passion of hidden inwardness), he also believes that to give only verbal assent to a true proposition is, in fact, not to have the truth at all. Ordinary instruction, then, in which the learner receives instruction directly from the teacher, may not evoke a passionate and personal response to truth. Instead,

11. Ibid., 114.
12. Kierkegaard, "On My Work as an Author," in *The Point of View*, ed. and trans. Howard V. Hong and Edna H. Hong (Princeton: Princeton University Press, 1998), 7.

the teacher must use indirect communication. In the *Postscript*, the pseudonymous author Johannes Climacus compares communicating indirectly to aiding someone who has consumed too much food: "When a man has filled his mouth so full of food that for this reason he cannot eat and it must end with his dying of hunger, does giving food to him consist in stuffing his mouth even more or, instead, in taking a little away so that he can eat?"[13] Climacus finds such a measure necessary "Because everyone knows the Christian truth, [and] it has gradually become . . . a triviality. . . . When this is the case, the art of being able to *communicate* eventually becomes the art of being able to *take away* or to trick something away from someone."[14] For Climacus, Europe is a bourgeois dinner party, and while the guests, who "have already gorged themselves," might demand yet more courses, someone who seeks instead to induce vomiting is their greatest benefactor.[15] Possessing the truth is not a matter of collecting more and more bits of unfiltered data, but rather of purging oneself (or being purged) of insignificant and ephemeral information and holding passionately onto (or being held by) the eternal.

In Kierkegaard's time, as now, consumerism thrived on middle-class comfort and complacency. Kierkegaard's age was, to him, marked by the bourgeoisie's ease of transportation, communication, and—most appallingly—salvation. Climacus wonders in the *Postscript* how someone as lazy as he could make a name for himself in such an age when industrious types, "the prized and highly acclaimed people" of the time, are

> making life easier and easier, some by railroads, others by omnibuses and steamships, others by telegraph, others by easily understood surveys and brief publications about everything worth knowing, and finally the true benefactors of the age who by virtue of thought systematically make spiritual existence easier and easier and yet more and more meaningful.[16]

13. Kierkegaard, *Concluding Unscientific Postscript to* Philosophical Fragments, vol. 1, ed. and trans. Howard V. Hong and Edna H. Hong (Princeton: Princeton University Press, 1992), 275, fn.

14. Ibid.

15. Ibid., 187.

16. Ibid., 186.

Climacus vows then "to make difficulties everywhere," so that life does not become so easy that the industrious no longer have any work to do.[17]

In the Climacus writings, Kierkegaard seeks to throw obstacles in the path of Enlightenment rationalism in order to save Christian belief. In *Works of Love* the project is similar: to salvage a distinctively Christian ethic of selfless giving from the economic model of exchange. In the former, Kierkegaard "takes away" pure rationality as an avenue toward religious truth. In the latter, he takes away this-worldly works righteousness—whereby an individual can be repaid for loving the neighbor through receiving acclaim or self-congratulation—and insists on the hidden, inward life of a love that does not seek recompense. Because secrecy is unthinkable unless people consider that the inner is distinguishable from the outer, keeping faith and love secret can shore up this distinction while de-commodifying the elements of Christian identity. Believers can protect faith and love from debasement only through the "necessary deception" of taking them off the market entirely, treating them as things so precious as to lie well beyond all price.

Although I argue Kierkegaard's Christian ethic of neighbor love aims at resisting a capitalist paradigm's encroachment on Christian life, Kierkegaard's critique is not aimed at capitalism *per se* in the way that Marx's contemporary critique was. Rather, as Merold Westphal points out, Kierkegaard aims his critique of capitalism primarily at the deification of society, and thus only accidentally at capitalism as an economic form with heavy influence on society.[18] My argument in this book, addressed as it is to an audience that lives in a society even more heavily determined by capitalistic thinking, is a critique of capitalism in the same way as *Works of Love* is. Kierkegaard's critique and mine are in a sense politically and economically neutral—if some other economic form dominated my society and threatened the integrity of Christian religious life, I would still criticize it. My hope is that this book shows a way, involving Christians' keeping distinctive features of their religious identity

17. Ibid., 187.
18. Merold Westphal, *Kierkegaard's Critique of Reason and Society* (Macon, Ga.: Mercer University Press, 1987; reprint, University Park, PA: Pennsylvania State University Press, 1991), 33–40 (page references are to reprint edition).

secret in their public lives, in which capitalism need not penetrate Christian thought and life.

"Love's Hidden Source"

Kierkegaard presents *Works of Love* as two series of "Christian deliberations in the form of discourses."[19] We see in the very first deliberation that Kierkegaard's critique of the encroachment of economic thinking on Christian love depends heavily on secrecy and other forms of hiddenness. In that first deliberation, titled, "Love's Hidden Life and Its Recognizability by Its Fruits," Kierkegaard establishes that Christian love (in Danish, *Kjerlighed*) depends on the distinction between the inner and the outer, a distinction that also stands as the *conditio sine qua non* for secret-keeping. Love originates in the inner, in the individual's relationship with God, but it must manifest itself in the outer, in works that someone *could* recognize, even if no one actually does. As the title of the deliberation indicates, love has a "hidden" source, but it must necessarily be recognizable "by its fruits."

Kierkegaard compares love at one point to a "secret compartment." "Just as the lid . . . looks as if it were the bottom," so the depths of love's origin are hidden to the observer (*WL* 10). It is perhaps more appropriate, though, to think of it as the hidden source of a spring, which, "however quiet in its concealment, is flowing nevertheless" (*WL* 10). Because love's origin is hidden (in God's love), neither the lover nor the beneficiary of the work of love can ever know with absolute certitude if a work is performed out of genuine love. It is impossible, then, to point to a work and say, "The one who does this unconditionally demonstrates love by it" (*WL* 13). In a later deliberation, Kierkegaard claims that while worldly forms of love are accompanied by visible signs—the spouse or friend or nation that is loved—"Christian love you cannot know even by

19. Kierkegaard, *Works of Love*, ed. and trans. Howard V. Hong and Edna H. Hong (Princeton: Princeton University Press, 1995), 1. Hereafter, all references to this volume will be parenthetical, *WL* and page number.

On the significance of the distinction between deliberations and discourses, see M. Jamie Ferreira, *Love's Grateful Striving: A Commentary on Kierkegaard's* Works of Love (New York: Oxford University Press, 2001), 14.

its loving the enemy, since this can also be a hidden form of embitterment, if someone does it in order to heap coals of fire on his
head" (*WL* 146). A work becomes a work of love not by virtue of
what it accomplishes, but by virtue of something unseen that could
be applied to *any* work. Just as the truth is in *how* the individual
holds it, a work is a work of love by virtue of *how* it is done (*WL*
13). Kierkegaard contends that we might very well have self-loving
or unloving motives for an apparent work of charity—we might
want to be praised as a magnanimous person, or we might want a
tax break. In such cases, the work is an element in the economy of
exchange, and the agent expects a return on the investment of his
or her time and effort.

Because of the inherent tension between hiddenness and recognizability, the life of love is a difficult balancing act. The Christian
must avoid the extremes of allowing love to collapse in on itself so
that it becomes a love affair with the divine that does not issue in
recognizable works, or of becoming too worldly and consequential-
ist, neglecting the inner life that nourishes love. The requirement
that love bear fruits does not mean that the fruits of love must be
material. Indeed, as I will show in the next chapter, having a merciful attitude toward someone in material need is a work of love in
the highest sense, even if someone can provide no material benefit
for the needy person (*WL* 324). Whether it provides material help
or not, the Christian love Kierkegaard advocates is inconspicuous.
It is not heralded by ruffles and flourishes. It is invisible, and yet it
paradoxically must manifest itself, but in such a way (as I shall also
show in the next chapter) as to be untraceable to any human agent.
The basic tension between love's hidden life and its recognizability by
its fruits, then, is reflected in the tension between that very recognizability and the need to avoid seeking recompense for one's altruistic
deeds. This latter tension results in a dilemma between needing to
ensure that one's works bear recognizable fruits, while at the same
time making one's agency in those works utterly unrecognizable.
For Kierkegaard, this dilemma is love's "greatest torment" (*WL* 11).
Most people know from experience this "torment" characteristic of
someone who keeps a secret, as a secret can eat away at the person
who holds it, almost as if the secret has a will to be told. Kierkegaard compares such a situation with that of a plant that withers

and dies because it will not allow itself to bear fruit. Because this is a self-contradiction, "it is not this way at all" with love (*WL* 11). While Kierkegaard will not deny that love must bear fruit, and "the fruit is the essential mark" of the tree (*WL* 11), the gospel does not say "that it is our task to know which trees are which."[20] Indeed, the fruits of love are purest, least tainted by reciprocity, when the person performing them ensures that they cannot be traced back to anyone at all.

"What Else Is Christianity but Inwardness!"

Although the life of love springs from a hidden source, such hiddenness is not the same as intentionally hiding something from another person. That is, it is not the same sort of secrecy that I have been discussing in this book so far. Cyril of Jerusalem could have told his baptismal candidates all about the sacraments at any point, but he thought there were good reasons not to do so. Love's hidden source in God's love is a different matter. This source is "unfathomable" by the human intellect.[21] It is a secret that could never be directly told, even if someone wanted to, because it could never be reduced to a linguistic or symbolic quantum that could then be reliably delivered to another person. Rather, someone could only ever be led (indirectly) toward this secret, accepting God's love from God himself. To distinguish this sort of secret from the kind of secret that does have a communicable content, we can call them "unsayable" and "sayable" secrets.[22] To know God's love, someone must accept that love, and to accept God's love is to have a relation to God in faith, which according to Kierkegaard is "eternally and always the saving secret" (*WL* 28). In my taxonomy, it is an unsayable secret.

Faith, for Kierkegaard, is a category of inwardness. Indeed, as *Fear and Trembling* indicates, Kierkegaardian faith and inwardness are identical. It is in his or her inwardness, the "sphere of the interior

20. Bruce H. Kirmmse, *Kierkegaard in Golden Age Denmark* (Bloomington and Indianapolis: Indiana University Press, 1990), 316.

21. Ferreira, *Love's Grateful Striving*, 22.

22. On this distinction, see Jonathan Malesic, "A Secret both Sinister and Salvific: Secrecy and Normativity in Kierkegaard's *Fear and Trembling*," *Journal of the American Academy of Religion* 74 (2006): 448–49.

secret,"[23] that the individual relates to God; no one is born with faith, and no one can acquire it through outward activity. We should also remember, for the purposes of understanding Kierkegaard's view of how Christians should present themselves in public life, that it is only by virtue of inwardness that the individual *is* an individual and not merely part of the faceless, two-dimensional crowd.

That does not mean, however, that observers would be able to pick Christians out of a crowd. In the deliberation "Love is a Matter of Conscience," Kierkegaard claims that Christianity makes an infinite change in a person "very secretly, because it belongs only to a person's hidden inwardness, the incorruptible being of the quiet spirit" (*WL* 138). Elsewhere in this deliberation, devoted to exploring the side of love that remains hidden in the human heart, he exclaims, "Indeed, what else is Christianity but inwardness!" (*WL* 137). The secrecy that Kierkegaard advocates, then, is not an accidental property that Christians could discard if it became inconvenient; rather, it reflects the unsayable secret at the very center of individuality and of Christianity, a secret that the individual Christian can do nothing about.

Even so, the unsayable character of Christian faith has not prevented faith from becoming the subject of the crowd's chatter. The fact that human faith and divine love are so often talked about is what warrants classifying them as secrets and not only as mysteries. Because people treat faith and love as things that *could* be told (as when they try to reduce the transcendent to domestic categories), someone like Kierkegaard can issue warnings to the denizens of Christendom that they *should not* be told. Kierkegaard thinks that Christians have frequently made the mistake of thinking that the unsayable secret of their relation to God could be told. Doing so collapses the all-important distinction between the inner and the outer, treating something inward and unsayable as if it were public and sayable. Although an individual's God-relation is unsayable, Christians must keep the relationship secret, protecting it as if it were sayable, in order to protect the faith from corruption by being equated with worldly ideas.

23. John Caputo, "Instants, Secrets, and Singularities: Dealing Death in Kierkegaard and Derrida," in *Kierkegaard and Post/Modernity*, ed. Martin J. Matuštík and Merold Westphal (Bloomington and Indianapolis: Indiana University Press, 1995), 221.

Even certain forms of concealment are not enough to protect the inner secret of Christianity adequately. For example, Kierkegaard argues in the deliberation titled, "Love is a Matter of Conscience" that monasticism is illegitimate: "there have in Christianity been times when it was thought necessary to betray the secret and provide Christianity with a worldly expression in the secular world" (*WL* 144). Kierkegaard sees entering a monastery as a very public expression of one's attempt at hiding from the world. To him, "The cloister's hidden occupant notified the world that he had hidden himself, . . . playing hide-and-seek" (*WL* 144). The monk ultimately remains within a public and reciprocal economy, because in exchange for his hiding away in the cloister, he receives worldly recognition among those who see in his renunciation something they "could never have the strength to do." The world can always potentially find the monk, because he has only moved away from the world *physically*.

Although Kierkegaard's target here is Roman Catholic monasticism, Protestant "this-worldly asceticism" falls before the same critique. Kierkegaard's critique, in fact, is similar to the critique of monasticism that Max Weber attributes to Kierkegaard's theological forebear Martin Luther. In Weber's account, the Lutheran contribution to the rise of capitalism was precisely this critique of monasticism. Luther, Weber claims, bequeathed the discipline of the monks to lay people by developing the notion of a secular "calling," which in turn became the seed of the Protestant ethic of industriousness and thrifty self-restraint that so easily weds "doing good" as a Christian to "doing well" as a capitalist. Weber claims that for Luther,

> The monastic style of life is now not only completely worthless as a means of justification before God (that much is self-evident), he also sees it as a manifestation of *unloving* egoism and an abdication from secular duties. In contrast, labor in a secular calling appears as the outward expression of Christian charity.[24]

The accuracy of Weber's characterization of Luther's theology is not relevant to my study. Kierkegaard would certainly agree with the first part of Weber's claim. To the extent that nineteenth-century

---

24. Max Weber, *The Protestant Ethic and the "Spirit" of Capitalism*, ed. and trans. Peter Baehr and Gordon C. Wells (New York: Penguin, 2002), 29.

Lutherans believed that their secular work was a sufficient expression of charity, however, Kierkegaard would disagree sharply with the second part. Both this-worldly asceticism and monastic asceticism mistake the outer for the inner, thereby risking mistaking an ascetical practice for Christian faith. Someone who hides her Christianness in her heart, "the hiding place of inwardness," on the other hand, and goes about the world appearing to be like everyone else, has hidden her most valued treasure much more securely, because while the world can see the monastery walls that conceal the monks, the world cannot see into a sincere human heart (*WL* 144). The world does not even know that the heart is concealing anything at all. The hiddenness incumbent upon the Christian by virtue of her inward faith requires her to keep that inwardness a secret, not "betraying" it through a public withdrawal from the world. Similarly, inwardness requires that the Christian not imagine that a secular occupation, with its visible accomplishments, is enough to fulfill Christian duties. Christians must be "weaned from the worldly point of view that insists on visible evidence" that a purpose has been accomplished (*WL* 145). Instead, "the essentially Christian . . . does not wish to bring about any external change at all in the external sphere; it wants to seize it, purify it, sanctify it, and in this way make everything new while everything is still old" (*WL* 145).

The source of the love that alone fulfills the love command arises from the individual's "conscientious" or "confidential" relationship with God. In the deliberation "Love is a Matter of Conscience," Kierkegaard indicates that "Love is a matter of conscience and therefore must be out of a pure heart and out of a sincere faith" (*WL* 147), echoing 1 Timothy 1:5. The "pure heart" required for the relationship of conscience is, as we would expect a Lutheran author to say, "bound to God" (*WL* 148). But Kierkegaard qualifies this bondage to God, claiming in another deliberation that the Christian is a "bond servant" to God in a "hidden," "secret," and "inward" way (*WL* 115). Although the inwardness of faith must remain concealed from the world, a sincere faith is, in its bondage to God, transparent before God, insofar as no one can keep secrets from God (*WL* 151), who sees in secret. As Martin Andic points out, Kierkegaard's conception of faith as confidence has three senses: "*disclosure* (confiding in or to), *concealment* (in confidence) and *trust* (with confidence, confidence in or that)."[25] Kierkegaard recognizes that secrets are signs of both inclusivity and exclusivity; in a relationship of confidence or conscience, the two parties are completely open with one another but cannot disclose the nature of their relationship to anyone else. The unsayability of this bond of trust "is precisely the sign that the relationship with God is the most intimate, the most confidential" (WL 152).

Because of his or her confidence in God, the single individual who is ready to practice genuine love walks around the world with a secret. Ferreira notes how in "Love is a Matter of Conscience," Kierkegaard expresses a notion that is very similar to a key idea from Fear and Trembling, that "the true knight of faith is not conspicuous in the world. . . . The real difference [between him and everyone else] is a matter of the hidden inwardness of conscience."[26]

Entering into the confidential relation to God that Kierkegaard advocates, though, appears to cause the Christian to risk ignoring the world—like Abraham, perhaps, who ignored his familial duties in favor of his duty to God. Amy Laura Hall voices this concern by claiming that the call to relate to God through inwardness can be misinterpreted in such a way that the individual does not open himself or herself up to another person, foreclosing the possibility of being lovingly criticized by the other.[27] For Hall, hiddenness is an ethically dangerous avenue to traverse if one wishes to practice works of love, because one's inwardness might not be accompanied by confidentiality with another. We can easily imagine how the Abraham story would have ended if Abraham had, after hearing the command to sacrifice Isaac, closed himself off from any further communication with anyone, God included. In that case, inwardness would become the "inclosing reserve" characteristic of the diarist in Kierkegaard's Stages on Life's Way. Inwardness transformed into inclosing reserve is, according to Hall, "destructive" and acosmic. Without the open disclosure of oneself to another in confidentiality, "Not knowing the one to whom we can turn for sustenance, not perceiving grace

25. Martin Andic, "Confidence as a Work of Love," in Kierkegaard on Art and Communication, ed. George Pattison (New York: St. Martin's Press, 1992), 162.

26. Ferreira, Love's Grateful Striving, 86.

27. Amy Laura Hall, Kierkegaard and the Treachery of Love (Cambridge: Cambridge University Press, 2002), 166–71.

simultaneous with the command, . . . we may burrow deep" within ourselves, neglecting the world and the command to love the other.[28] Hall, in her criticism, is right to point out that Kierkegaard does not advocate a solipsistic inwardness, in which the self is always kept under tight wraps—even Kierkegaard thinks that one can go *too* far into oneself. The requirement that one's love bear recognizable fruit can be a safeguard against such solipsism. Still, this fruit must be nourished by the deeper relation between the two poles of hiddenness (from the world) and self-disclosure (to God) that is characteristic of faith's confidentiality.

"The Secret of Faith"

Although withdrawing entirely from the world might be appealing to some Christians, the vast majority will always live in the secular. Necessarily, then, they will have contact with the people and ideas of the world as they work, socialize, rear children, become educated, buy and sell things, be entertained, travel, vote, and volunteer. The world is the one field for all of the worthwhile activities of public life. It is also, naturally, the only place where one is going to find the neighbor, whom Christians are commanded to love.

But contact with the world is not entirely benign—this truth is what motivated minority religious groups in America to found Catholic schools, Hillel centers, and the like. A Christian today, in her secular life, will at times follow purely worldly principles in guiding her actions. For example, if she is a shopkeeper, she will want to maximize her profits, and so she will try to find the cheapest source for the goods she sells in her shop. In principle, the profit motive and the work it takes to find better prices pose no threat to her religious faith. She could very well love God above all things and her neighbor as herself while having a moderate desire to make money through her business. But if the profit motive proves time and again to succeed, the shopkeeper may begin to apply its principles elsewhere in her life. She may seek friendships that she can "get more out of" or find activities that will be "good investments" of her children's time. She might leave her church for one that "offers more" to her soul

28. Ibid., 168.

and lifestyle. Eventually, the light garment of the profit motive may well become a Weberian iron cage, in which the woman's Christian faith is trapped and enervated.

In a Kierkegaardian view, the dangers the world presents to Christian faith stem from the confusion or collapse of the distinction between the inner and the outer. Even more dangerous are the inroads worldly thinking has made into a complacent Christian church, so that there is no escape from worldliness and the confusion of the inner and the outer even in ostensibly Christian institutions. As Kierkegaard writes,

> The world is always diametrically opposed; where Christianity wants to have inwardness, worldly Christendom wants outwardness, and where Christianity wants outwardness [e.g., in the sacrament of baptism], worldly Christendom wants inwardness—which can be explained by the fact that wherever the essentially Christian is found it is accompanied by offense. (WL 146)

As this quotation shows, Kierkegaard is not advocating a form of Christianity that is stripped entirely of the outward, the bodily, or the communal. Indeed, it is the worldly corruption known as "Christendom" that wants to reduce the decisive sacramental experience of receiving "the water in Baptism" (WL 146) to one of inward feeling. The world is as wrong about this point as it is about love. The world, which thinks only in terms of external (and often selfish) benefit in evaluating the merits of an outward activity, neglects the inward character of *how* an outward work is done. Rather than doing away with the external, then, Kierkegaard wants to keep the distinction between it and the internal clearly defined. Doing so, though, is not simply an intellectual exercise, a matter of having the right philosophical categories. As we saw in the last section, Kierkegaard thinks that Christians should conceal their Christianness in their hidden inwardness so that the world cannot find it and so that Christians themselves will not exploit it for worldly gain. Kierkegaard also thinks that not all Christians do this; if some did not allow worldliness to taint their faith, Kierkegaard would have no need to remind them to protect their faith. Thus it is not simply the case that the outer has nothing to do with the inner, such that there can never be any communication between them. In this respect, Kierkegaard differs from Luther, who contends that no external work could have the slightest effect on the individual soul.[29] Kierkegaard rather thinks that there is a natural separation between the outer and the inner, but that it is easy to invert or collapse this distinction. Kierkegaard must think that outward contact with the secular can affect the inward relation to God in faith; otherwise his many warnings against secular thought, which I will explore in this section, would make little sense.

Because the threat that worldliness poses to Christianity is a threat to the inner/outer distinction, Kierkegaard's response to that threat is to reaffirm that distinction and ensure that properly inward things are treated as inward. In the deliberation titled, "You *Shall* Love," he does so by enjoining Christians to "keep the secret of faith" when dealing with the world. The world, Kierkegaard warns, is filled with people who are trying to "trick" individuals "out of the highest . . . by continual comparison with other people, by habit, and by externals" (*WL* 27). In other words, worldly existence can cause you to think that outwardness is all there is, so that even being a Christian becomes only a matter of outwardness—measuring your piety against others', going through the motions of a Christian life, and making loud declarations of faith. Kierkegaard tells his reader therefore to "Beware of people" and to "keep the secret of faith" as ways to resist the world's distortions of Christianity's essential inwardness (*WL* 27). To do so, Christians must be both vigilant and savvy in protecting their faith: "You are not to use the wisdom of serpents in order to make faith into something else, but, wise toward people, you are to use the wisdom of serpents to shield the secret of faith within you and be on your guard against people" (*WL* 28).

Despite what the hypocrites say, "the highest" will not be found in anything outward. In the next deliberation, Kierkegaard explains that for Christianity, "the shortest way to find the highest" is to "shut your door and pray to God—because God is surely the highest" (*WL* 51), echoing Jesus' instruction in Matthew 6:6: "whenever you pray,

---

29. Martin Luther, *The Freedom of a Christian*, trans. W.A. Lambert, ed. and rev. Harold J. Grimm, vol. 31 of *Luther's Works*, ed. Helmut T. Lehmann (Philadelphia: Fortress Press, 1957), 347.

go into your room and shut the door and pray to your Father who is in secret; and your Father who sees in secret will reward you." The highest, then, which is in secret, can be found only by those who secret themselves away from the world. Given that Christians cannot and should not avoid being in the world entirely, they must make a closet of their hearts, both to relate to God and to protect their faith against clever, worldly deceivers, or indeed against worldly self-deception.

Kierkegaard's claim that keeping the secret of faith will protect Christians against the "indolence of habit" (WL 27) does not imply that faith necessarily requires great exertion. Faith's interiority keeps it from being something that only busy or vociferous people can accomplish. If faith is a secret, and not a matter of comparison, habit, and other externals, then Christians can keep the faith when they have become weak and incapacitated as equally as they can when they are in good health: "when you lie weak on your sickbed and cannot move a limb; when you cannot even move your tongue, you can still have this secret within you" (WL 28).

This discussion of "the secret of faith" is a means for Kierkegaard to explain how Christianity can counter modernity's worship of "objectivity." Both of the world's avenues for collapsing the distinction between the inner and the outer—speculative philosophy and bourgeois society—depend entirely on objectivity for making judgments and claims. That is, they claim that all truths can be known by the objective means of empirical measurement and logical deduction. This reliance on objectivity can deeply distort Christian faith, which Kierkegaard believes is necessarily subjective—something that exists within the individual's being as a subject.[30] In religious matters, an objective point of view—in both its philosophical and cultural forms—can only see the outer and infer whether or not faith exists in a person. According to speculative philosophy, faith is either a

---

30. This does not mean that Kierkegaard thinks that truth is *purely* subjective. His emphasis on inwardness and subjectivity should remind us of Augustine's similar emphases. For Kierkegaard, as for Augustine, the journey inside oneself leads to the discovery of a truth beyond one's own subjectivity. Charles Mathewes explains this point in Augustine very well in *A Theology of Public Life* (Cambridge: Cambridge University Press, 2007), 50. See also Daphne Hampson, *Christian Contradictions: The Structures of Lutheran and Catholic Thought* (Cambridge: Cambridge University Press, 2001), 268.

practical postulate for the sake of ethics or the inevitable outcome of universal dialectic—if you're a thinking person, then you must be Christian, because Christian faith is one outcome of purely rational thought. Kierkegaard thought that the culture of nineteenth-century Europe likewise made being a Christian objective. According to the culture's logic, all Danes are Christian, so if you are a Dane, you must therefore be Christian. As Kierkegaard's pseudonym Johannes Climacus rather ironically puts it, "Don't you tend to your work in the office as a good civil-servant; aren't you a good subject in a Christian nation, in a Lutheran-Christian state? So of course you are a Christian."[31] Such are the words of the worldly deceivers who trick Christians out of "the highest" by encouraging complacency where passion is needed. The age in its lazy objectivity "wants to set the generation in place of the single individuals, wants to make the generation the recipient and the single individuals automatically sharers by virtue of that" (*WL* 27). As I will show in a later chapter, the replacement of the individual by the nation as the primary locus of Christian identity is for Dietrich Bonhoeffer a principal mistake that contributes to the cheapening of grace.

If Christianity is objectively universal in the ways that philosophy and culture think it is, then Christianity can be taken for granted and become something that no one needs to be passionate about. We can only be passionate about things that are distinctive, or different from the things around them. It makes no sense to be passionate about having 206 bones in your body, because everyone else has the same number. Likewise, nationalism is only possible if there are other nations against which to compare one's own. If everyone is Christian, then, and we know this objectively, then Christianity ceases to be distinctive, and if it is not distinctive, there can be no passion about it. And without passion, there can be no faith in the Kierkegaardian sense. In fighting against objectivity, Kierkegaard is fighting for the distinctiveness of Christian faith and love. Thus he laments that "now when Christianity is presupposed, presupposed as known, as given, and is implied . . . now this Law of love is repeated by everyone as a matter of course" but few ever "earnestly and gratefully" consider

31. Kierkegaard, *Concluding Unscientific Postscript to* Philosophical Fragments, vol. 1, 51.

"what his condition might be if Christianity had not come into the world" (*WL* 24). The fact that Christianity is ubiquitous does not mean thereby that it is not distinctive, because even if all of Europe (in the objective sense that history books consider) long ago converted to Christianity from paganism, "it is indeed not so very long since both you and I, my listener, were pagans—that is, if we have become Christians" (*WL* 26). Even though Christianity has existed for eighteen centuries and Europe has become synonymous with "Christendom," the fact that being a Christian is not a matter of objectivity, and that faith is not directly communicable from one person to another, makes Christianity constantly "original." Objectively, Denmark is a Christian nation because it has an established national church. This has no bearing, however, on the subjective state of an individual Dane's soul. Christianity maintains its originality through each individual who becomes a Christian.

Christianity can even remain original if every single individual became a Christian in Kierkegaard's inward, subjective sense. In order to demonstrate how the individual nature of Christian faith keeps it original, Kierkegaard compares Christianity's originality to a secret password. He asks, "Is a password no secret because everyone knows it individually when it is confided to everyone and is kept as a secret by everyone?" (*WL* 28). The answer to this rhetorical question is that the password can still be a secret, even if everybody knows it, as long as everybody keeps it like a secret and avoids telling anyone else the password or trying to find out if someone else knows it. If the secret is simply *kept* in this way, then no one could ever know that, in fact, everyone knew the password. Someone who knew would have to suppose that not everyone knew it, and if there were nothing to be gained by telling the secret, then protecting the password would be the most important duty.

In comparing faith to the password (as we shall see later, Kierkegaard does think faith can be passed on—indirectly), Kierkegaard emphasizes the individuality of faith against the objectifying view promoted by philosophy and bourgeois society. People should not take Christianity for granted, even in a putatively "Christian" nation, because no one can see inside of others' hearts to determine if faith is present there. Christianity is original in every single individual in the same way that a secret can remain a secret even when everybody knows it: through a lack of presumption and a focus on whether *you*—and not your social acquaintances, business associates, or political rivals—have faith. If the Christian faith is to become universal, it must become so subjectively, one individual at a time. The demonstrations of the philosophers do not make it universal; neither does state sponsorship of a national church. Every time someone becomes a Christian, it is as if he or she is the first one to have discovered Christianity, because faith can only be acquired from God, the same way the first apostles acquired their faith.

There is a difference between faith and a secret password, however: "The secret of the password, however, is one thing today and another tomorrow, but it is the essence of faith to be a secret, to be for the single individual" (*WL* 28). There is nothing inherent in a given word that makes it a password—a password is purely conventional, and it can change if necessary. But Christian faith is secret in its essence. It cannot be changed in case Christian leaders fear that it has been compromised. It cannot be directly communicated from one individual to another at all. If someone has faith, then he or she has received it from God, just as every other Christian has. Again, it is not important to keep track of who has faith and who does not, but rather to ensure that you persevere in the faith.

Someone could object that by emphasizing the individuality and noncommunicability of faith, Kierkegaard is ruling out the possibility of two or more Christians self-consciously forming a Christian community. The existence of a church is predicated not only upon people having faith, but also upon their knowing that others share their faith. If every Christian guards the secret of faith as closely as Kierkegaard advises, then no Christian could ever be certain that another person was a Christian, and could not provide others with any visible sign that he or she is a Christian. Following Kierkegaard's advice to keep faith like a secret seems to lead to an "anti-social" stance in which "there is only the God-relationship," to which "all other relationships are reduced," thereby rendering any community, Christian or otherwise, pointless.[32] We need not interpret the fact

---

32. Peter George, "Something Anti-social about *Works of Love*," in *Kierkegaard: The Self and Society,* ed. George Pattison and Stephen Shakespeare (New York: St. Martin's Press, 1998), 75.

that faith is "for the single individual" this way, however. Kierkegaard allows that Christians can confess their faith, but even then
he offers a dire warning that if faith "is not kept as a secret by every
individual, even when he confesses it, then he does not believe" (*WL*
28). In other words, you can confess your faith (as in the recitation of
the creed in a church service), but you must not do so in such a way
that you think that confession is the same as faith. The individuality
of Kierkegaardian faith does not necessarily mean that there cannot be a church, but it does mean that nominal membership in the
church is not enough to make someone a true Christian; the God-
relationship must not be reduced to social relationships. True faith
is concealed in the individual's heart, and objective, external signs
like wearing a cross on a necklace chain, praying in public, or even
reciting the creed in church do not necessarily spring from true faith.
As I have already mentioned, even an action as seemingly genuine as
"loving the enemy" can be done out of secret "embitterment," and
not Christian love (*WL* 146).

Kierkegaard's closest approximation to an answer to the charge
that he makes Christian communal life difficult is to say that Christians must rely on the fact that those who believe in love can recognize
love (*WL* 16), and that they can understand the metaphorical use of
language (*WL* 209), in which meaning is hidden in plain sight, understandable to those who hold the "key" to interpreting the verbal
code. Kierkegaard explains that

> in one sense the spiritual person and the sensate-psychical person
> say the same thing; yet there is an infinite difference, since the latter
> has no intimation of the secret of metaphorical [*overført*] words
> although he is using the same words, but not in their metaphorical
> sense. There is a world of difference between the two; the one has
> made the transition or let himself be carried over [*føre over*] to the
> other side, while the other remains on this side; yet they have the
> connection that both are using the same words. (*WL* 209)

In playing on the meaning of "metaphor" in Greek, Kierkegaard suggests a similitude between metaphorical signification and the initiation undergone by the person who passes from "sensate-psychical"
(i.e., aesthetic, worldly) existence into "spiritual" (i.e., religious) ex-

istence. He implies that the religious individual seems, from outward appearances, to be no different from the aesthete, but the religious individual's identity is recognizable to other religious individuals by virtue of the words he or she uses—and, more important, *how* these words are used. That is, the religious incognito is not such that the individual's faith is absolutely hidden; it is, however, hidden from those who do not know what to look for.

Conclusion: Suspect Community

But Kierkegaard might not have wanted anyone to come to his defense regarding his ethic's alleged anti-sociality. As Mark Dooley points out, communities are exclusive and self-interested; "the logic of 'mine and yours,' or 'ours,' perpetuates . . . a *communio*,"[33] whereas the universality of neighbor love shatters a competitive logic in which "ours" is always at odds with "theirs." Kierkegaard believes that Christianity aims at what Dooley calls a "loosely bound kingdom of neighbors," determined not by competitive relations, but by forgiveness.[34] Furthermore, Kierkegaard saw in his own city how a Christian community can easily devolve into an institution like any other, concerned purely with externals. Here we see perhaps the greatest difference between Cyril and Kierkegaard—Cyril kept secrets from his baptismal candidates partly to encourage moral reform in them, but also partly to form a communal identity in them. In Cyril's homilies, there is always clearly an "us" (orthodox, baptized Christians who had access to the sacraments) separated by secrecy from "them" (the heterodox or unbaptized) and from "you" (the candidates themselves, in the process of passing from "them" to "us"). The individual for Cyril is always part of a group; the members of that group bear responsibility for each other and for the traditions. Although Kierkegaard certainly encourages his readers to take responsibility for their neighbors, he has little to say in *Works of Love* about the Christian community of the church. At least, he has little good to say about it. Indeed, in nineteenth-century

---

33. Mark Dooley, *The Politics of Exodus: Kierkegaard's Ethics of Responsibility* (New York: Fordham University Press, 2001), 243.
34. Ibid., 234.

Copenhagen, in which it would be hard to find an unbaptized person or a schismatic, Kierkegaard thinks that some of the greatest dangers to an authentic Christian faith were in the church itself.

We see Kierkegaard's concern about worldly ideas creeping into the church in later deliberations. In "Love is a Matter of Conscience" he claims that it is a "misunderstanding of Christianity" to think that Christianity demands that one "betray the secret" by expressing "in a worldly way" how neighbor-love supersedes all familial and political attachments and duties (WL 144). In light of Kierkegaard's warnings to keep the secret of faith safe from corruption by the world, someone does not betray the secret simply in expressing neighbor-love's indifference to personal inclinations and obligations, but in doing so "in a worldly way," by expressing this truth in a way that makes Christianity accessible to worldly reason and categories. This notion of betrayal is echoed in a screed found in the last deliberation of the first series:

> Woe to the one who betrayed and broke the secret of faith and perverted it into public wisdom because he took away the possibility of offense! Woe to the one who could comprehend the secret of the Atonement without perceiving anything of the possibility of offense, and once again woe to him for thinking that thereby he would do God and Christianity a service. (WL 200)

Objectifying the faith cheapens it as surely as flooding the market would cause the price of spices to drop: "There are certain things, particularly the secrets of inwardness, that lose by being made public" (WL 136). The response to this problem must be to keep the faith hidden from the public, inaccessible to speculative philosophy or bourgeois morality. These do not make Christians anyway.

4

How Kierkegaard's Secret *Agape* Subverts Bourgeois Culture

Seeing oneself as a member of a community is not a distinctively Christian vision of society. Seeing each person as "the neighbor" is. At the beginning of a deliberation on "the neighbor," Kierkegaard takes care to "give to Christianity what is Christianity's, love of neighbor, of which no intimation is to be found in paganism" (*WL* 44). To be fair, I should note that Kierkegaard does not think paganism is devoid of love; he attributes erotic love and friendship entirely to paganism. But these forms of "preferential" love are in fact forms of self-love, in which the other is no more than an "*other I*" (*WL* 53). For Kierkegaard, you do not love the neighbor and therefore do not love in the distinctively Christian way if, in Robert Gibbs's words, you "can count on some preference and reciprocity of [your] special feelings."[1] Christian love is likewise distinguished from the "lower view of love" that is modeled on the practices of reciprocity that obtain in "the commercial world" (*WL* 237). To maintain their

1. Robert Gibbs, "I or You: The Dash of Ethics," in *The New Kierkegaard*, ed. Elsebeth Jegstrup (Bloomington: Indiana University Press, 2004), 144. Gibbs also rightly points out that the two greatest commandments, given in Matt. 22:37–40, including the command to love the neighbor, "are CHRISTIAN commandments because they were Jewish." Gibbs, 146.

peculiar Christian identity in their public lives in consumer-capitalist societies, then, Christians must ensure that their love is nonreciprocal. They must police themselves, so they do not undertake works of love in order to receive something in return. Such self-suspicion is necessary for a fallen humanity always ready to seek the lesser goods offered by the world in favor of those offered by God.

The present chapter explores a means for Christians to carry out this self-suspicion by rooting out the possibility that their neighbor love—which should govern all their actions in public life—is done in order to receive some worldly repayment. As I will demonstrate, concealing one's agency when performing a work of Christian love provides just such a means. This sort of concealment aims, like the concealment of Christian identity in public life that I am advocating in this book generally, to maintain the distinctiveness of Christian identity in modernity. The aim is accomplished by separating distinctively Christian moral norms from the prevailing economic norms of Christendom.

It might be easy to mistake Kierkegaard's suspicion of reciprocity for a disdain for all forms of self-love. In that case, a critic of Kierkegaard could see his position as at least problematic for Christians and at most untenable. While the model of Christian love is self-sacrificing, the merit of self-sacrifice hinges on the inherent value placed on self-preservation. Self-sacrifice for the sake of another is not equivalent to self-hatred. Moreover, Christian faith must be driven by a "self-interested" desire for beatitude and self-fulfillment in God. One can "find" one's life in Christ (Matt. 16:25). Kierkegaard does in fact recognize this. As Ferreira points out, Kierkegaard's relentless criticism of self-love is actually aimed at "selfish self-love," and that Kierkegaard recognizes "proper self-love" at the heart of the command to love the neighbor as yourself.[2] So although Christians do "find" themselves, they only do so if they first "lose" their life for Christ's sake, and not if they "want to save their life" (Matt. 16:25). Sacrificing selfishness comes before self-fulfillment. We also must not forget that Kierkegaard always wrote out of and for his own historical context, a context that is nonetheless basically similar to ours. Middle-class Europeans in Kierkegaard's time did

2. M. Jamie Ferreira, *Love's Grateful Striving: A Commentary on Kierkegaard's* Works of Love (New York: Oxford University Press, 2001), 31–36. See also *WL* 18 and 151.

not need to be reminded to love themselves. Indeed, a hallmark of modern Christendom is the view that God is purely providential: his "purpose" is to promote for you precisely the worldly goods you would seek for yourself anyway.[3] To Kierkegaard, the problem was that the modern bourgeoisie's narrow, materialistic conception of self-love was a far cry from a self-love that is genuinely compatible with Christian selflessness. Preaching any form of self-love to such an audience runs the risk of reinforcing a bad concept that in fact drives them further away from real Christian love.

Kierkegaard's desire to convince his contemporaries to replace an inferior form of self-love with a Christian one places him in concert with Pope Benedict XVI, who in the encyclical *Deus Caritas Est* maintains that Christianity rehabilitates forms of love it shares with non-Christians, putting them in proper order. Thus in Benedict's view, the Old Testament criticized Greek *eros*, but it

> in no way rejected *eros* as such; rather, it declared war on a warped and destructive form of it, because this counterfeit divinization of *eros* [in Greek religion] actually strips it of its divinity and dehumanizes it. . . . [E]ros needs to be disciplined and purified if it is to provide not just fleeting pleasure, but a foretaste of the pinnacle of our existence.[4]

Kierkegaard, then, writes in the tradition of the biblical authors when he tries to discipline modern self-love and to purify it of the selfishness upon which the modern economy is built. Kierkegaard acknowledges an appropriate Christian sense of self-love, but it would be futile to advocate it before sharply criticizing non-Christian, selfish self-love.[5] The fact that Kierkegaard called the various essays in *Works of Love* "deliberations" indicates that he hoped to remove defective ideas about love and replace them, not tinker with notions that were already basically sound. In his taxonomy, a "deliberation"

3. Taylor, *A Secular Age* (Cambridge, MA: Belknap Press, 2007), ch. 6. See especially p. 230.

4. Pope Benedict XVI, Encyclical Letter *Deus Caritas Est* (2005), 4.

5. Daphne Hampson shows that the ideas of proper self-love and the individual's self-fulfillment in God's love are present in Kierkegaard's thought to a far greater extent than his critics acknowledge. To Hampson, Kierkegaard's view of the self's relation to God in love is more "Catholic" than that of Luther and the Lutherans Rudolf Bultmann and Anders Nygren. See Hampson, *Christian Contradictions*, 249–84.

is intended for someone who is unacquainted with the subject of the deliberation.[6] It must be rhetorically forceful in order to shake its readers out of complacent unawareness of their mistaken notions. Like his answers to many modern problems, Kierkegaard's response to Christendom's distorted view of love sounds extreme (recall his image of indirect communication as one of inducing vomiting) because so much needs to be cleared away before modern people can begin to appropriate the truth. To the extent that Christians in a consumerist American society continue to hold to distorted views of love, Kierkegaard's bitter therapy is needed here, too, before proper self-love can flourish. In what follows, "self-interest" and "self-love" refer to the idea of distorted, "selfish" self-love prevalent in the modern West.

Forsaking Reciprocity

Trying not to receive credit or payback for good deeds goes well against the inclinations of people who are immersed in consumer capitalism. Because capitalism's principles—seek self-interest, maximize efficiency, negotiate shrewdly, acquire more than your competitors—work so well in raising people's standards of living,[7] it stands to reason (though deliberate thought has little to do with it) that these principles would be effective in other arenas, including moral life. The sociologist Robert Wuthnow showed in his 1991 book *Acts of Compassion* that although Americans volunteer at very high rates (forty-five percent of adults give five or more hours per week), they also expect their volunteer activity to be compensated in some way. Among those Wuthnow surveyed, "91 percent registered agreement with the statement, 'When you help someone in need, you get as much from it as they do.' Only a slightly smaller portion (78 percent) agreed with the statement, 'If I help others, it is likely that someone will help me when I am in need.'" This does

6. Ferreira, *Love's Grateful Striving*, 14.
7. See, for example, research by Angus Maddison, as cited in Dierdre McCloskey, "Avarice, Prudence, and the Bourgeois Virtues," in *Having: Property and Possession in Religious and Social Life,* ed. William Schweiker and Charles Mathewes (Grand Rapids: William B. Eerdmans, 2004), 326–28.

not necessarily mean that people volunteer primarily because they hope to be compensated, but it does strongly suggest that people think about volunteering in very much the same terms as they think about buying and selling and working. Religion seems to be doing little to counteract this basically consumer-capitalist paradigm for volunteer work. Although church programs are the outlets for much of Americans' volunteer spirit, people in Wuthnow's sample "were at a loss for words when asked to describe any specific religious teachings that might be relevant to their efforts to be kind and compassionate." Few, however, had difficulty explaining ways in which their volunteer work helped themselves, even if it led simply to some form of personal "fulfillment." One woman claimed in an interview that "it's a good bargain" if serving your self-interest happens to help another person.[8]

Wuthnow wonders how Americans can give so much of their time to others and yet be a nation of individualists who value self-interest above all else. Kierkegaard might answer that America has perfected the bourgeois ethic that weds Christianity to capitalism, such that giving to others is a "good bargain" because it fulfills both the love command and the desire to do well for oneself.

To sever just such a connection between commerce and Christian ethics, Kierkegaard places a number of obstacles in the way of the defective form of love he calls "*Gjenkjerlighed*," a word he coins by joining *Gjengjeld* (repayment) and *Kjerlighed*[9] (Christian neighbor love) in a term the Hongs translate as "reciprocal love" (*WL* 349). In condemning *Gjenkjerlighed*, Kierkegaard thereby demands that the Christian relinquish self-interest in practicing *Kjerlighed*. To Kierkegaard, "self-denial . . . is Christianity's essential form" (*WL* 56). The law of love "must be self-sacrificing and therefore without the requirement of any reward" (*WL* 130). One way to ensure that Christian love is self-sacrificing is to "remain in love's debt" to the neighbor. By insisting that we owe an infinite debt of love to others, Kierkegaard takes away the possibility for any sense of reciprocation or exchange: "When the left hand never finds out what the right

8. Robert Wuthnow, *Acts of Compassion: Caring for Others and Helping Ourselves* (Princeton: Princeton University Press, 1991), 56, 158, 38.
9. Ferreira, *Love's Grateful Striving*, 216.

hand is doing, it is impossible to make an accounting, and likewise when the debt is infinite" (*WL* 178).

Several additional obstacles Kierkegaard places in the way of reciprocity—thereby ensuring good works' distinctively Christian character—involve keeping aspects of the works hidden from the public. In the penultimate deliberation, Kierkegaard contends that recollecting the dead is one of "the two greatest good works" (*WL* 349), and it has the additional distinction of being an utterly unselfish work.[10] As Kierkegaard sees it, "When one wants to make sure that love is completely unselfish, one can of course remove every possibility of repayment. But this is exactly what is removed in the relationship to one who is dead" (*WL* 349). Kierkegaard's inclusion of a "work" that few of us would think of when asked to name a good deed incumbent upon Christians shows how he thinks that nonreciprocity is absolutely essential to maintaining the Christian character of moral activity. The dead provide an opportunity to "test yourself as to whether you love unselfishly" (*WL* 350–51). Recollecting them is a silent, unostentatious way of doing good for the dead, in contrast to the "crying and clamor" characteristic of those who love the dead "inordinately" and perhaps seek repayment from the crowd in the form of pity (*WL* 351). By loving the dead unselfishly, someone can gain valuable practice and experience in loving the living in such a way that one does not expect repayment. There is nothing the dead can offer us; we get no "return" on our investment of emotional or moral "capital" in them. The secular economy of reciprocity is broken down in the relationship to one who is dead by virtue of the veil (penetrable only from one direction) that stands between the living and the dead. As the proverb goes, "dead men tell no tales": the kindness shown to the dead by recollecting them will never be made known to another living soul.

Not surprisingly, Kierkegaard has been criticized for placing Christians' duties toward the dead so prominently near the top of the list of works of love; Theodor Adorno writes that Kierkegaard "demands that love behave toward all men as if they were dead."[11] Adorno also

10. The other greatest work, "to give a human life," is repaid with the joy parents take in their children (*WL* 349).

11. Theodor W. Adorno, "On Kierkegaard's Doctrine of Love," in *Søren Kierkegaard: Modern Critical Views*, ed. Harold Bloom (New York: Chelsea House, 1989), 23.

criticizes Kierkegaard for another of his means to forestall reciprocity for Christians' works of love: the invisible "gift" of mercifulness, which *"has nothing to give"* and *"is able to do nothing"* (WL 317, 323) and thereby does not on its own improve the material situation of the person to whom it is shown.[12] Others have shared Adorno's evaluation of these works of love.[13] Critics' offense regarding the deliberations on recollecting the dead and on mercifulness shows just how strange Christian ethics is, how far Christianity departs from worldly common sense. Christians are identified in part by the duties they incur that non-Christians do not. For example, Christian merchants have a duty to charge fair prices, but it is not their Christianness that imposes the duty; the fact that a good reputation is good for business makes it incumbent on all merchants to charge fair prices. We can, in fact, derive such a duty from self-interest alone, as Kant demonstrates.[14] Furthermore, redistribution of wealth is a Christian duty, but it is not a distinctively Christian one. Indeed, the duty can be derived without any appeal whatsoever to Christian principles, as Marx and Engels were doing while Kierkegaard was writing *Works of Love*. What the communists cannot derive from reason and history, however, is mercifulness.[15]

Kierkegaard places mercifulness ahead of even generosity. But what is the difference between them? Isn't it always merciful to give generously to the poor, whose obvious material lack causes them so much suffering? Not in itself, for relief to the poor can be given in an unloving or unmerciful way. Mercy is distinctively Christian, while generosity is not. Generosity is outward and worldly. It is conspicuous. The redistribution of wealth that generosity effects

12. Ibid., 28–29.

13. See Ferreira, *Love's Grateful Striving*, 292, note 3, for a catalogue of the critics of Kierkegaard's discussion of recollecting the dead.

14. Immanuel Kant, *Groundwork of the Metaphysics of Morals*, ed. and trans. Mary Gregor (Cambridge: Cambridge University Press, 1997), 11.

15. Kierkegaard claims in an 1847 journal entry that the deliberation "about mercifulness is also properly aimed at communism" (though *The Communist Manifesto* appeared a year later and Kierkegaard had only a vague idea of what communism was). Kierkegaard admits that he is keen to articulate a distinctively Christian view: in this deliberation, "the matter is given a completely different twist and a Christian one to be sure." Kierkegaard, *Papirer* VIII 1 A 299, as cited in Kierkegaard, *Papers and Journals: A Selection*, trans. Alastair Hannay (London: Penguin, 1996), 272. See also Joakim Garff, *Søren Kierkegaard: A Biography*, trans. Bruce H. Kirmmse (Princeton: Princeton University Press, 2005), 486, 503.

could even be mandated by law, with the ungenerous subjected to punishment. The distinctively Christian virtue of mercifulness, on the other hand, is inward and hidden. It can only be mandated by God, because God alone can recognize it and reward it and punish those who do not practice it. An example of mercifulness is "a poor woman who gives another the only bread she has" (WL 324). Giving the bread, something any observer can witness, is not in itself merciful; indeed, Kierkegaard insists that a person could be merciful even if he or she had nothing to give, perhaps by offering "a silent prayer sighed to God" on another's behalf (WL 324). But unless this poor woman tells someone else that she has given her *only* piece of bread away, no one will know that she mercifully relieved another person's hunger, possibly at the cost of going hungry herself. A painter could depict "that it is one piece of bread but not that it is the only one she has" (WL 325). The work's greatness derives from something that remains hidden in the secret recesses of the poor woman's subjectivity. Betraying that secret would no doubt invite either the replacement of the recipient's hunger with guilt, or else some kind of material repayment, as wealthy people might give the poor woman money or food out of pity, guilt, or congratulations. In either case, the result of the woman's mercy being public severely mitigates the mercifulness of the action, and so the woman's mercy must remain her secret. Mercifulness, as unseen, is an element in the "hidden life" of love—the life originating in God the unseen seer, conveyed through the inwardness of the individual—that provides the ground and justification for love's secrecy.

The fact that Kierkegaard emphasizes mercifulness over generosity does not mean that he thinks Christians do not have a duty to be generous. Their generosity, however, is not what marks them as Christians. Kierkegaard here seeks only to guard against people using their generosity alone as evidence of their practicing neighbor love. If a rich man announces that he has forgiven a debt owed by a poor man, he has acted generously—even magnanimously—and wins the acclaim of the public. The rich man has received his reward. But mercifulness makes a person "willing to give yet unwilling to make the confession that it is charity, as is the person who averts his face in order not to have the shame of having *others see* that he has honor from it, or as is the person whose left hand actually does not know what his right hand is doing" (*WL* 316–17). Here, it is not quite that Christian identity is intentionally concealed from the public, but rather that Christian identity is the intentional *concealment* of essential characteristics of the work.

Hiding Moral Agency "in a Dash"

Recollecting the dead severs ethics from the economic paradigms that hold sway in public life in one way, by giving quietly to people who are absolutely unable to repay their benefactors. Mercifulness does so in another, by giving nothing. Both of these ways involve secrecy insofar as the agent maintains reserve where he or she could easily make the work highly visible and gain pity or applause from people. In both cases, being ostentatious about the work would render it no longer a genuine work of Christian love, but rather a work of self-service, as the agent receives something in return for the work. A third and more radical way is to perform a work but to conceal one's agency in performing it, thus forestalling the possibility that the gift could be repaid because the beneficiary could not know whom to repay. Kierkegaard explores this third way in the deliberation "Love Does Not Seek Its Own."[16]

In "Love Does Not Seek Its Own," the "secret working" of love is tied intimately to the realization of the highest ethical and religious goods. Specifically, Kierkegaard claims, it is the common highest goal in both "civic" and "spiritual" life "to become one's own master" (*WL* 274), a slave neither to capital nor to sin. If this is "the highest," then "in love to help someone toward that, to become himself, free, independent, his own master, to help him stand alone—that is the greatest beneficence" (*WL* 274). Kierkegaard immediately attaches a qualification to this claim regarding the greatest beneficence: "the one who loves" must also know "how to make himself unnoticed so that the person helped does not become dependent upon him—by owing him the greatest beneficence" (*WL* 274). Love, then, is asymmetrical. I have a duty to accomplish the highest for another person and remain in love's debt to my neighbor, yet I must not allow the

16. My argument in this section is richly informed by Robert Gibbs's insightful essay, "I or You: The Dash of Ethics," in Jegstrup, ed., *The New Kierkegaard*, 141–60.

other to become indebted to me or expect the highest in return. Here is one of the many points where Ferreira has shown affinities between Kierkegaard and the twentieth century Jewish philosopher Emmanuel Levinas.[17] The difference between Kierkegaard and Levinas, however, is in the metaphors used. Levinas describes this asymmetry in terms of height—the other is "above" me because he can command me to serve him, yet also "below" me because he is destitute and desperately needs my help.[18] Kierkegaard puts this relationship in economic terms, and the choice of metaphor is not arbitrary, as he is once again attempting to block consumer-capitalist thinking's inroads into Christian moral thought.

Insofar as it is a part of Kierkegaard's project of purging Christian ethics of economic paradigms, performing the greatest beneficence is a form of indirect communication. "[T]he greatest beneficence, to help the other to stand alone, cannot be done directly" (WL 274) because the benefactor has to protect the autonomy of the beneficiary. If I publicly help another to stand by himself or herself, then I will almost assuredly be thanked profusely by that person. He or she will feel indebted to me and therefore will not truly stand by himself or herself, because it will be recognized that I propped the person up. In that sense, if, for instance, I publicly resolve to help an alcoholic overcome his addiction, I have released that person from slavery to alcohol, but I have become the person's master in its place. I have not performed the greatest beneficence, because—even if I am a less destructive master than liquor had been—the recovering alcoholic is still not his own master. Kierkegaard articulates this problem with a simple *argumentum reductio ad absurdum*: "The greatest benefaction, therefore, cannot be done in such a way that the recipient comes to know that it is to me that he owes it, because if he comes to know that, then it simply is not the greatest beneficence" (WL 275).

"On the other hand," Kierkegaard continues, "if someone says, 'This person is standing by himself—through my help' and what he says is true, well, then he has done for this person the highest that one human being can do for another, has made him free, independent,

---

17. Ferreira, *Love's Grateful Striving*, 163, 216–22.

18. See Emmanuel Levinas, "Transcendence and Height," in *Basic Philosophical Writings*, ed. Adriaan T. Peperzak, Simon Critchley, and Robert Bernasconi (Bloomington and Indianapolis: Indiana University Press, 1996), 11–31.

himself, his own master, and just by hiding his help has helped him to stand by himself" (*WL 275*). One might reasonably ask what the difference is between "This person is standing by himself through my help" and "This person is standing by himself—through my help." Kierkegaard answers this question with a meditation on the significance of a typographical em dash: in Danish, a *Tankestreg*, which literally means, "thought-line." Here the thought-line signifies that what follows in the quotation is thought but not spoken. It is an intentional mental reservation, a quantum of knowledge disclosed to no other person. In other words, the dash indicates the presence of a secret. This secret—that it is "through my help" that this other stands by himself or herself—is the very qualification that distinguishes the greatest beneficence from lesser forms of beneficence.

It is not difficult at all to avoid saying that another person stands by himself through my help, but that secret can easily be discovered if my actions are obvious enough. To counter the possibility of such a discovery, then, Kierkegaard demands that Christians use this dash not only to stop themselves from taking credit for good works, but to hide their agency in practicing the works themselves, placing a veil of secrecy between their agency and those whom it aids. If Christians can do this, then the neighbor truly can become his own master, for he can see no one to whom he might owe a debt.

This *is* difficult, and to some, laughably so. The theologian Kathryn Tanner ridicules this sort of notion in a parody of postmodern analyses of the "impossibility" of gift-giving. To ensure a gift's "purity of motive," there must be "no possibility of a return of any sort—not even gratitude, not even self-congratulation." Therefore, "Complete anonymity in giving is a must. . . . In case [recipients] find out who gave it to them, it would be a good idea if the gift were not appreciated; the recipients should not like their presents—no temptation to make a return, then!" The effort to forestall reciprocity must be absurd, Tanner thinks, because "No one else benefits, and you don't either."[19] While Kierkegaard is not named as Tanner's target here, he may be guilty by association with a theorist of gift-giving like Jacques Derrida, who Tanner *does* name and whose book *Given Time* is seen

19. Kathryn Tanner, *Economy of Grace* (Minneapolis: Augsburg Fortress, 2005), 61.

by many as having deep affinities with *Works of Love*.[20] But it is not necessary to interpret the impossibility of performing the greatest beneficence anonymously in the way that Tanner interprets Derrida's theory of gift-giving. Rather, as Ferreira explains, Kierkegaard's repeated insistence on the impossibility of fulfilling the love command (whether because the debt is infinite or because anonymity must be total) must be understood in the context of the command's already being fulfilled by Christ and the consequent availability of the grace Christians need to fulfill the command themselves.[21] Kierkegaard wants his readers to avoid complacently assuming that they have ever "done enough" to fulfill the command and to be "appropriately 'humbled' to know our total reliance on grace."[22] This sort of impossibility is not meant to discourage Christians from trying to conceal their identity when performing beneficent works, but to point out to them that this kind of work is unlike the ordinary works they undertake in their secular lives. Ordinary work accomplishes the possible. Distinctively Christian works of love accomplish the impossible—with God's help.

Still, we can imagine a few concrete examples of works done in this fashion. If, for instance, someone happens upon another person who needs medical help but who cannot get to the hospital, a work of love would be, clearly, to take the person to the emergency room. Someone who helped another in this way would be a latter-day Good Samaritan. But to fulfill Kierkegaard's requirement that the benefactor hide his or her agency, he or she would have to resist the temptation to visit the beneficiary in the hospital later on. Such a visit would present little benefit for the sick person, but it could have great benefit for the person paying the visit: the sick person might thank his or her benefactor, praising him or her up and down as a living saint. Similarly, if someone wanted to help a poor family, one could find out who their landlord was and pay their rent for them. There is no need to let the family know who helped them; telling them would in fact be gratuitous, again inviting a form of worldly repayment.

20. E.g., Gibbs, "I or You," 143; Ferreira, *Love's Grateful Striving*, 164–67; Dooley, *The Politics of Exodus: Kierkegaard's Ethics of Responsibility* (New York: Fordham University Press, 2001), 194–246.
21. Ferreira, *Love's Grateful Striving*, 121–24.
22. Ibid., 123.

As a test for determining the rightness of one's actions within a certain moral context, the dash plays a role in Kierkegaardian ethics analogous to the categorical imperative's role in Kant's ethical system. Because the categorical imperative is objective, knowable purely from the *a priori* exercise of reason, it is decidedly not a secret to anyone. It is utterly common knowledge, and in principle, no one would need to be taught the categorical imperative as one should be able to figure it out on one's own. As a publicly accessible test for maxims of action in the public realm of the ethical, the categorical imperative is the gold standard for the Enlightenment moral economy. Kant's examples of the categorical imperative in action, such as setting honest prices for goods or promising to repay a creditor, show that it dovetails well with bourgeois public life.[23] But Kierkegaard fears that the intimate relationship between Protestantism and capitalism that Enlightenment ethics reflects has been bad for Protestantism, resulting in the banalities of liberal theology and the elevation of good manners as the highest ethical expression of Christianity. Kierkegaard's standard, self-concealment, accomplishes the same as Kant's standard, but whereas Kantianism serves as an effective social lubricant in bourgeois society, Kierkegaard refuses to allow Christianity to be subordinated to culture. Unlike the safeguard against immoral action that Kant prefers, the shining light of putatively objective reason, the dash (like mercifulness and the silent recollection of the dead) indicates the hidden inwardness of the individual's subjectivity as the decisive force in determining a course of moral action.

Kierkegaard highlights the difference between Christian ethics and even the most virtuous secular ethic by introducing the example of Socrates. Because Kierkegaard and Socrates (or at least, Kierkegaard's Socrates) share a similar view about the necessity of concealing one's agency in helping another person, Kierkegaard can say with confidence, "In this understanding of what it is to help another human being, the one who truly loves and that noble rogue [Socrates] agree" (*WL* 276). Kierkegaard imagines Socrates, too, hiding himself in a dash, speculating that

23. Kant, *Groundwork of the Metaphysics of Morals*, 11, 32.

when the work [of helping another to be free] was completed, he said very softly to himself: Now this individual is standing by himself. But then we come to the dash, and with the dash a smile comes upon the lips of that noble, yet roguish one, and he says, "Now this individual is standing by himself—through my help." He keeps to himself the secret of this indescribable smile. (*WL* 277)

For Socrates, secret agency is "the art, to have been able to do everything for the other person and pretend as if one had done nothing at all" (*WL* 277). But there is a difference between saying something "very softly" and not saying anything at all. And there is a difference between smiling and displaying no outward reaction at all. Socrates smiles and congratulates himself for helping the other to stand by himself. As noble and virtuous as Socrates is, he remains a rogue who wants to be paid back—even in a small way, even only through self-congratulation—for his good works.

Christians, Kierkegaard thinks, must hold themselves to a more rigorous standard. The genuine lover who hides her love has one additional qualification that Socrates lacks: "for the loving person this dash means something different from a smile. . . . [T]he dash . . . (but please note that it is not noticeable) is like a heavy breath, *almost* like a deep sigh" (*WL* 277, my emphasis). It is the silent sigh of hidden inwardness, distinct from the self-satisfied smile the noble rogue flashes. The next sentence contains a surprising double reference to the pseudonymous literature that gives some sense of what is contained in that sigh: "In this dash are hidden the sleeplessness of anxiety, the night watch of work, the almost desperate exertion; in this dash is hidden a fear and trembling that has never found any expression and for that very reason is all the more terrible" (*WL* 277). *The Concept of Anxiety* is signed by a pseudonymous night watchman (Vigilius Haufniensis); *Fear and Trembling* reports on the hidden trial Abraham underwent. In each of these pseudonymous texts, the author maintains that the invisible sign of the single individual is his or her hidden inwardness, whether that inwardness takes the form of anxiety or silence. Hence, the difference between Socratic secret agency and Christian secret agency is the additional secret—signaled by the inaudible sigh—of hidden inwardness that the Christian lover bears.

To bear this secret is also to bear responsibility. Although it is the greatest beneficence to help another to become his or her own master, "the one who loves . . . has also understood the danger and the suffering in the midst of the work, and above all the terribleness of the responsibility" (*WL* 277–78) to help another realize his or her full autonomy. Secrecy renders this responsibility all the more solemn, as the beneficiary should have no idea whom to blame or call into account if the benefactor's attempt fails. Worldly justice is indeed suspended here, though only in this one respect, for the secrecy Kierkegaard advocates for the greatest beneficence is ordered toward realizing the highest ideal of justice in giving to each person the self-mastery he or she deserves as a bearer of God's image.[24] This deliberation implies that a purely liberal notion of justice, in which every action is accounted for in plain sight so that reward and punishment can be meted out in perfect proportion to each person's desert, cannot attain "the highest" ideal of civic or spiritual life, for it cannot permit the secrecy required to enable the greatest beneficence. In chapter 7, I will explore in more detail how secrecy dovetails with the responsibility to care for others and suspends responsibility as the duty to uphold the moral law.

The gift of self-mastery is at the same time a second—and also noneconomic—gift, in which the giving of it does not cause the giver to lose what he or she already has. This kind of giving is, if not uniquely Christian, then at least directly counter to the worldly economy that is based on competition over scarce resources. As Tanner observes, "giving to others and having oneself are simply not in competition with one another in a theological economy."[25] Someone who practices works of love "possesses" faith—he has God as "his confidant" (*WL* 279). Because the lover already has a relationship (of conscience or confidence) with God, and has it in full, and not only latently, then in helping the other to stand, the lover is secretly acting to initiate the other into the relationship with God that the lover already has. In Martin Andic's

24. Mark Dooley argues that Kierkegaard shares with Jacques Derrida a conception of justice that suspends legalism, in certain cases, in order to achieve the ideal of realizing higher forms of justice for "the lowliest, whose singularity (hidden and secret) has been crushed by the law and who are urgently in need of some justice." Dooley, *The Politics of Exodus*, 220.

25. Tanner, *Economy of Grace*, 83.

words, "more fully knowing ourselves as we truly are in knowing and being known by God, requires us to help others to this truthfulness and knowledge, just as loving and being loved by him requires helping others to this love."[26] One of the chief moral dangers secrecy poses, according to liberal accounts of morality—namely, that initiatory secrecy can rob another person of his or her autonomy by preventing the person from knowing everything he or she would need to make a fully informed, voluntary decision[27]—is completely inverted in this initiation. In this process, the true practitioner of love completely gives away the power he or she holds by virtue of the secret, thereby granting full autonomy (self-mastery) to the beneficiary of the work and retaining no ability to coerce and no means of receiving credit for the service rendered.

By making one's own agency invisible, one leaves the other nowhere to turn in gratitude for having received uprightness except to God. By virtue of hiding "in a dash," the practitioner of this initiation "is completely and wholly transformed into simply being an active power in the hands of God. This is why his activity cannot be visible. His activity, after all, consisted in helping another or other persons to become their own masters, something they in a certain sense were already" (WL 279). The gift, self-mastery, "looks as if it were the recipient's property" (WL 274). In this manner, all works of love originate in the secret of faith, but, through this initiatory aspect to the greatest beneficence, the works also return to the secret of faith, enabling another to receive what the practitioner of the work has also been given. It is a deception, to be sure, but a necessary one, to help people attain the highest goods, for "*to help another person to love God is to love another person; to be helped by another person to love God is to be loved*" (WL 107, italics in original).

Conclusion: Secrecy against Christendom

A major aim of Kierkegaard's entire authorship was to reinvigorate and revalue Christian faith in a time when bourgeois modernity had

26. Martin Andic, "Confidence as a Work of Love," In *Kierkegaard On Art and Communication*, ed. George Pattison (New York: St. Martin's Press, 1992), 175.
27. E.g., Sissela Bok, *Secrets: On the Ethics of Concealment and Revelation* (New York: Vintage, 1982), 56–58.

rendered faith a breezy and flimsy willow branch. The historical situation meant that someone who doubted whether he might be Christian would be sent to the "geography book," which showed very clearly that "the predominant religion in Denmark is Lutheran-Christian."[28] Kierkegaard feared that modernity, through philosophy, government, and economics, had cheapened Christianity, and his proposed solution was to make the individual the primary locus of returning Christianity to authenticity. It should be obvious by now that Kierkegaard employs this tactic in *Works of Love*, providing a challenging program for the individual to have an authentic faith and to practice Christian neighbor love, even if the culture encourages spiritual laxity.

Or even if the church does. Recall Kierkegaard's screed against the "apologists" within the church who "ingratiatingly" remove the harshness and offense of the essentially Christian. Kierkegaard has plenty of venom for "the one who betrayed and broke the secret of faith and perverted it into public wisdom because he took away the possibility of offense" (*WL* 200).[29] According to Bruce Kirmmse, Kierkegaard's polemic against "Christendom" hinges upon his desire to maintain the distinction between "inner" and "outer"—the distinction on which secrecy and, to Kierkegaard, Christianity itself, hinges. Christianity, then, becomes endangered when secrecy, too, is endangered, when the age becomes superficial enough to believe that outwardness is all, that those things that do not appear to the senses or to the naked "I think" do not have existence. As Kirmmse writes,

> For SK, the incognito of Love must be maintained—despite the fact that this leads to misunderstanding, incomprehensibility, and opposi-

---

28. Kierkegaard, *Concluding Unscientific Postscript to* Philosophical Fragments, vol. 1, ed. and trans. Howard V. Hong and Edna H. Hong (Princeton: Princeton University Press, 1992), 50.

29. Bruce Kirmmse contends in *Kierkegaard in Golden Age Denmark* that the diatribe is aimed at the rationalist theologian Martensen (an early intellectual rival who quickly surpassed Kierkegaard as a scholar) and at the dispenser of "cheap grace," Bishop Mynster (the Kierkegaard family's longtime pastor). Both Martensen and Mynster represented, for Kierkegaard, the complete alliance of Christianity with German philosophy and bourgeois capitalism. Kirmmse, *Kierkegaard in Golden Age Denmark* (Bloomington: Indiana University Press, 1990), 322–23.

tion in the world—or all would be lost for Christianity. In fact, if all could be seen outwardly in a fixed relation to the inward, Christianity would no longer be possible, SK asserts.[30]

To the extent that the church gives up on the distinction between inner and outer, gives up on offense, gives up on the idea that there is something decisive in being Christian, it ceases to be Christian. In that case, according to Kierkegaard, "we should not hesitate . . . to preach **against** Christianity in *Christian*—yes, precisely in *Christian* sermons" (*WL* 198).

Clearly, Kierkegaard's anger toward the Danish Lutheran Church of his time was strong, and it was so largely because the church had, Kierkegaard thought, discarded the principle that enables one to recognize the difference between Christianity and culture. His displeasure with the Danish Lutheran Church was perhaps best illustrated in the incident when, on his deathbed, Kierkegaard refused to receive communion from a pastor (his own brother!) who visited him, claiming that "The pastors are the servants of the Crown and have nothing to do with Christianity."[31] In his view, Europe would be able to see Christianity in its distinctiveness and its offensiveness only through reform of the inner: the individual, the inward, the world of human conscience. Without first reclaiming this secret realm, Christianity cannot even begin to form itself as a church in, but not of, the world.

Kierkegaard believed that he lived in a time dominated by technological, cosmopolitan consumerism. In fact, he was living proof. Perhaps we should read *Works of Love* as Kierkegaard's way of struggling with his own relationship to the economic system of his day (and to his merchant father), which, after all, provided so well for him. Kierkegaard's anger at the church is one facet of his anger at everything smacking of the bourgeoisie out of which he came—and came into money.

One night after speaking with Kierkegaard, the pastor and scholar C. J. Brandt wrote of being struck by his friend's "conclusion that

30. Ibid., 317.
31. Account of Emil Boesen, Oct. 19, 1855, *Encounters with Kierkegaard: Alice as Seen by His Contemporaries*, trans. Bruce H. Kirmmse and Virginia R. Laursen, ed. Bruce H. Kirmmse (Princeton: Princeton University Press, 1996), 125–26.

from now on he was going to read only 'writings by men who had been executed.'" Brandt seems to have been convinced by Kierkegaard that "there is something to be learned only from those who have offered their lives for their convictions." Although Brandt in this note refers to Kierkegaard as "the ironist," he seems not to have entirely picked up on the irony of Kierkegaard's remark. Brandt writes that here "it is of course quite obvious to think of Christianity: all the way from our Savior himself to the least of the martyrs, they indeed offered their lives for what they said."[32] But Jesus left no writings. Neither did Socrates, the other executed figure who haunts all of Kierkegaard's work. But if we take Kierkegaard at all seriously here, the anecdote indicates that the writings of Dietrich Bonhoeffer, hanged by the Gestapo in April 1945, would have passed the test and been worthy of reading. Indeed, in Bonhoeffer's project of developing a "religionless Christianity" appropriate to public life in modernity, he seems to preach "against Christianity in Christian" writings. As we shall see, this version of Christianity in public life, too, demands disciplines of secrecy.

---

32. Diary of C. J. Brandt, Sept. 1, 1843, in Kirmmse, ed., *Encounters with Kierkegaard*, 59.

5

Bonhoeffer's *Arkandisziplin*

Christian Confession in a World Come of Age

A martyr (*martyros* in Greek) is a witness. Christian martyrs witness to the truth of Christianity through their willing submission to death in the face of worldly persecution. To Athanasius in the fourth century, the prevalence of Christian martyrdom was nothing less than a complete proof that Christ has decisively defeated death and opened the door to eternal life. If there were no hope for resurrection, he thought, no one would willingly submit to death.[1] Martyrdom need not be associated with a bloody death, however; the crowns used in Orthodox marriage rites suggest martyrdom—the couple's visible witness to Christ's love.[2] Neither sense of martyrdom is conceivable apart from a Christian identity visible to the world beyond the confines of the church.

1. St. Athanasius, *On the Incarnation* 27, ed. and trans. a religious of C.S.M.V., introduction by C. S. Lewis (Crestwood, NY: St. Vladimir's Seminary Press, 1993), 57–58.

2. Paul Evdokimov, *The Sacrament of Love: The Nuptial Mystery in the Light of the Orthodox Tradition*, trans. Anthony P. Gythiel and Victoria Steadman (Crestwood, NY: St. Vladimir's Seminary Press, 2001), 154–55, as cited in Eugene F. Rogers, Jr., ed., *Theology and Sexuality: Classic and Contemporary Readings* (Oxford: Blackwell, 2002), 53.

One twentieth-century Christian readily and widely considered a martyr is Dietrich Bonhoeffer, the German Lutheran theologian and pastor who was imprisoned and executed by the Nazis for participating in a plot to assassinate Hitler.[3] Bonhoeffer is frequently praised for the seamless unity of his thought and action, particularly in his tragically true profession that "Whenever Christ calls us, his call leads to death."[4]

Given Bonhoeffer's widely accepted (if not canonical) status as one whose witness to Christ led him to die like Christ at the hands of a brutal power with imperial aspirations, it would be easy to suppose, as Stanley Hauerwas does, that Bonhoeffer in his theology wants Christians to be unambiguously upfront about their Christian identity. It would be easy to assess his total theological and political project as "the attempt to reclaim the visibility of the church as the necessary condition for the proclamation of the gospel in a world that no longer privileged Christianity."[5]

It would also be incorrect. While it is certainly true that Bonhoeffer frequently calls for Christian visibility in the world, he does not make visibility into a normative category that thereby excludes hiddenness altogether.[6] Secrecy is a highly important theme in Bonhoeffer's theology, at least as important as public witness is, such that no assessment of Bonhoeffer can be complete without acknowledging the need he sees to conceal Christian liturgy, prayer, and moral action. In fact, Bonhoeffer taught and wrote—in his university and seminary lectures,

---

3. For a study of Bonhoeffer's participation in the German resistance and the plot against Hitler, see Larry Rasmussen, *Dietrich Bonhoeffer: Reality and Reistance* (Louisville: Westminster John Knox, 2005).

4. Bonhoeffer, *Discipleship*, vol. 4 of *Dietrich Bonhoeffer's Work*, ed. Geffrey B. Kelly and John D. Godsey, trans. Barbara Green and Reinhard Krauss (Minneapolis: Fortress, 2003), 87. Hereafter, references to this volume will be parenthetical, *D* and page number.

The more famous—but less faithful—translation, "When Christ calls a man, he bids him come and die" is from Dietrich Bonhoeffer, *The Cost of Discipleship*, rev. ed., trans. R. H. Fuller (New York: Macmillan, 1963), 99.

5. Stanley Hauerwas, *Performing the Faith: Bonhoeffer and the Practice of Nonviolence* (Grand Rapids: Brazos, 2004), 34.

6. The manifold and seemingly contradictory strains in Bonhoeffer's theology contribute to the wide divergence of projects for which Bonhoeffer's thought has been employed since his death: liberal, conservative, radical, pacifist, secularist, and so on. See Stephen R. Haynes, *The Bonhoeffer Phenomenon: Portraits of a Protestant Saint* (Minneapolis: Augsburg Fortress, 2004).

in the most important book he completed, and in his prison letters to Eberhard Bethge—that making one's identity as a Christian *invisible* to secular public life was the "necessary condition" Hauerwas seeks. In what we can read as a concise summary of Bonhoeffer's belief that conditions in modernity necessitated Christian secrecy, he wrote to Eberhard Bethge's newborn son from Tegel prison that

> Our church . . . is incapable of taking the word of reconciliation and redemption to mankind and the world. . . . It is not for us to prophesy the day (though the day will come) when men will once more be called so to utter the word of God that the world will be changed and renewed by it. . . . Till then, the Christian cause will be a silent and hidden affair, but there will be those who will pray and do right and wait for God's own time.[7]

Together, the hidden prayer, liturgy, and moral life of the church as it actively waits "for God's own time," when everything will be revealed in the Eschaton, comprise the *Arkandisziplin*, a ruling category for the stance Bonhoeffer thought Christians should take toward the modern world.

Bonhoeffer's *Arkandisziplin* means that Christians confess their Christian identity in secret and conceal that identity in public. The ways they confess that identity can take the form of verbal professions of faith, prayer, and the liturgy and sacraments. As I will show in this chapter, all of these forms of confession are meant to be done entirely behind closed doors, made visible only to other Christians. These forms of confession are the characteristic activities of the Christian "public" (to use again Alan Wolfe's sense of the term[8]), highly relevant to the dominant public life of the secular nation and economy but not thereby thrown open to it. The next chapter covers the distinctively Christian form of public life that Bonhoeffer calls "being for others"—actively ministering

7. Dietrich Bonhoeffer, *Letters and Papers from Prison*, enlarged ed., ed. Eberhard Bethge (New York: Touchstone, 1997), 300. Hereafter, references to this volume will be parenthetical, *LPP* and page number.

8. Wolfe, "Public and Private in Theory and Practice: Some Implications of an Uncertain Boundary," in Jeff Werntraub and Krishan Kumar, eds., *Public and Private in Thought and Practice: Perspectives on a Grand Dichotomy* (Chicago: University of Chicago Press, 1997), 198.

to the specific needs and sufferings of people in the secular sphere through "extraordinary" or "righteous" deeds. While this activity must be visible in the same sense that Kierkegaard insisted that Christians' works of love should bear visible fruits, the Christian identity of the one who exists for others must not be intentionally revealed. We will see that this latter requirement does not necessarily mean that no one will find out that the person doing the work for others is a Christian, but the Christian must never become so self-conscious that he or she ever tries to make his or her Christian identity known. Both aspects of the *Arkandisziplin* are measures that protect the "costliness of grace" and prevent Christians from seeking righteousness in the eyes of other human beings rather than in the eyes of God.

As we have seen already with Cyril's use of secrecy in the liturgy and Kierkegaard's advocacy of secrecy for Christian moral life, secrecy is a strategy meant to address the church's need to preserve its members' distinctive identity at a specific moment in the history of its contact with the secular. The same is true for Bonhoeffer's call for secrecy. Although many of the deeds that have contributed to Bonhoeffer's historical significance were done in secret to prevent Nazi authorities from disrupting them—for example, his teaching at an underground seminary for the Confessing Church and his participation in the *Abwehr* conspiracy against Hitler—Bonhoeffer's call for the *Arkandisziplin* did not occur in a time when Christians were incessantly persecuted by the state. While some Christians, including some in Bonhoeffer's circle, were imprisoned, sent to concentration camps, and put to death, this persecution was not widespread and did not remotely approach the systematic oppression and murder of millions of Jews. Bonhoeffer's fairly consistent advocacy of the *Arkandisziplin* from 1932 to his last extant writings in 1944 suggests that the point of secrecy was not to protect Christians against political persecution. Indeed, secrecy would not have been necessary at all for very many Protestants early in the Third Reich; its usefulness as a safeguard against persecution would have been limited primarily to pastors or those seeking leadership positions in the Party in later years. As the historian Richard Steigmann-Gall has argued, "the anticlericalism of the Nazis was not simply the product of an ideological opposition to all Christian religion."[9] Rather, Bonhoeffer's immediate historical context was one in which, despite the vocal anti-Christian paganism of some prominent Nazis, many Nazi leaders considered themselves and their agenda to be basically Christian. Furthermore, Germans overwhelmingly remained (tax-paying) members of their churches during the Third Reich. Any Nazi campaign against Christianity had little noticeable effect at all on church membership, the most reliable historical indicator of Nazism's effect on ordinary German Christians.[10] In these respects, Bonhoeffer's context shares much with Kierkegaard's, as Christianity could still be assumed as the religious substructure of the nation, and even with Cyril's, as rank-and-file Christians did not need to fear persecution. Bonhoeffer himself also shares with Cyril and Kierkegaard considerable social privilege—he was a professor, quite cosmopolitan, and the son of a prominent physician—and so we can see his theological critique as (like theirs) a form of bourgeois self-understanding, an attempt to show Christians who want to remain privileged how to do so without thereby reducing Christianity to bourgeois morality or the norms of the prevailing public sphere.

The eschatology that suffuses much of Bonhoeffer's writing makes his context also appear far broader than the confines of Nazi Germany. The references in his letters to the "world that has come of age" (*LPP* 327) indicate that he is addressing a "religionless" modernity in which enterprises like art and science thrive without appeal to God. To Bonhoeffer, this is a welcome development, as it frees the church from having to regulate every human social and intellectual endeavor. Moreover, as the above quotation from Bonhoeffer's baptismal address to Dietrich Bethge indicates, the historical context that matters the most is the church's position in the time before "God's own time." The *Arkandisziplin*, then, must be considered as a temporary measure, but not temporary in the sense of, "until the fall of Hitler." It is temporary until the secular passes away entirely, in history's ultimate moment. Until then, Christianity may continue

9. Richard Steigmann-Gall, *The Holy Reich: Nazi Conceptions of Christianity, 1919–1945* (Cambridge: Cambridge University Press, 2003), 264.

10. Doris L. Bergen, "Nazism and Christianity: Partners and Rivals? A Response to Richard Steigmann-Gall, *The Holy Reich: Nazi Conceptions of Christianity, 1919–1945*," *Journal of Contemporary History* 42 (2007): 29.

to be part of the rhetorical toolkit of the power-hungry. But Christians can do much to preserve the integrity of their faith and even halt the rise of deeply unjust regimes if they begin to consider, as Bonhoeffer did, the concealment of Christian identity in public life as normative, though with limits in the most extreme cases.

One final introductory note. In this chapter I do not translate the word *Arkandisziplin* except when quoting another author, in order to distinguish Bonhoeffer's concept from the ancient practice of the "discipline of the secret"—a term that would be the most accurate English rendering of *Arkandisziplin*. Any other concise English translation of the German word is misleading. "Secret discipline" suggests that it is a church discipline (like catechesis or confession) that is being kept secret; this captures only part of Bonhoeffer's notion, as gaining proficiency or mastery in the activity of keeping things secret is a large part of what the discipline is about. "Arcane discipline" suffers from the additional shortcoming of connoting intellectual obscurity—like number theory or wizardry—more than intentional concealment of something otherwise intellectually graspable. Only "discipline of the secret" would do. It is true, as we shall see, that Bonhoeffer's notion of *Arkandisziplin* drew from the parallel notion in antiquity. But we shall also see that his *Arkandisziplin* is very much his own, and it should rightly be distinguished from the practice of Cyril and his contemporaries. John W. Matthews's rendering, "responsible sharing of the mystery of Christian faith,"[11] seems exactly right, as it captures the *Arkandisziplin*'s note of caring for the tradition and its ultimate aim of revealing and passing on Christian identity at appropriate times; it is a bit too cumbersome, however, to be repeated frequently.

One Week in 1944: A Way into the Question

Most scholarly attention to the *Arkandisziplin* begins by noting two places where the term appears in letters Bonhoeffer wrote to Bethge

11. John W. Matthews, "Responsible Sharing of the Mystery of Christian Faith: *Disciplina Arcani* in the Life and Theology of Dietrich Bonhoeffer," *Dialog* 25 (1986): 19–25.

over the course of a single week during Bonhoeffer's imprisonment in Tegel. On the face of it, this hardly seems like enough warrant for declaring the *Arkandisziplin* to be essential to Christian discipleship. But Bonhoeffer wrote about the idea of intentionally concealing the confession of faith, using the term *Arkanum* in an early lecture on ecclesiology, as far back as 1932. He then used the term *Arkandisziplin* in his 1935–36 lectures at Finkenwalde, so that the idea's appearance in the prison letters is really a reappearance. Furthermore, the idea is closely related to the hiddenness of Christian life that Bonhoeffer writes about in his 1937 book *Discipleship*. Bonhoeffer also fleshes out the idea without mentioning it by name in other letters from Tegel. In L. Gregory Jones's words, "The significance of the term far exceeds the two brief references to it in the *Letters*."[12] I will draw in this chapter from all of the above-mentioned sources, but to set out the basics of the *Arkandisziplin*, I begin where most other scholars do.

One of the "brief references" comes in Bonhoeffer's letter of April 30, 1944. Shortly after his oft-quoted litany of questions about what a "religionless" theology, sermon, and church could be, Bonhoeffer asks, "Does the secret discipline, or alternatively the difference . . . between penultimate and ultimate, take on a new importance here?" (*LPP* 281). Bonhoeffer's next sentence is, "I must break off for today," so we get no immediate elaboration of the point. The second reference to the *Arkandisziplin* comes in the May 5, 1944, letter to Bethge. Bonhoeffer, still wrestling with the meaning of the "non-religious interpretation," criticizes Karl Barth's "positivist doctrine of revelation," saying that it "isn't biblical." Rather, Bonhoeffer writes, "There are degrees of knowledge and degrees of significance; that means that a secret discipline must be restored whereby the *mysteries* [*Geheimnisse*] of the Christian faith are protected against profanation" (*LPP* 286).

The entire issue of the *Arkandisziplin* arises while Bonhoeffer seeks to explain his "non-religious interpretation" of Christianity, in which otherworldly and individualistic concerns are shorn away

12. L. Gregory Jones, "The Cost of Forgiveness: Grace, Christian Community and the Politics of Worldly Discipleship," in *Theology and the Practice of Responsibility: Essays on Dietrich Bonhoeffer*, ed. Wayne Whitson Floyd, Jr., and Charles Marsh (Valley Forge, PA.: Trinity Press International, 1994), 160.

for the sake of ministering to the suffering masses of this world. But insofar as the *Arkandisziplin* is a protective discipline, whereas nonreligious Christianity seeks to love without reserve, the two ideas seem to complement each other dialectically. Bethge himself notes in his monumental biography of Bonhoeffer that the *Arkandisziplin* serves as "the indispensable counterpoint of nonreligious interpretation" of Christianity: it protects the distinctiveness of Christian doctrine and "guarantees [Christian] identity."[13] The need for protection and guarantees arises because of the danger that the worldliness that "religionless" Christianity demands could easily become indistinguishable from secular rationalism or the common sense of the *Zeitgeist*. For Bethge, the relationship between worldliness and the *Arkandisziplin* as mutual correctives prevents them from becoming "meaningless and banal. Arcane discipline without worldliness is a ghetto, and worldliness without arcane discipline is nothing more than a boulevard."[14]

It is clear that the letters place *Arkandisziplin* and religionlessness in relation, and *Arkandisziplin* is certainly ordered toward protecting Christian identity in the Christian's public life. But in spite of Bethge's attempt to lend clarity to the two puzzling references in the letters to him, his own interpretation stands in need of clarification. The relationship between concealment and hiddenness in Bonhoeffer's theology is not simply that Christians have a hidden life behind the walls of the church and a public one beyond them, for the sake of which the Christian leaves the trappings of his or her Christian identity entirely behind in the church's vestibule. As I will demonstrate, there is disclosure within the boundaries set up by the *Arkandisziplin*, and the Christian's public ethical activity is qualified by a secrecy that shrouds the Christian identity that the individual Christian carries into public life. Thus the counterpoint appears as much *within* Christians' ecclesial lives and *within* their public lives, as it does *between* their ecclesial and public lives. Furthermore, both the confession of faith in secret and concealment in public life serve the same end of maintaining the distinctiveness of Christian identity

13. Eberhard Bethge, *Dietrich Bonhoeffer: A Biography*, rev. ed., ed. Victoria A. Barnett, trans. Eric Mosbacher, et al. (Minneapolis: Augsburg Fortress, 2000), 881, 880.
14. Ibid, 884.

in the face of a secular world that is both independent of the church and badly in need of transformation.

Perhaps the dialectic between Christians' obligation toward the world and their obligation toward their own tradition culminates in a single duty derived from Christians' understanding of Christ himself. To Andreas Pangritz, Christians were saddled with two primary obligations in dealing with the historical situation in twentieth-century Germany: an ethical requirement to maintain a public silence in response to their failure to obey the "concrete command" to resist fascism, and the ecclesiological requirement to fortify the church's distinctive identity and forbid an overly close association with the world. Both of these are taken up in the christological requirement to understand Jesus as the "man for others" to whom alone Christians owe their allegiance.[15]

It is often hard to separate Christology from eschatology in Bonhoeffer's thought,[16] but it would be a mistake to allow the essential question about Christ to obscure the fact that the *Arkandisziplin* hinges on an understanding of time that is not finally reducible to an answer to the question of Christ's identity. We see the temporal orientation of the *Arkandisziplin* in remarks like the one already quoted: that for now, "the Christian cause will be a silent and hidden affair, but there will be those who will pray and do right and wait for God's own time" (*LPP* 300). The focus on eschatology has been suggested by Rachel Muers, who understands Bonhoeffer's theology of God's and humans' silence not only christologically, but also in terms of the distinction between the penultimate and the ultimate. Bonhoeffer saw secrecy as a requirement only in the peculiar historical conditions of the "penultimate" stage in salvation history. Beginning from Bonhoeffer's equation of the ultimate as "the last word" and the penultimate as a period of God's silent listening, Muers argues in part that human practices of silence, including patient listening to others, can participate in this divine

---

15. Andreas Pangritz, *Dietrich Bonhoeffers Forderung einer Arkandisziplin: eine unerledigte Anfrage an Kirche und Theologie* (Köln: Pahl-Rugenstein Verlag, 1988), 467–68.

16. For a summary of Bonhoeffer's Christology that wrestles with the difficulty of defining what Christology even means for Bonhoeffer, see Pangritz, "'Who is Jesus Christ, for us, today?'" in *The Cambridge Companion to Bonhoeffer*, ed. John W. de Gruchy (Cambridge: Cambridge University Press, 1999), 134–53.

silence.[17] While we must bear in mind that silence and secrecy are not equivalent, and so Muers's interpretation of Bonhoeffer will not map perfectly onto mine, we can see that the eschatological approach attends closely to the *limits* of secrecy and Christians' public lives: the times and even the places where Christians must dispense with secrecy in order to preserve their integrity and identity (I address this issue in the next chapter). In the prison theology and in *Discipleship*, we will see Bonhoeffer work out the conditions under which Christians must make themselves and their specifically Christian commitments known in public life.

Confessing Christian Identity in Secret: Hidden Liturgy and Prayer

In the May 5 letter, Bonhoeffer acknowledges that the *Arkandisziplin* is not his invention, but a restoration of an older way of thinking: "a secret discipline must be restored whereby the *mysteries* of the Christian faith are protected against profanation" (*LPP* 286). Although this sentence is meant to count against Barth's so-called "positivist doctrine of revelation," in which every Christian doctrine is equally obscure to the ungraced mind, Bonhoeffer's remark calls attention to the theological principle that the liturgical discipline of the secret rests upon—namely, the recognition that there is a limit to what the unbaptized should be taught. Bonhoeffer's earlier writings show an abiding interest in the liturgical discipline of the secret practiced in the ancient church. In light of this interest, his proposal for the modern *Arkandisziplin* appears to share both the form and the purpose of practices like the ones Cyril of Jerusalem employed to negotiate the relationship between Christian identity and public life. The call from Tegel is in fact an echo both of this ancient tradition and of Bonhoeffer's scholarly work in the 1930s: Christians must conceal their liturgical and prayer lives in order to protect Christian identity from being corrupted by Christians' importing into the church the patterns of worldly thinking—including economic paradigms, status-consciousness, and advantage-seeking—that hold sway in public life.

17. Rachel Muers, *Keeping God's Silence: Towards a Theological Ethics of Communication* (Malden, MA: Blackwell, 2004), chs. 3, 4, and 6.

In lectures on ecclesiology delivered at Berlin in 1932, Bonhoeffer places confession at the heart of what it means to share a Christian identity with other members of the church. This confession contributes to the liturgy's role in separating Christians from non-Christians: "No religious service should be without the confession of faith. This differentiates the community from the general public."[18] The identity maintained by confession "ought to be clear and unequivocal," not only for the community itself, but for the sake of "nonbelievers . . . so that we don't drive them away from the church."[19] We can already see that Bonhoeffer's ecclesiology shares emphases with Cyril's. For both thinkers, the liturgy, both preaching the Word and celebrating the sacrament, is a site for the articulation of Christian identity. There is a strong line of distinction between believers and nonbelievers. Faithful ministry to nonbelievers will include refraining from preaching to them about the sacraments, the creed, and other Christian formulas, which nonbelievers could not truly understand. Furthermore, the church's obligation to care for its traditions benefits not only the church's members, but also those who are not (or are not yet) members.

For my purposes, the most significant affinity between Bonhoeffer's ecclesiology and Cyril's is that in these lectures, Bonhoeffer places the distinguishing characteristics of church membership behind a veil of secrecy: rather than being "propaganda" in a campaign against the world, "The confession of faith belongs . . . to the 'Discipline of the Secret' (*Arkanum*) in the Christian gathering of those who believe. Nowhere else is it tenable."[20] It is not meant to be shared in "dialogue" with unbelievers (or, for that matter, in witness of the gospel to the worldly). Verbal revelations of Christian identity should be reserved strictly for times when Christians are only with each other. They are inappropriate for public activity, as non-Christians lack the means to make spiritual use of such formulations.

One difference between Bonhoeffer and Cyril is in the content of the confession. Bonhoeffer in these lectures explicitly states that the

18. Dietrich Bonhoeffer, "The Nature of the Church," in *A Testament to Freedom: The Essential Writings of Dietrich Bonhoeffer*, rev. ed., trans. Geffrey B. Kelly, ed. Geffrey B. Kelly and F. Burton Nelson (San Francisco: HarperSanFrancisco, 1995), 85.

19. Ibid., 86.

20. Ibid.

Apostle's Creed, "The Bible, the Our Father, and baptism . . . are not the confession of faith."[21] Rather, the confession is a "religionless" (and strikingly evangelical) one, consisting in "immediate presence" before God, to whom the individual states only, "I acknowledge and confess your truth, O God."[22] In spite of this religionless interpretation of the confession, baptism remains a decisive marker of Christian identity for Bonhoeffer. Baptism grants the ability to perform a dual confession. Baptized Christians confess to the church in the "word of recognition between friends":[23] a watchword, perhaps, in the fashion of Cyril's use of the creed as a secret password in the *redditio symboli* rite. Baptism also enables Christians to confess to the world by means of wordless deeds.[24] I will explore the latter sort of confession in the next chapter.

Later lectures display a continuing concern with concealing liturgy and confessions of faith from the public. When he was a seminary professor, Bonhoeffer taught about the discipline of the secret and commended its recovery to his students. In his 1935–36 homiletics course at the illegal Confessing Church seminary at Finkenwalde, Bonhoeffer correctly identifies the Eucharist, the creed, and the Our Father as forbidden to catechumens and other outsiders in antiquity. In citing 1 Corinthians 14:23 in support of the discipline of the secret, Bonhoeffer suggests that maintaining the offense of Christian belief, prayer, and sacrament need not entail actively inviting public scorn.[25] Throwing open the doors of a church in which Christians are speaking in tongues unintelligible to outsiders would in fact damage the faith by giving non-Christians the perverse impression that the Christians were insane or drunk.[26] In two lectures on catechetics given in February 1936, Bonhoeffer traces the history of the catechumenate from Tertullian to Augustine and beyond, acknowledging Cyril of Jerusalem as a significant contributor to the development

21. Ibid.
22. Ibid.
23. Ibid.
24. Ibid.
25. Dietrich Bonhoeffer, *Werke*, vol. 14, *Illegale Theologen-Ausbildung: Finkenwalde 1935–1937*, ed. Otto Dudzus and Jürgen Henkys in collaboration with Sabine Bobert-Stützel, Dirk Schulz, and Ilse Tödt (Gütersloh: Chr. Kaiser Verlag, 1996), 526.
26. See Raymond F. Collins, *First Corinthians*, Sacra Pagina, vol. 7 (Collegeville, MN: Liturgical Press, 1999), 509.

of the catechumenate and the discipline of the secret. Bonhoeffer emphasizes how ancient catechumens were led through a succession of stages that culminated in their receiving the sacraments.[27] By having catechumens pass through these stages, presenting different prayers, doctrines, and rites to them at each successive stage, the ancient church acknowledges the "degrees of knowledge and degrees of significance" that Bonhoeffer affirms in the May 5 letter (*LPP*, 286). Eschewing a "positivist doctrine of revelation," then, is the doctrinal prerequisite for the liturgical discipline of the secret, in which one is led by degrees into the mysteries of Christian life and doctrine.

Bonhoeffer's concern in these lectures eventually goes beyond description and turns to recommending a restoration of the discipline of the secret for the twentieth-century church. Bonhoeffer laments that while "the Catholic Church has in some respects retained the discipline of the secret," Lutherans "have given it up."[28] He sees the contemporary practice of only allowing the confirmed to share the Lord's Supper as "a last feeble remnant" of the discipline of the secret.[29] But Bonhoeffer hopes that this remnant will grow. By relating the discipline to Luther's liturgical practices, which required that a penitential rite or an "examination of faith" based on the catechism precede the Lord's Supper, Bonhoeffer in the second lecture attempts to justify finding a place for the discipline in the Lutheran worship of his own time.[30]

It is tempting to think that Bonhoeffer's advocacy of the discipline of the secret in 1935–37 is purely the product of his immediate context of teaching at an illegal seminary and training pastors for an underground church. Although Bonhoeffer mentions in a lecture on catechetics that persecutions sometimes demanded that secrecy surround Christian prayer and worship in antiquity, he indicates later in the same lecture that the discipline of the secret was primarily meant as a means of preventing the church from squandering its inheritance.[31] Like Cyril of Jerusalem did, Bonhoeffer proposed the

27. Bonhoeffer, *Illegale Theologen-Ausbildung*, 546–51.
28. Ibid., 550. My translation.
29. Ibid., 551. My translation.
30. Ibid., 551.
31. Ibid., 549, 550.

concealment of the liturgical markers of Christian identity not to protect Christians from persecution, but to prevent them from allowing the world—including Christians' own public lives—to compromise the liturgy's integrity, a perennial need for the church.

Nurturing Disciples in Secret

Bonhoeffer's published work from this period exhibits a similar interest in recovering the liturgical discipline of the secret in modernity. In *Discipleship*, published in 1937, Bonhoeffer finds a place for the discipline of the secret within his larger theological project of expounding the meaning of following Christ. Here the discipline of the secret is a means to safeguard costly grace—"grace as God's holy treasure which must be protected from the world and which must not be thrown to the dogs" (*D* 45). Paradigmatically, this discipline is necessary in periods of rapid Christianization. After lamenting the ease with which Germany became a "Christian" nation, Bonhoeffer writes,

> Is the price that we are paying today with the collapse of the organized churches anything else but an inevitable consequence of grace acquired too cheaply? We gave away preaching and sacraments cheaply; we performed baptisms and confirmations; we absolved an entire people, unquestioned and unconditionally; out of human love we handed over what was holy to the scornful and unbelievers. We poured out rivers of grace without end, but the call to rigorously follow Christ was seldom heard. What happened to the insights of the ancient church, which in the baptismal teaching watched so carefully over the boundary of the church and the world, over costly grace? (*D* 53–54)

Bethge echoes Bonhoeffer's words here in stating in a 1977 article that "Hitler never forbade the preaching" of a gospel of cheap grace. In the Nazi era, "Forgiveness of sins was preached in such a way that the whole thing petered out to nothingness," without any acknowledgement of "God's justice over against" human beings.[32] To Bonhoeffer and Bethge, the church fell short in its mission

---

32. Eberhard Bethge, "Prayer and Righteous Action in the Thought of Dietrich Bonhoeffer," *Currents in Theology and Mission* 4 (1977): 198.

to Germany—centuries ago and in the contemporary period—by failing to sift out the essentially Christian from the pagan. This church erected no boundaries and demanded nothing in the way of discipleship. It presumed, perhaps, that grace would turn Germans into disciples after they were already baptized and confirmed, and it failed to recognize that baptism already ought to be discipleship. Bonhoeffer equates costly grace with a boundary, for without the boundary, the grace the church dispenses through the sacraments cannot be costly. Indeed, "The expansion of Christianity and the increasing secularization of the church caused the awareness of costly grace to be gradually lost. The world became Christianized; grace became common property of a Christian world. It could be had cheaply" (D 46).

In bemoaning cheap grace, Bonhoeffer is by no means advocating works righteousness. Rather, the cost in discipline and suffering accompanies the reception of grace; it is not a payment for it. The idea that grace can be earned—and the ensuing search for cheaper, more efficient means to acquiring that grace—is, in fact, worldly thinking of the sort that Kierkegaard criticized. Costliness of grace, then, is the recognition that grace is not for sale at all. Giving one's life to—or for—Christ *is* grace. As Bonhoeffer writes later in *Discipleship*, "In baptism we receive both community with Christ and our death as a gift of grace" (D 208).

The secularization of Europe in modernity offers the churches an opportunity to call once again for people "to rigorously follow Christ," with the recognition that this must entail intentionally keeping people at an arm's length from the sacraments, concealing them, not until the people "earn" the grace of the sacraments, but until they have passed through the stages of spiritual development that lead from unbelief to curiosity and finally to genuine faith and the desire to follow Christ.[33] Bonhoeffer, then, calls for an honest reckoning with the difficulty of becoming a disciple, and the harm

---

33. Bonhoeffer, *Illegale Theologen-Ausbildung: Finkenwalde 1935–1937*, 551. Incidentally, conversion *from* Christianity to thoroughgoing Nazism was seen by Heinrich Himmler as requiring a slow process through stages for much the same reason. As Himmler wrote in 1937, Nazi officials should take their time in leaving the church, so as to do so "out of true conviction, [rather] than for someone to follow a fashion, and do it only externally." As cited in Steigmann-Gall, *The Holy Reich*, 221–22.

that can be done to both the church and the would-be disciple if grace is seen as the common possession of a church with many public privileges. Bethge believes that the church in Germany missed its chance to reform after the war, but instead of following the example of the Confessing Church Bethge and Bonhoeffer belonged to and "depend[ing] totally on free-will offerings," it remained the beneficiary of taxes levied in return for the service it rendered to the nation.[34] But recognizing that Bonhoeffer addressed his theology to a broad modern context and not only to mid-century Germany reveals that in all periods, whether the world is adopting or giving up Christianity, the church must always have a specific identity to transmit to its members, an identity that grows out of the "concrete demand"[35] laid on those who follow Christ.

The two references to baptism in the passage about costly grace from *Discipleship* suggest that Bonhoeffer thinks that the sacraments are important enough markers of Christian identity to be placed behind the veil of the *Arkandisziplin*. In the April 30, 1944, letter to Bethge, Bonhoeffer asks, "What is the place of worship and prayer in a religionless situation?" right before asking if the *Arkandisziplin* "take[s] on new importance here," suggesting that liturgy should be kept hidden. In the May 5 letter, he refers to the *Arkandisziplin* protecting "the *mysteries* of the Christian faith." These "mysteries" likely include not only the doctrines of the Trinity and the virgin birth that Bonhoeffer mentions in the same paragraph, but also the sacraments, which, as we saw in chapters 1 and 2, were concealed from catechumens in antiquity by bishops whose word for "sacrament" was "*mystērion*."[36] Recall that the creed also was subject to the discipline of the secret, and that bishops like Cyril of Jerusalem warned baptismal candidates that they should keep the formula of the creed secret, lest "any heretic pervert any of the traditions."[37] Bonhoeffer, like the bishops of the ancient church, wants to keep the world out of the church, so that authentically believing, professing,

---

34. Bethge, "Prayer and Righteous Action in the Thought of Dietrich Bonhoeffer," 197.

35. Bonhoeffer, "The Nature of the Church," 83.

36. The German word translated as "*mysteries*" in the April 30, 1944, letter is "*Geheimnisse*," which means both "secrets" and "mysteries."

37. Cyril of Jerusalem, *Catechesis* 5.12–13.

and practicing Christians would not have their traditions distorted by worldly opportunists seeking cheap grace and public benefits for a nominal Christianity without discipleship. Furthermore, any honest account of the sacraments and Christian verbal formulas must recognize that those who lack faith only deceive themselves into thinking they understand and can make positive spiritual use of the sacraments and formulas; indeed, even those with faith often fail to comprehend the purposes of God's grace.

Bonhoeffer's continued advocacy of the *Arkandisziplin* in light of his study of the historical discipline of the secret suggests that his 1932 statement that "The Bible, the Our Father, and baptism . . . are not the confession of faith"[38] should not be taken to mean that Bonhoeffer saw these as inessential or as things that should be shared openly with the world. The less evangelical-sounding Bonhoeffer of *Discipleship* and the prison letters recognizes that the sacraments are important markers of Christian identity; they, too, are parts of the "confession of faith" that distinguishes Christians from non-Christians and is subject to the *Arkandisziplin*.

Like the liturgy and the rites of Christian initiation, prayer is an action that confesses Christian faith and that Bonhoeffer believes ought to be done in secret. Bonhoeffer's fullest explanation of the necessary hiddenness of prayer appears in the section of *Discipleship* in which he explains how the model of discipleship presented in the Sermon on the Mount can take shape in modernity. There, Bonhoeffer sees all prayer as petitionary; the one praying hopes to receive something, but as Jesus teaches in Matthew 6, that person can receive what he or she wants either from God or from other people. Because "Genuine prayer . . . is the request of the child to the heart of the Father" who already knows what the child needs, "prayer is never demonstrative, neither before God nor before ourselves, nor before others. . . . Prayer is necessarily hidden. It is the opposite of a public act in every way" because it is addressed to God and never to any human being (*D* 153). When prayer receives a human audience, it "degenerates into empty phrases." Even solitary prayer can lose its authenticity by receiving a self-conscious audience of the one praying. Echoing the theme of Matthew 6, Bonhoeffer warns

---

38. Bonhoeffer, "The Nature of the Church," 86.

Christians against receiving any kind of earthly reward for their piety. A self-conscious prayer runs a similar risk of degenerating as a prayer on a street corner could. Bonhoeffer states that in self-conscious prayer, "I hear myself. Because I do not want to wait for God to listen to me, . . . I construct my own hearing of my prayer. I observe that I prayed piously, and this observation provides the satisfaction of being heard. . . . Because I have given myself the reward of public acclaim, God will give me no further reward" (D 154). The confession of faith in God's providence that comes in petitionary prayer, then, must, to remain genuine, be so concealed from a human audience as to be concealed even from self-reflection. The left hand must not be allowed to learn what the right is doing. The antidote to self-consciousness is humility: the death to self and to the worldly expectation of reward, which allows Christ to live and pray within the Christian (D 154, 160–61).

Conclusion

Despite this very high standard of ensuring that prayer is not demonstrative, Bonhoeffer recognizes that Christians must pray together. But their prayer together must not become an occasion for self-righteous posturing or campaigning for influence within the church—doing so is a classic example of bringing worldly thought and behavioral patterns into the church where they don't belong. Jesus in the Sermon on the Mount sets righteousness before other human beings and righteousness before God in competition; either way, one will receive one's reward. Because of the danger of the self-deceptive quest to appear righteous before others, Christians must instead remain chastened by the teaching against hypocritical public prayer: "Although genuine prayer is hidden prayer, that does not exclude the possibility of community prayer, provided that it has become clear how great are the dangers of common prayer" (D 154). This points to a limit on the *Arkandisziplin*. The discipline is in certain rare circumstances inappropriate, and, as I shall show in the next chapter, ultimately gives way to supreme visibility.

6

The Limits of *Arkandisziplin* and of the Secular

The complement to confessing Christian identity in secret is concealing it in public life. The discipline of conducting Christian liturgy and prayer behind closed doors, addressed in the previous chapter, is intentional: the boundary between the church and the world must be maintained through vigilantly ensuring that baptism is not conferred lightly and that Christian prayer seeks the benefits of God's providence and not of worldly recognition. But this discipline is the prerequisite for the unreflective, unintentional discipline of secrecy that we have already seen Bonhoeffer advocate for prayer, and which obtains all the more in Christian moral life. Moral life, preeminently neighbor love, is the primary mode of Christians' activity in the public sphere, and thus can be the gateway to compromising the distinction between Christian identity (especially a "religionless" Christian identity) and worldliness. If their religious identity fully informs their lives, then Christians will seek to bring their positions on political matters, their purchases and investments, the way they do their jobs, and even the way they interact with strangers on the bus into coherence with the Christian moral tradition. But adhering to this moral tradition will often not result in worldly success. The temptation to depart from or debase the tradition is no doubt great when it seems to conflict with the natural imperative to provide for one's family. Still, Bonhoeffer is confident that the demands of the gospel do not "have to be rejected by people who work and worry about their daily bread, their jobs, and their families," as if those demands were "the most godless tempting of God" (*D* 38). There must be a way for Christians to care for the tradition they have been charged with while participating in the secular life of politics, the economy, and the workforce. This chapter begins by showing how Bonhoeffer thought it was possible. In short, it can only be done if Christians conceal their Christian identity in public, cultivating a paradoxical "disciplined unconsciousness" about that identity. Later in the chapter, I show how the *Arkandisziplin* takes account of its—and the world's—limits, yielding ultimately to the revelation of Christian identity.

Recall that Cyril's liturgical discipline of the secret was done in part to encourage newly baptized Christians to maintain their moral purity. Recall as well that Kierkegaard insisted that Christians' secret faith and prayer must issue in works of love, which themselves are meant to be secret. For both authors, the secret of liturgy or prayer leads to the secret of Christian ethics (though in neither case is it accurate to say that they *terminate* in ethics). The same is true of Bonhoeffer, who, with respect to secrecy, may be the *Aufhebung* of Cyril and Kierkegaard, the one who reveals that these two are, despite their differing outlooks and emphases, indeed each part of a single Christian tradition. For these thinkers, the relationship between a Christian's liturgical and moral life is not that the former is hidden while the latter is manifest. Rather, secrecy must guide Christian moral life, too. In Bonhoeffer's thought, the *Arkandisziplin* requires the Christian to conceal the distinctively Christian character of his or her good works. This protects the costliness of grace by forestalling the possibility of seeking a worldly reward for the works. In this way, the Christian can follow Christ by being entirely "for others" (*LPP* 381) in his or her public activity, liberated by selflessness from the temptation to make something of his or her identity as a Christian.

The call to conceal Christian identity in Christians' public activity of good works came throughout Bonhoeffer's career, as we shall see through a review of the same sources I drew upon in the previous chapter. The constancy of Bonhoeffer's call for an *Arkandisziplin* that encompasses Christian morality, along with the idea's close relationship with Bonhoeffer's ecclesiology, eschatology, and theology of justification by faith, shows that the *Arkandisziplin* is much more than a passing notion Bonhoeffer had during one week in Tegel. It is in fact a category that should govern the whole of Christian life.[1]

Concealing Christian Identity in Public: Deeds of Hidden Righteousness.

In the 1932 lectures on ecclesiology, after noting that the "confession of faith" is only "tenable" when it is guarded by secrecy "in the Christian gathering of those who believe," Bonhoeffer grants that Christians do have something to confess to the world:

> The primary confession of the Christian before the world is the deed which interprets itself. If this deed is to have become a force, then the world itself will long to confess the Word. This is not the same as loudly shrieking out propaganda. This Word must be preserved as the most sacred possession of the community. This is a matter between God and the community, not between the community and the world. It is the word of recognition between friends, not a word to use against enemies.[2] This attitude was first learned at baptism. The deed alone is our confession of faith before the world.[3]

In this passage we see, in highly compressed form, the dialectical relationship between confessing Christian identity in secret and concealing Christian identity in one's public activity. Here, Bonhoeffer places the verbal confession of faith strictly within the Christian assembly and demands that Christians' public witness be done with wordless

---

1. On "life" as a guiding theme in Bonhoeffer's religionless Christianity, see Rolf K. Wüstenberg, *A Theology of Life: Dietrich Bonhoeffer's Religionless Christianity*, trans. Doug Stott (Grand Rapids: Eerdmans, 1998), esp. 112–46.

2. The translation glosses over a sentence here that translates, "In the ancient church one had if anything to guard against enemies." See Bonhoeffer, *Das Wesen der Kirche*, in *Gesammelte Schriften*, vol. 5, ed. Eberhard Bethge (Munich: Chr. Kaiser, 1972), 259.

3. Bonhoeffer, "The Nature of the Church," in *A Testament to Freedom: The Essential Writings of Dietrich Bonhoeffer*, rev. ed., trans. Geffrey B. Kelly, ed. Geffrey B. Kelly and F. Burton Nelson (San Francisco: HarperSanFrancisco, 1995), 86.

deeds. To be sure, "the deed which interprets itself" is an odd locution. It is clearer in the German, in which "It interprets itself" is a separate sentence.[4] The lack of a comma between "deed" and "which" in the above translation seems to imply that Bonhoeffer is distinguishing these deeds from deeds that do not interpret themselves. But in that case, Bonhoeffer has written a sizable hermeneutical IOU, as he still needs to explain what kinds of deeds do not interpret themselves. The simplest way around this problem is to maintain the comma between "deed" and "which," thereby placing "which interprets itself" in apposition to "the deed," as John Matthews does in his rendering: "The primary confession of the Christian community is the deed, which interprets itself. When the deed becomes a powerful thing, then the world will inquire about the verbal confession behind such deeds."[5] "The deed," then, is distinguished from "the Word," or perhaps simply from words of confession that could be used to interpret Christians' deeds in the world. Christians need give no explanation for their righteous deeds in the world; they need not tell the world, "I am doing this because I am a Christian." Another commentator straightforwardly equates "the deed which interprets itself," the "*arcani disciplina*," and "prayer and righteous action in the world."[6] As I have been trying to show, there is greater nuance to the relationship among these three elements: the *Arkandisziplin* ensures that the dual demands of prayer (which is done in secret) and righteous action (which needs no word of explanation) do not break down the distinction between the church and the world and thereby compromise Christian identity.

Furthermore, deeds alone, done in silence, are a Christian's mission to the world, drawing persons to a willingness to make the verbal confession of faith. Bonhoeffer, then, shares Kierkegaard's confidence in neighbor love's ability to transform the neighbor. Limiting one's mission to deeds has two advantages over "loudly shrieking out propaganda." First, it preserves the tradition's distinctiveness by refusing to reduce it to terms that the worldly could appreciate.

4. "Das erste Bekenntnis der christlichen Gemeinde vor der Welt ist die Tat. Sie interpretiert sich selbst." Bonhoeffer, *Das Wesen Der Kirche*, 259.

5. John W. Matthews, *Anxious Souls Will Ask. . .: The Christ-Centered Spirituality of Dietrich Bonhoeffer* (Grand Rapids: Eerdmans, 2005), 66.

6. Peter Selby, "Christianity in a World Come of Age," in *The Cambridge Companion to Dietrich Bonhoeffer*, ed. de Gruchy, (Cambridge: Cambridge University Press, 1999), 243.

Even "dialogue" with nonbelievers does too much, in Bonhoeffer's view, to accommodate the gospel to worldly ears. There is in fact no good reason to tell non-Christians that one is a Christian at all. The primary duty to them is to love them.

The verbal confession of faith that comprises the community's relationship with God, then, identifies Christians to each other: a password or watchword (in German, *Parole*), of sorts, for people who keep a secret from the world but who share secrets with each other. The intimacy of members of the church must be that of close friends, like Bonhoeffer and Bethge, for whom "it would be silly to have any secrets from" each other, but who carry out a secret correspondence (*LPP* 319).[7]

Eschewing propaganda in favor of a mission of deeds has a second advantage in forestalling self-righteousness. "While the church is in the world and is even a bit of the world," and thus the temptation to claim all of the world's high ground as its rightful territory is acute, the church "cannot hope to represent itself as a visible communion of saints. Secularity means renunciation of the ideal of [moral] purity." That is, the church has work to do in the world, but it must not set itself above the world or "justify itself . . . before the world."[8] It can only hope to be counted as justified *coram deo*—before God. What Daphne Hampson has said of Luther is equally true of Bonhoeffer: "the attempt to be righteous *coram hominibus* may lead a person further from God!"[9]

Secrecy about a Christian's religious identity, then, acts as a measure against the temptations to flout the gospel's "extraordinary" moral demands, to forget that one is a sinner, and to seek righteousness *coram hominibus*. This is why the lessons of Matthew 5, to live visibly holy lives, are followed by the exhortations to secrecy in Matthew 6. Bonhoeffer recognizes that these two chapters "collide hard against each other" (*D* 149). In exploring the seeming conflict between them in *Discipleship*, Bonhoeffer deepens the theology he gives in succinct form in the lectures on ecclesiology. In *Discipleship*, he maintains that Christians witness to the world through

7. See also Rachel Muers, *Keeping God's Silence: Towards a Theological Ethics of Communication* (Malden, MA: Blackwell, 2004), 203.
8. Bonhoeffer, "The Nature of the Church," 87.
9. Hampson, *Christian Contradictions*, 39.

deeds—here characterized as "extraordinary," sharply distinct from ordinary worldly actions—but keep the secret of their Christian identity through a disciplined unselfconsciousness. Bonhoeffer later characterizes this sort of faith as *fides directa*; he associates it with the faith of newly baptized children, but claims that it can be reacquired by adult Christians.

The section on Matthew 6, titled "Hidden Righteousness," is strikingly similar in both theology and tone to Kierkegaard's *Works of Love*, not least because Bonhoeffer is here dealing with the gospel's paradoxical demands. For Kierkegaard, love issues from a "hidden source" into works that make it "recognizable by its fruits," though the agency of the one doing those works must in turn be hidden. Bonhoeffer notes in this section that in the righteousness demanded of Christian life, "something has to be visible, but—paradoxically: beware that it does not happen for the sake of being seen by people" (D 149). The very distinctiveness of Christian moral life, "that which steps away from the world" (D 146), can become a fetish. Christians take their identity from the fact that their lives are supposed to rise "above the world" (D 146), opening the door to a triumphalist desire to defeat or deny the world, not heal and transform it. The way through this paradox is to conceal Christians' righteousness. The will to demonstrate to others that one is righteous is nothing extraordinary at all; it is rather a typical aim in worldly existence. Thus "Jesus," in demanding the extraordinary, "calls a halt to our thoughtless, unbroken, simple joy in what is visible" (D 148). Those who follow him need to "watch out for" extraordinariness, ensuring that it does not "happen in order to be seen" (D 148).

Bonhoeffer is not calling here for people to conceal their entire personal identity when doing righteous works in public, as if they need to perform these works only behind their beneficiaries' backs. Bonhoeffer is, however, calling for the specifically Christian character of Christians' deeds—their extraordinariness—to be hidden. But "from whom should the visibility of discipleship be hidden?" Bonhoeffer answers, "Not from the other people, for they are to see the light of Jesus' disciples shining. Rather, it should be hidden to those doing the visible deed of discipleship" (D 149). His answer makes it seem at first that Christians have license, and even the obligation, to make their identity as Christians utterly apparent to the public, yet somehow hidden from themselves. But we soon learn that hiddenness from self and hiddenness from others are not in competition. In fact, hiddenness from self is primary simply because it *encompasses* hiddenness from others. If a man commits an "extraordinary" act, but he remains unaware that the act is one of Christian discipleship—that is, he takes no satisfaction in thinking that it is "the Christian thing to do" because to him it is the *ordinary* thing to do—then he surely is not making known to others that the act was done for the sake of discipleship. How could he? In order to tell another person that he feeds the hungry because that is how one follows Christ, then the man would necessarily also have to be self-conscious about the distinctively Christian character of the act. By ruling out self-consciousness, Bonhoeffer also rules out intentionally displaying one's discipleship to others.

Bonhoeffer's position here recalls Kierkegaard's contention in *Works of Love* that Socrates' efforts at helping another to stand by himself were not "the greatest beneficence" precisely because Socrates became self-satisfied. Also as with Kierkegaard, for whom "there are no *mine* and *yours* in love" (WL 265) because all belongs to God, Bonhoeffer sees no ground for self-satisfaction, because "You should not know your own goodness," for otherwise "it will really be *your* goodness, and not the goodness of Christ" (D 150–51). Because all goodness is ultimately Christ's, "the goodness of discipleship takes place without awareness. The genuine deed of love is always a deed hidden to myself" (D 151).

Bonhoeffer's position is distinguished from Kierkegaard's in that the former is not advocating the *active* concealment of Christian identity in moral matters. Rather, in maintaining that discipleship should be hidden from oneself, he is advocating a cultivated unreflectiveness with respect to Christian discipleship. This unreflectiveness is born of a healthy self-suspicion about the un-Christian uses to which Christians can put their identity. Christians are saddled with a paradoxical task, as they need to develop the habits of extraordinary behavior, but in doing so, they must not think that there is anything extraordinary about it: "reflection . . . needs to be guided so that we do not stray into reflection about our extraordinariness. Our paying attention to our righteousness [in Christ] is supposed to support our not paying attention to our righteousness" before the world (*D* 149). In place of reflection on their righteousness (which is not properly theirs, anyway), "[t]he only required reflection for disciples is to be completely unreflective in obedience, in discipleship, in love" (*D* 150). They become this way by not reflecting on themselves at all. Instead, disciples "look only to their Lord and follow him" (*D* 150).

Bonhoeffer reiterates the need for disciples to "look only to their Lord" in a later chapter in *Discipleship* on "The Saints." Although such a statement can seem platitudinous, the contrast between the activities of "looking" versus "speaking" highlights how careful Bonhoeffer is to ensure that Christians remain unostentatious about their religious identity in public life. As with the fruits of righteousness, "the fruit of sanctification" will be seen in works of love (*D* 268). No one could deny the results of the works: the truth was spoken, the naked were clothed, the grief-ridden were comforted. Such works are necessarily visible. But what need not be visible is the Christian identity or the motivation of the person who undertakes these works. Bonhoeffer here says that "especially" at the moments when Christians are being most sincerely praised by the world (when "the world . . . is compelled to say . . ., 'See how they love one another'"), Christians "*look* exclusively and constantly" to the Lord (*D* 268, my emphasis). They do not *speak* of the Lord, something that would give away their Christian identity immediately. If they speak at all, it is to "ask for the forgiveness of their sins" (*D* 268). They remain confident that their deeds will interpret themselves.

Forgetting oneself and looking only to Christ is an act Bonhoeffer calls (following earlier Protestant dogmatics) *fides directa*, a faith that points simultaneously back toward baptism and forward toward the Eschaton. In a letter from Tegel dated July 27, 1944, Bonhoeffer asks Bethge whether there might be such a thing as "'unconscious Christianity,' with which I'm more and more concerned." He then raises the distinction between "a *fides directa* and a *fides reflexa*," which are "related . . . to the so-called children's faith, at baptism" (*LPP* 373). Indeed, Bonhoeffer explored this distinction and its relation to infant baptism in his 1931 dissertation, *Act and Being*. There, *fides directa* is "the act of faith which, though taking place in the consciousness of the person, cannot be reflected in it."

146

In this direct act of faith, the person "sees only Christ, as his Lord and his God."[10] This unreflective faith may be the "attitude . . . first learned at baptism" that enables both sides of the *Arkandisziplin*—sharing the Word with other Christians and witnessing to the world in "deed alone"—as Bonhoeffer articulated it in the 1932 lectures on ecclesiology.[11] The baptismal *fides directa* carries eschatological significance as well, as it is the ground for Christians' justification. Bonhoeffer relates "unconscious Christianity" with "the left hand does not know what the right hand is doing" in a brief note from July or August, 1944 (*LPP* 380). Bonhoeffer probably is referring to Matthew 25:34–40, in which those whom Jesus counts as righteous at the last judgment (those "on his right") did not know that they were righteous.[12] The paradox is that it takes discipline and self-reflection to become unreflective about one's faith. The genuine selflessness of Christian good works can be guaranteed only by Christians' becoming unconscious of their being Christian.

"The Difference between the Ultimate and the Penultimate": The *Arkandisziplin*'s Eschatological Orientation

As we have already seen, especially in Cyril, secrets are always kept with their disclosure in mind: whether I keep a secret from you in anticipation of revealing it to you later, or in fear of your finding it out, I cannot help but imagine how the secret might be disclosed. In Christian thinking, secrecy cannot be an end in itself. In the biblical language Bonhoeffer uses in the section from *Discipleship* on hidden righteousness, "There is nothing hidden which will not be revealed" (Matt. 10:26) (*D* 151). This does not mean, however, that Christians have warrant for revealing their righteousness to the world. God alone will reveal the Christian's righteousness, so any revelation of that righteousness to oneself or another usurps God's role as judge:

10. Bonhoeffer, *Act and Being*, trans. Bernard Noble (New York and Evanston, IL: Harper & Row, 1961), 181.

11. Bonhoeffer, "The Nature of the Church," 86.

12. John de Gruchy sees similarities between "unconscious Christianity" and Karl Rahner's "anonymous Christianity." De Gruchy, "The Development of Bonhoeffer's Theology," in *Dietrich Bonhoeffer: Witness to Jesus Christ,* ed. de Gruchy (London: Collins, 1988), 40.

There is no difference whether they seek [recognition] in the cruder form, in the presence of others, or in the more subtle form, in the presence of themselves. Whenever the left hand knows what the right hand is doing, whenever I myself become aware of my own hidden goodness, whenever I want to know about my own goodness, then I have already prepared for myself the public reward which God intended to store up for me. (D 151)

God's judgment of the world is, as Bonhoeffer maintains in his unfinished *Ethics*, "the final word"—the ultimate.[13] If Christians try to speak this word themselves, during the penultimate time, then they usurp God's lordship not only over judgment, but over time and being as well. Maintaining the distinction between the penultimate and the ultimate humbly acknowledges humans' subordinate position with respect to God. As Muers says of God's position as the ultimate, "The 'last word' . . . is both the free act of God compelled by nothing that precedes it and in contradiction to all existing understandings of continuity, and the act of God that establishes the reality of what precedes it."[14] The penultimate, then, is both distinct from and contingent upon God. By virtue of this contingency, it is not in competition with the ultimate in any sense. David Ford sees this fact as essential to Bonhoeffer's religionless project:

Religion, as Bonhoeffer understands it, sets up dualisms and boundaries which are inappropriate to the reality of the world which is affirmed, judged and reconciled by God—dualisms of sacred and secular, God and the world, heaven and earth, inwardness and the public world. In *Ethics* Bonhoeffer used the dynamic concept of the penultimate and ultimate to undermine such dualisms while preserving necessary distinctions.[15]

The distinction between the ultimate and the penultimate, then, shares secrecy's purpose of sorting or sifting things out, recognizing that not all things, including historical moments, should be ap-

13. Bonhoeffer, *Ethics*, ed. Clifford J. Green, trans. Reinhard Krauss, Charles C. West, and Douglas W. Stott (Minneapolis: Augsburg Fortress, 1996), 149.

14. Muers, *Keeping God's Silence*, 87.

15. David F. Ford, *Self and Salvation: Being Reconciled* (Cambridge: Cambridge University Press, 1999), 262.

proached in the same way. This concept also reflects the logic of secret-keeping, as concealment (penultimate) gives way to the promise of disclosure (ultimate), although such a disclosure might give way to the recognition of a further secret.

By equating the *Arkandisziplin* with "the difference . . . between penultimate and ultimate" in the April 30, 1944, letter (*LPP* 281), Bonhoeffer reveals the *Arkandisziplin* to be a practice conditioned by Christians' historical situation in the times before the end. God's lordship of all time means that no historical era could be in competition with him, but it does not abolish the distinction between history's secular "duration" now and its consummation in the future.[16] The *Letters* indicate that Bonhoeffer did not think that secrecy was essential to Christianity per se, but rather essential to Christianity in the period between the Fall and the Eschaton. In his December 5, 1943, letter to Bethge, in which he affirms that theology and belief must recognize that we live in "the last but one," and not quite yet "the last" (*LPP* 157), Bonhoeffer explains that secrecy is a consequence of the fall into sin:

> After all, "truthfulness" does not mean uncovering everything that exists. God himself made clothes for men; and that means that *in statu corruptionis* many things in human life ought to remain covered. . . . Exposure is cynical, and although the cynic prides himself on his exceptional honesty, or claims to want truth at all costs, he misses the crucial fact that since the fall there must be reticence and secrecy. (*LPP* 158)

In this quotation, Bonhoeffer is referring to the concealment of sin by noting that Adam and Eve needed to conceal the source of their shame, once they sinned. On its own, this quotation establishes a necessary connection between the Fall and secrecy, but it does not necessarily link the Fall to secrecy about Christian identity.

Other writings, however, show that for Bonhoeffer living in the penultimate means that even good works, prayer, and hope ought to be concealed. At the conclusion of the chapter in *Discipleship* titled "The Visible Church-Community," Bonhoeffer affirms an es-

16. The notion of the secular as "duration" is an overriding theme in Mathewes, *A Theology of Public Life* (Cambridge: Cambridge University Press, 2007).

sential *invisibility* of the Christian community—at least for now. By confessing their Christian identity in secret and concealing it in their public activity by cultivating an unconscious *fides directa* that recalls the faith they acquired at baptism, Christians make their lives' conform to the model of the course of salvation history. Bonhoeffer writes that Christians'

> true life has not yet been revealed; it is still hidden with Christ in God (Col. 3:3). . . . What is visible here is nothing but their dying—their hidden, daily dying to their old self, and their public dying before the world. They are still hidden even from themselves. The left hand does not know what the right hand is doing. As a visible church-community, their own identity remains completely invisible to them. They look only to their Lord. He is in heaven, and their life for which they are waiting is in him. But when Christ, their life, reveals himself, then they will also be revealed with him in glory (Col. 3:4). (D 251)

This same confidence that God will reveal the righteousness of the righteous also entails confidence that any unrighteous persons who present themselves as righteous will be found out in time. Thus there is no need to investigate members of the community who might be impostors, who give verbal confession of faith but conceal "dark intent in the cloak of Christian piety." These may be "seeking power and influence, money, fame by [their] own thoughts and prophecies," and they believe they can get away with it because they know "that Christians are easy to fool" because "Christians are prohibited from judging" (D 177). Their bad intent "will reveal itself in due time. . . . The time to bear fruit will come, the time of open difference will come" (D 177). Secrecy, then, is not ultimate in Bonhoeffer's view. God will dispense with it at the end of the world's duration. As I will show in the next section, there are also limited circumstances in which Christians will have to dispense with it themselves.

Bonhoeffer also emphasizes how secrecy for now goes along with Christians' patient eschatological hope in his May 1944 "Thoughts on the Day of the Baptism of Dietrich Wilhelm Rüdiger Bethge." Here Bonhoeffer writes that "our being Christian today will be limited to two things: prayer and righteous action among men" (LPP 300). Until the day when a new Christian language can be spoken and people will be ready to hear it and live it, "the Christian cause will be a silent and hidden affair, but there will be those who pray and do right and wait for God's own time" (*LPP* 300). There is no timetable for this day's arrival—at least, no timetable of which humans could be aware. That day when a new language is spoken may be the last day, and until then, genuine Christians will have to be caretakers of their tradition in silence. If secrecy is a religion's defense against "the perceived cultural threat of an outside Third's penetration"[17] during a transitional period between historical ages (to stretch Paul Johnson's categories a bit here), then the penultimate is one long transition during which the *Arkandisziplin* is appropriate. This time precedes Christianity's becoming fully and finally public in the ultimate.

By being baptized, Dietrich Bethge had become a stakeholder in the Christian tradition and as such, he is responsible to be a caretaker of the tradition and protect it against the world, even though he is simultaneously duty-bound to serve the world. It's significant that Bonhoeffer puts this explicit call for Christian secrecy in a baptismal homily. The sacraments are of course visible signs of the invisible reality they bring about, making grace known within the Christian community of worship. The sacraments are also the means by which the Christian tradition is transmitted—the church heeds Jesus' commission to go and baptize, it remembers the Last Supper and distributes the body of Christ to its members, it ordains priests and bishops and confirms lay adults through laying hands upon them in an unbroken line of apostolic succession, and it sanctifies conjugal love and the raising of children through marriage. Bonhoeffer recognizes what Cyril recognized—that receiving the sacraments entails a responsibility to be a caretaker of the tradition of the community that provides one's Christian identity. Just as grace itself is "worth" enough to be passed on carefully through institutionalized sacraments, so must the tradition be passed on with equal care. If the tradition is in danger of losing its integrity or distinctiveness, then the tradition's caretakers have a responsibility to protect the tradition by concealing it. As Cyril also recognized, baptism initiates the Christian into a secret. In Ford's words, "The 'secret'" for Bonhoeffer "is the hidden reality of the crucified and risen Jesus Christ,

17. Johnson, *Secrets, Gossip, and Gods: The Transformation of Brazilian Candomblé* (New York: Oxford University Press, 2002), 5.

and to know this is of ultimate significance. When one participates in it one cannot live in a religious sphere separate from the world; but neither can one live without worship."[18] The Christian's responsibility to the tradition will for now entail concealing worship and verbal confessions of faith and eschewing "noisy and loquacious" piety (*LPP* 298) in order to purify the tradition of the dross of accumulated worldly thinking. This is precisely what Gregory Jones has argued is the aim of the secret discipline: to purify Christian language through silence and hiddenness, with the ultimate aim of being better able to proclaim the costliness of grace.[19]

The Limits of the *Arkandisziplin*

By placing secrecy in the category of the penultimate, as a Christian activity appropriate for now but not essential to all historical moments, Bonhoeffer puts a limit on the *Arkandisziplin*. Even within the period he designates as the penultimate, there are limits on the duties to confess Christian identity only in secret and to conceal it always in public. Even in the *Letters*, where Bonhoeffer calls very explicitly for an *Arkandisziplin*, he also makes claims that seem to undercut secrecy. These claims should be read, however, not as repudiations of the *Arkandisziplin*, but as, first, safeguards against reducing Christian discipleship to an attitude, and second, recognitions that there are (rare) historical circumstances in which Christians' care for their tradition requires an explicit public witness to—or even against—the world.

One example of Bonhoeffer's seeming denial of any form of Christian secrecy comes in his July 8, 1944, letter to Bethge, in which he writes that "the Bible does not recognize our distinction between the outward and the inward" (*LPP* 346), the very distinction on which the possibility of secrecy rests and which Kierkegaard believed was essential to the Christian critique of modern culture. And we have already seen how visibly "extraordinary" actions are essential to

18. Ford, *Self and Salvation*, 263.
19. L. Gregory Jones, "The Cost of Forgiveness: Grace, Christian Community and the Politics of Worldly Discipleship," in *Theology and the Practice of Responsibility: Essays on Dietrich Bonhoeffer*, ed. Wayne Whitson Floyd, Jr, and Charles Marsh (Valley Forge, PA: Trinity Press International, 1994),163.

Bonhoeffer's vision of Christian discipleship. He states that "The extraordinary . . . cannot remain hidden. The people have to see it. The community of Jesus' disciples . . . is the visible community" (*D* 145). Perhaps no remarks are more damning to the *Arkandisziplin*'s requirement that confession be done in secret than the claims that "There is no following Jesus without living in the truth unveiled before God and other people" (*D* 131) and "To flee into invisibility is to deny the call. Any community of Jesus which wants to be invisible is no longer a community that follows him" (*D* 113). In an essay on Bonhoeffer, Stanley Hauerwas takes this latter line as a ruling principle for Bonhoeffer's ecclesiology.[20] Indeed, Bonhoeffer's statement certainly seems unambiguous.

But these claims can be read as admonitions against making Christian identity into an emotional or mental state that has no effect on the Christian's outward actions. In that respect, in his insistence on Christians' visibility, Bonhoeffer is simply reminding his readers that justification by faith does not obviate the duty to perform good works. He in fact echoes Kierkegaard's insistence on the visibility of the fruits of love. The fruits must be deeds, not feelings: "Of course, what is extraordinary does have to become visible, it does have to happen, but—beware that you do not do it *in order* for it to become visible" (*D* 149). Christians do not simply "see the world differently" or "feel differently" from the way the rest of humanity sees and feels; they actually are supposed to do different things. For Bonhoeffer, it should in principle be possible to judge whether someone is a Christian purely by examining his or her moral behavior. It may nonetheless not be desirable to do so; Bonhoeffer is adamantly against what he calls "clerical" nosiness in the July 8, 1944, letter (*LPP* 345). Although he refuses a purely interior Christianity, Bonhoeffer does not want Christians to go to the opposite extreme, making themselves noisily known in the world. Such behavior would draw attention to them and away from God, who rightly should get the glory for Christians' deeds (Matt. 5:16). None of the "extraordinary" actions brought up in *Discipleship*—forgiving transgressions, foreswearing lust, telling the truth—need to involve making Christian identity explicit. They can all simply be done without any explanation (they

20. Stanley Hauerwas, *Performing the Faith: Bonhoeffer and the Practice of Nonviolence* (Grand Rapids: Brazos, 2004), 44.

"interpret themselves"), without any public appeal to Christ's teaching. The call to visibility is tempered, then, by the warning against making an idol out of visibility.

In addition to the general limit on the secrecy of the *Arkandisziplin* imposed by the requirement to perform visible actions, Bonhoeffer recognizes a specific limit in the need occasionally to protest publicly against the world in defense of the Christian tradition. Bonhoeffer's time certainly offered many opportunities to test this limit. During the Third Reich's early period, he believed that the Aryan laws' requirement that Christian ministers with Jewish backgrounds leave their posts constituted a *"status confessionis,"* a situation in which conscientious Christians must publicly protest the state's interference with the church by, in this case, publicly leaving the state-supported church.[21] Bonhoeffer addresses the need to make such a dramatic gesture in *Discipleship*, where he acknowledges that "in living out their secular vocations, Christians come to experience very definite *limits*, and . . . in certain cases the call into a secular vocation must of necessity be followed by the call to leave that worldly vocation" (*D* 245). This occurs "whenever there is a clash between the space the body of Christ claims and occupies in this world for worship, offices, and the civic life of its members, and the world's own claim for space" (*D* 245–46). Christians' response at such moments must be "to make a visible and public confession of faith in Christ," and then the world will have to choose "wisely to withdraw or to resort to violence" (*D* 246). Despite the overtones here that point to the particular *status confessionis* over the Aryan laws, we can draw the general conclusion that Bonhoeffer recognized that there have been and will again be times when the church must witness publicly and vocally against specific worldly events or policies. Individual Christians will have to walk off the job, resign from office, boycott companies or nations, go on hunger strikes, and even be led to the gallows in witness against the world, especially when worldly powers seek to dictate church discipline. But a simple principle that underlies the

---

21. John Moses, "Bonhoeffer's Germany: The Political Context," in de Gruchy, ed., *The Cambridge Companion to Dietrich Bonhoeffer*, 19; Ruth Zerner, "Church, State, and the 'Jewish Question,'" in de Gruchy, ed., *The Cambridge Companion to Dietrich Bonhoeffer*, 192–96; and Victoria Barnett, *For the Soul of the People: Protestant Protest Against Hitler* (New York: Oxford University Press, 1992), 125–33.

power of secrecy—that revealing knowledge only rarely and after a long delay enhances the effectiveness of the revelation—implies in this case that such public assertions of Christian identity ought to be reserved for truly extreme cases.

The conditions under which Christians confess their religious identity in public have to be extreme in order to prevent Christian protest from losing its strength through overexposure. I said at the beginning of chapter 5 that Bonhoeffer wrote his theology for the modern, secular West, and not only for the Nazi period. Had he not lived and died under the Third Reich, his theology would lack the enormous influence it currently carries. Yet restricting Bonhoeffer to that context forces any theologian who hopes to show Bonhoeffer's relevance today to make the highly dubious claim that we suffer under another Nazi regime.[22] But if Bonhoeffer's theology is in fact a response to conditions in modernity and in human nature itself that made—and may still make—such regimes possible, then his call for Christians to make a public witness to their faith only in the specific conditions of the Aryan laws and the eventual genocide of millions of Jews shows just how high the bar must be for Christians to abandon the *Arkandisziplin*. The historical situation of the church would have to be very close to the "ultimate"—as was the case of the church under the Third Reich—to warrant Christians' being "drawn into public suffering" (*D* 246). The "new language" Bonhoeffer hopes young Dietrich Bethge will one day hear will only "shock people" (*LPP* 300) if it is born out of a long Christian silence.[23] A Christian language spoken by everyone at all times as if the one speaking were the equivalent of a Bonhoeffer or Martin Luther King, facing the same extreme historical challenges as they faced, would be just as banal as the pious platitudes uttered casually—or calculatedly—by politicians stumping for the "Christian vote."

22. This is, however, precisely the claim that some activists have made, in marshalling Bonhoeffer to the cause of bombing abortion clinics. See Stephen R. Haynes, *The Bonhoeffer Phenomenon: Portraits of a Protestant Saint* (Minneapolis: Augsburg Fortress, 2004), 172–73.

23. Charles Marsh, heavily informed by Bonhoeffer and by the American civil rights movement, argues this point in *Wayward Christian Soldiers: Freeing the Gospel from Political Activity* (New York: Oxford University Press, 2007).

Conclusion: The World "Come of Age"

Bonhoeffer addressed his theology to Christians living in a "world that has come of age" (*LPP* 327). In such a world, "everything gets along without 'God'—and, in fact, just as well as before" (*LPP* 326). The sciences can flourish without the church's oversight. The political order need not make appeal to God's authority. This world, in itself and apart from the kinds of clashes discussed in the last section, poses no threat to the church or to divine truth because God and the world are not in competition with each other, fighting to fill the "gaps" in human knowledge and experience (*LPP* 311). "God in Jesus Christ" remains "the centre of life" (*LPP* 312), but, as Muers puts it, the secularity of the world means that God is, in effect, silent for now. This fact means that asserting Christian identity in the world should "not necessarily give rise to an endless battle between competing human voices—and, at the same time, . . . assertions about the decisive significance of the resurrection do not necessarily result in the silencing of all other voices by a triumphalist Christian proclamation."[24]

The *a priori* absence of competition between God and the world does not mean that the world cannot pose an indirect threat to the church. In modern secularism, worldly ideas often influence religious ideas, as Christians import worldly thinking and norms into their and the church's thoughts, moral outlooks, and practices. Much less rarely does the opposite occur. Bonhoeffer's view of secularity implies that if Christians are going to transform the world, then it will be done morally from within the world, not by making the world accommodate Christian thought or practice. As I have argued in previous chapters, the specific danger that Christians' public lives pose for their tradition does not come directly from the world. Activities like participating in politics or the worldly economy, listening to secular music, or attending public schools do not, on their own, threaten the Christian tradition in the least. The true threat to the tradition comes from Christians themselves. When they make the secular economy into their model for Christian morality, or when they trade off of their identity as Christians in order to gain standing

24. Muers, *Keeping God's Silence*, 86.

in public life, they harm the tradition by cheapening it, making it about something less than the forgiveness of sins through the death and resurrection of Jesus Christ. Because the threat to the tradition comes from the individual Christian's dual status—a member of the church who also has a public life in the secular—Bonhoeffer wants these Christians to erect a boundary of secrecy within themselves, self-consciously unconscious of their religious identities as they live and work in public.

Thus a Christian in public life has to be on the watch against his or her own attitude toward worldly culture. The Western world has come of age by virtue of its secular independence of the church, as culture (including politics and economics) is no longer mediated principally by Christianity. There is no use in seeing this state of affairs as an unfortunate divergence that can be corrected by a straightforward return to a premodern cultural or metaphysical model. Bonhoeffer rightly saw this as impossible and undesirable (*LPP* 327). To him, the challenge of secularity is to find ways of being Christian in the face of this world, neither capitulating to nor seeking to abolish the secular. Because Christ is Lord of all time, this is possible. Between these two extremes, there are, to be sure, models for the relation between Christianity and the world that encourage making Christian identity overt in most if not all circumstances. But the world come of age confronts the Christian as a place to help transform, and in which Christians must be for others and provide for their families; here, Christian identity need not be maximally visible to the public outside the church. In fact, it ought rather to be hidden from public view, because its publicity adds nothing to the Christian's primary tasks in the world or even to the distinctive deeds that constitute Christian "extraordinariness," like foreswearing vengeance and forgiving enemies. These works can be simply done, without announcing that they are motivated by faith. Christians' focus in public life ought to be on the ones they are serving and on Jesus Christ, not on themselves. The disciplined unconsciousness about Christian identity in public life that Bonhoffer recommends maintains the distinction between what is Christian and what is worldly without simply cutting Christians off from all contact with the world. He believes that the best defense against the temptations toward self-interest is to become unreflective about one's faith in public. If someone is not thinking about his or her religious identity, then it will not become a publicly traded commodity. Christian identity still ought to be expressed and performed, so that it does not wither and disappear entirely, but it should be done only in secret, in activities that presuppose a shared Christian identity as the very ground for the activities being coherent at all. When these two sides of the *Arkandisziplin* are being done, Christians' religious identity ceases to be "religious" in Bonhoeffer's sense of religion as a human-made, self-serving system of imaginary escape from the suffering and ugliness of this world. It can instead become authentically Christian.

Part Two

Concealment of Christian Identity in Contemporary America

7

The Secret-Keeping Self and Christian Responsibility for the Other

Who keeps secrets?

If we understand this question in the most straightforward way, then the answer is obvious: everyone. But there could be more to it than that. The question could be asking about the human subject, and so giving an adequate answer will require articulating the conditions within the human self that make the secret-keeping I have been discussing so far possible. But "who" can be plural, too, so we could consider what kind of human community can be built around a commitment to secret-keeping. What would such a community value? How would it grow? What aspects of human communal life would it leave out? The question, "Who keeps secrets?" can also be taken as an implied rebuke: in an age in which morality and politics are thought to require maximal access to information relevant to the interests of those whom our actions affect, who would be villainous enough to keep secrets from others? Isn't secrecy radically at odds with the better modern moral and political projects: liberalism, informed consent, and democracy?

The purpose of Part One of this book was to demonstrate that a tradition of thought exists in Christianity that encourages Christians to conceal essential aspects of their religious identity in their public lives. As my attention to Cyril of Jerusalem, Kierkegaard, and Bonhoeffer has shown, this is not an isolated tradition, but one that can be seen in a variety of Christian confessions: from the highly liturgical and communal, to the individualistic and pietistic, and finally to a version of Protestantism that draws from both of these extremes. We also saw that this tradition cuts across historical lines, as advocacy for secrecy is associated with periods of transition in a religion's public status. This accounts for the gap of fifteen centuries between my historical sources in Part One. On a grand scale, the church in Europe did not undergo a transitional period to or from the cultural margins during the Middle Ages, so we should not expect to find calls for secrecy in that period. I have for the most part avoided discussing mysticism and monasticism, two significant aspects of Christianity in the Middle Ages with secret-like features, but which do not fit the definition of secrecy as the intentional concealment of Christian identity that I favored in Part One.

The church's place in European culture has rarely seen long-term stability since the Reformation and especially since the French Revolution. Thus, we can find much more advocacy for secrecy in the past few centuries, including the debates between Protestants and Catholics over the *disciplina arcani* in the seventeenth century, the call for "reserve" made by John Henry Newman and the Oxford Movement, the "mystery theology" of Dom Odo Casel, and the recovery of the adult catechumenate after Vatican II. Modernity may be a long transitional period for the relationship between the church and the public life of the West; unless that relationship eventually becomes as settled as it was prior to the sixteenth century, Christian claims to secrecy will continue to be heard.

The purpose of Part Two is to explain what secrecy about Christian identity in the public life of contemporary America would mean. The present theoretical chapter articulates the nature of the responsibility Christians bear as secret-keepers. This responsibility grows naturally out of a conception of selfhood that underlies both an individual's capacity to conceal aspects of his or her identity and the self-searching interiority characteristic of the monotheistic religions that see Abraham as an ancestor. The next chapter explores the communal life of a church whose members keep their religious identities secret in public. The final chapter argues—contra a major contemporary theological account of Christians' position in American public life—that concealing Christian identity in public life better serves the Christian tradition in contemporary America than publicizing Christian identity does.

This chapter aims to answer two versions of the question, "Who keeps secrets?" First: what is the human self, that it can keep secrets about its identity? To answer this question, I show how the modern notion of an interior self, an understanding highly compatible with Western monotheistic religions' notion of a self that stands under divine scrutiny, is a necessary condition for secret-keeping about religious identity. Both Western monotheism and secrecy invite suspicion from the universalistic ethics of the Enlightenment, and for similar reasons. Both are seen as impediments to a public life liberated from sectarianism and dependent upon individuals' ability to make fully informed decisions about matters of interest to them.

For this reason, the second question I answer in this chapter is this: what does the interiority of selfhood mean for ethics and public life, given that secrecy is typically considered a violation of the standards that obtain in the public life of a secular democracy? As a corollary to this question, I ask if Christians' concealing their religious identities in public life thereby violates the openness and self-disclosure that are supposed to animate the public sphere. We will see that the answer to this question is yes, in a significant sense, but this does not mean that Christians abandon ethics entirely. Christians' public ethical lives in fact grow out of their God-formed interior selfhood. Their radical responsibility both *to* a God from whom the self cannot keep secrets and *for* the neighbor who stands before the self replaces their public duty to uphold universal *a priori* moral maxims. In so doing, Christians can be moral citizens, though not on the same grounds as their secular counterparts. In answering these questions, my argument in this chapter proceeds through linking elements into a chain connecting modern selfhood to radical responsibility for others via secrecy and a consideration of the paradigmatic monotheist and disciple, Abraham.

The Expedient of Interiority

Up to this point, I have referred many times to Christian identity but not to the self that has such an identity. In this chapter I explore a paradox central to the call for Christians to protect the distinctiveness of their tradition by concealing their religious identity in public: that recognizing an interior depth to selfhood opens the self up to responsibility for another. To begin addressing this paradox, we need to understand the relationship between identity and interiority, a relationship that has caused considerable controversy in academic circles.

Claiming that human beings have identities is not controversial. We all identify ourselves by physical and social characteristics, memberships, allegiances, and circumstances. Many identities come to the person through historical accidents—nationality, race, gender, and religion, to name a few—though many others (including religion, often enough) result from a person's choices. Identities face outward toward the world; they are recognizable, even if they are not recognized. As Charles Taylor contends, an identity orients the person toward a good, granting the individual a "framework" within which he or she can make value judgments and conduct his or her outward life.[1] Identities are cultural products, placing the individual in a community—a small-scale "public" like a family, ethnicity, or church—but also arising out of a recognition of difference, as not everyone has the same identity. The groundedness of identity in community and the orientation of identity toward the good open the self up to higher things and, therefore, to being judged by the standards of the higher.[2] Thus identities enable people to aspire to greater things and to recognize their own failings. This fact is extremely important for Christians practicing secrecy, as they need a check against their secrecy devolving into sectarianism. I will address this point more fully in the next chapter.

While the presence of exterior identities is uncontroversial, the presence of an interior space beneath identities is another matter. The notion of interiority has taken quite a beating in the last several

1. Charles Taylor, *Sources of the Self: The Making of the Modern Identity* (Cambridge, MA: Harvard University Press, 1989), 25–32.
   2. Ibid., 138–39.

decades, as theorists of performativity, neo-Marxist historicists, and historians of religion all agree that the inner/outer distinction and the concomitant privilege given to interiority are constructs serving ideological purposes.[3] Furthermore, these thinkers, along with neo-virtue ethicists, argue that the description of the self as inward ignores the individual's rootedness in the public life, the communities, and the narratives that sustain him or her. The inward self appears then to be a false refuge from history's power plays and ambiguities, blinding the person to the responsibility to allow oneself to be properly formed, and not merely self-discovered. These disparate thinkers have therefore redescribed the self in largely exterior terms, in order to give greater pride of place to collective action and communal life, to correct long-standing intellectual biases in favor of heroic individualism and the esoteric, and to enable greater moral wholeness for those marginalized by the inner/outer distinction.

Redescribing the self in such a manner seems to address the moral and political problems posed by modern individualism and heterosexism and the privilege given in religions to the mystical and esoteric over the mundane and public. The appeal of this redescription is therefore understandable, but it in no way avoids modernity's moral and political problems altogether. Rather, it runs directly into the philosophical anthropology that underlay the greatest political problem of the twentieth century and continues to underlay a chief problem in the public life of North America today: the reduction of the individual to one of his or her exterior, historically visible identities. Combining such a move with a narrative of racial or national purity fed the genocides of the last century and continues to feed them today. Combining it with advertising narratives—whether political or commercial—yields the banal, consumerist public life from which our country now suffers. Absent a notion of an interior self, individuals become nothing more than their identities. Indeed, in such a case, they would cease to be individuals at all, as they recede into the communities from which their identities emerged. Such groups then fall prey to demagoguery,

---

3. See, e.g., Eve Kosofsky Sedgwick, *Epistemology of the Closet* (Berkeley: University of California Press, 1990); Judith Butler, *Giving an Account of Oneself* (New York: Fordham University Press, 2005); Steven M. Wasserstrom, *Religion after Religion: Gershom Scholem, Mircea Eliade, and Henri Corbin at Eranos* (Princeton, NJ: Princeton University Press, 1999).

racism and tribalism, sexism, class warfare, and a host of other movements that exploit ossified identities. Mass culture poses a problem to justice and public morality not because it doesn't orient people toward a putative good. Rather, it poses a problem because if the crowd robs a person of the internal debate about goods that happens within the self, then an impediment to the pursuit of certain supposed goods, like racial purity or material acquisitiveness, is also lost. So even granting that the inner/outer distinction is a construct, we must see it as one of such great usefulness in addressing large-scale contemporary problems that it is worth retaining.

This distinction also enables us to make sense of the experience of being able to conceal aspects of our identity in particular contexts. The fact that, for better or worse, a person can conceal a sexual, religious, or political identity suggests that exterior appearances in a single context do not exhaust the person. Somehow, an individual can shuffle his or her identities, placing some "below" others to serve some end: survival, treachery, decorum. It can even be done for the sake of one of the person's identities. And the individual can imagine (fearfully as well as hopefully) shuffling a suppressed identity toward the top. Thus an inner space within the self is a forum for debate among the various goods presented to it by the identities available to it—in other words, for negotiation among the demands imposed by memberships in various "publics." As Taylor has shown, this conception of selfhood has ancient roots but flourished in modernity, aided by thinkers as seemingly disparate as Descartes, Locke, and Freud. The self, in the modern view, also serves as a stable character in the narrative of a single human life and the shifts in identity that narrative may feature. Although identities are publicly recognizable, the modern self is inaccessible to others in any way—neither intersubjective relationships nor scientific methods can give a definitive account of selfhood.[4] In fact, the self is not definitively accountable to oneself either, for if others' discursive practices are inadequate to giving an account of one's self, then one's own discursive practices are equally inadequate to this task, which requires one to treat oneself as another.[5]

---

4. In his more recent book, *A Secular Age* (Cambridge, MA: Belknap Press, 2007), Taylor calls this characteristic of the self its being "buffered" from outside scrutiny and influences. See, e.g., 41–42.

5. Rowan Williams, *On Christian Theology* (Malden, MA: Blackwell, 2000), 241.

The issue of Christian identity is central to this book. Religious identities, like all other identities, have some ground or fact that gives the person warrant for claiming the identity: characteristics at birth provide grounds for claiming racial and gender identity, while experience and personal choice ground identity as a biker or a Democrat. These grounds are not equivalent to an identity, however, as the case of Christian identity makes clear. Exhibiting a Christian identity entails claiming to be a Christian and doing distinctively and visibly Christian things like going to church, reciting prayers, doing good works in Jesus' name, or the like. But Christian theology holds that God saves not those who exhibit Christian identity, but those who have faith.[6] Faith is the unspeakable ground for this identity, just as being born female is the ground for a feminine identity; in both cases, however, it is possible to claim the identity without having the ground.

In these terms, my overall argument is for Christians to retain the ground for their religious identity and to exhibit the identity only in specific contexts: when one is among members of the community out of which that identity arises and doing the actions that distinguish that community from others. Such a context can be identified as Christian because it would cease to make sense without the ground for the community members' common Christian identity. In the contexts of public life, however, individuals' Christian identity should be concealed. One way to determine which contexts are which is to ask if a particular context would dissipate if the ground for Christian identity were removed. While removing the ground for Christian identity makes a sham of the community of the church, public life would persist without that ground just as it would persist without the ground for Irish-American identity or the ground for Green Bay Packers fan identity. The church is not merely a collection of people who believe. A subway car filled with people, all of whom happen to

6. The Roman Catholic formulation, "faith formed by charity," suggests that it may in fact be difficult to exhibit Christian identity consistently without eventually acquiring the ground.

Note, too, that on my account here, Rahnerian "anonymous Christians" would have the ground for Christian identity but claim that identity neither in public nor within the community of the church, because they do not recognize the ground as a ground for claiming a Christian identity.

be devout Christians, is not in itself the church. Such a collection of selves lacks the Spirit of Christ, because they are not gathered "in [his] name" (Matt. 18:20). They are gathered in the name of getting to work. Their being on the subway car is every bit as intelligible as it would be if they happened not to be Christians or if there were no such thing as Christian faith. In any public arena in which the ground for Christian identity is not a condition for the existence of that arena, Christian identity ought to be left below the surface, while the ground for it remains within the self.

Interiority and Monotheism

The transcendence asserted by monotheistic faith is linked to interiority by its resistance to attempts to explain it through historical discourse. Although the Western monotheisms are historical religions, they are not reducible to history, as the very reason they are called historical is because they profess that history is the site for the interruption of a transcendent God into the world. It is thus worth exploring to what extent transcendence and interiority mutually imply each other. Doing so will help show how an ethic of responsibility is implied in a Christian account of a "deep" self.

The genealogists of selfhood—Nietzsche, Foucault, Taylor, Bernard Williams—agree that once upon a time human beings defined themselves in purely exterior terms such as their rank or class within a (perhaps rudimentary) society. Then at some point (they disagree about exactly when) human beings began to define themselves in terms of interior things: moods, moral statuses, desires, intentions. For better and for worse, a shift occurred that had both immediate and far-reaching consequences, as it gave birth to Platonism (according to Williams and Taylor), Christianity (Nietzsche), and scrupulous sexual mores (Foucault). We modern human beings still live with the consequences of that shift.

The Bible's genealogy of interiority is not, in its narrative structure, much different from these others. In Genesis 2, the first human beings—credulous and seemingly incapable of deception—have a direct and unproblematic relationship with each other and with God. Their identities are role-based, determined by external, visible fac-

168

tors: their nakedness means that there can be no doubt who is a man and who is a woman. But then a decisive shift occurs. Immediately after eating the fruit of the tree of knowledge of good and evil, the humans begin to conceal things that had formerly been out in the open. They cover their naked bodies with fig leaves, and they hide themselves from God "among the trees of the garden" (Gen. 3:8). At the same time, their world becomes invested with moral meaning; the humans themselves become moral beings who can look into themselves and see good or evil. But even as God punishes the humans for transgressing his law, he endorses their capacity for secret-keeping, giving them leather garments to conceal their nakedness.

Genesis 4:3–4 presents religious worship—in the form of Cain's and Abel's sacrificial offerings—as beginning in the generation following the advent of secrecy. Although it would be wrong to equate monotheism with interiority, it seems that interiority is at least a necessary precondition for biblical religion.[7] Theologians and critics of Western monotheism alike have recognized this direct link from the advent of the interiority that enables secret-keeping and the birth of Western religion. Religion as Friedrich Nietzsche knew it was born of "internalization," the repression of violent instincts that becomes incumbent upon human beings shoehorned into society and placed under law. These instincts could not simply go away, so they inevitably turned against the self, but their doing so gave birth to the self's infinitely interesting interior life: "The entire inner world, originally as thin as if it were stretched between two membranes, expanded and extended itself, acquired depth, breadth, and height."[8] This internalization enabled the "bad conscience" Nietzsche sees as the *conditio sine qua non* for the eventual advent of the "holy God" of Judaism and Christianity.

Nietzsche's genealogy points out something Christians should already recognize in their theological tradition. Much of the ethic espoused in Pauline literature and the Sermon on the Mount is incomprehensible apart from the existence of an inner depth to the

---

7. On the other hand, Steven Wasserstrom argues that scholars' perception of interiority as normative for Western monotheisms is in fact a distortion. See his *Religion after Religion*.

8. Friedrich Nietzsche, *On the Genealogy of Morals*, trans. Walter Kaufmann and R. J. Hollingdale (New York: Random House, 1967), 84.

person.[9] Furthermore, the Christian individual comes to understand himself or herself before God through the introspective activities of self-scrutiny, self-reflection, and self-suspicion—activities that attempt to imitate God's activity of knowing and loving, but also judging, the person. The Christian paradigm here is Augustine, whose *Confessions* accomplished the intellectual wedding of Platonic introspection to the Pauline divided self. Augustine also demonstrates the consequences of that intellectual development in discovering his nature as a person created by God with a purpose of returning to God through Christ only when he begins looking within his own memory of himself. In his conversion, Augustine did not gain a new self, but a new identity—a new orientation toward the good, granted to him by God through a Christian worshipping community.

In Islam, too, the religious self is necessarily an interior one. It looks inward and keeps secrets, even if it cannot keep them from God. Ruqayya Yasmine Khan has shown that the Qur'an presents the self as utterly incapable of keeping secrets from God, who has complete power over secrecy and revelation.[10] Still, the Qur'anic self is a chamber of secrets, as the "breast" is frequently called a "hiding place" (see 3:29, 11:5, 28:69, 40:19, 64:4, 67:13, 100:9–10). A ninth-century *Book of Concealing the Secret and Holding the Tongue* by the moralist al-Jahiz reiterates this view of selfhood, acknowledging as well that keeping a secret is a burden, for "It is part of the breast's nature (considered not as a bodily vessel but as a gathering agent) through a power of God which human beings do not understand that it becomes constricted around what it contains and finds what it bears heavy." Yet this burden should not be blithely shrugged off, as al-Jahiz warns against "forfeiting a secret by broadcasting it."[11]

Islam shares inwardness with Judaism and Christianity in part because these three religions all are founded on belief in a historical revelation that occurred in a particular place and time and given

9. See Rowan Williams, *On Christian Theology*, 253–64.

10. Ruqayya Yasmine Khan, "Secrecy and Selfhood in Early Arabo-Islamic Canons," presentation at American Academy of Religion annual meeting, Philadelphia, Pa., November 19, 2005. Khan also explores similar patterns of secrecy regarding intimacy and sexuality in later nonreligious Arabic literature in her article, "On the Significance of Secrecy in the Medieval Arabic Romances," *Journal of Arabic Literature* 31 (2000): 238–53.

11. al-Jahiz, *Nine Essays of al-Jahiz*, trans. William M. Hutchins (New York: P. Lang, 1989), 14, as cited by Khan, "Secrecy and Selfhood."

to a particular person or finite group of persons. The three Western monotheisms also share Abraham, the model of a person who received a particular revelation from God and who, by doing so, violated the universal ethical norms of Enlightenment thought. The Abraham story as recounted in Genesis 22 and dialectically poetized by Søren Kierkegaard illustrates the close connectedness of interiority, monotheistic religion, secrecy, and responsibility for the other. Although Islam does not share the same account of Abraham's trial—significantly, Abraham in Surah 37:102 does not conceal the sacrificial plan from Ishmael—Islam does share a view of the religious self as the bearer of secrets that can be kept from other humans but not from God. In any case, the historical particularity and interiority of Abraham's selfhood remains something unthematizable by the ethics that underlies modern public life. Understanding Abraham's selfhood and ethical status, then, will go a long way toward understanding the ethical status of modern Christian disciples who conceal their religious identity in public life. But first, we need to be clear about why secrecy of any sort seems incompatible with modern public life.

The Ethical Status of Secrecy

Secrecy reveals the rift between revealed religion and secular moral philosophy as readily as specific historical revelation does. Secular ethics like Immanuel Kant's arose out of an attempt to secure certain of Christianity's goods through means other than allegiance to the God of Abraham who addresses the particular, choosing Abraham out of all the people in the world without any apparent regard for merit. The secular moralists did not question the Christian moral code, however. To them, the churches were right to proclaim Christian morality as universal law, binding on all individuals and a solid base on which to construct society. Thus in the conflict between the particular address of the Abrahamic covenant and the apparently universal address of the morality issuing from that covenant, the secular moralists decided in favor of universalism and sought to base something very much like Christian morality on immanent grounds.

171

While Enlightenment philosophers wanted to differentiate their projects from Christianity, now that Western civilization has largely accepted some secular version of ethics that, at minimum, underlies public life, the task has turned to theologians to differentiate Christianity from the secular. If Christianity and secularism have converged since the Enlightenment, then it is not because the secular has been reabsorbed into Christianity, but rather because the Christianity preached and practiced in Europe and North America has ceased to pose a legitimate alternative to secularism. This is not intended as simply a predictable complaint against liberal theology. Or rather, it is meant as a complaint against all theologies, academic and popular, and including many that tout themselves as "orthodox" or "traditional," that line up too tidily with a single secular economic, political, or social program.[12] Like Dorothy Day's Catholicism, Christianity in America ought to feel some unease with all confessedly secular projects, even while cooperating with them. If Christians never advocate what the nations see as folly, then they are not preaching Christianity.

To an Enlightenment ethic, secrecy is not simply foolish, but is *prima facie* immoral. It is a close relative of lying, which Kant absolutely condemns. He frames his condemnation in terms of avoiding any responsibility beyond the demands the moral law makes upon one's own actions. From Kant's perspective, my decision to lie renders me responsible "for the consequences, however unforeseeable," of the actions undertaken by the person to whom I have lied.[13] Implicit here is the view that we execute all our actions based on information we gather through our senses and thought and through reliance on what others tell us. If someone commits a particular act because of something false I deliberately told him or her, and he or she would not have committed the act had I told the truth, then I have, in effect, made the decision for that person. In my lie, my autonomous decision to provide false information substitutes my autonomy for the other's.

---

12. Marsh argues that the Christian right in America actually espouses a highly accommodationist, and hence liberal, theology. See *Wayward Christian Soldiers: Freeing the Gospel from Political Activity* (New York: Oxford University Press, 2007), 96–119.

13. Kant, "On a Supposed Right to Lie from Altruistic Motives," in *Critique of Practical Reason and Other Writings in Moral Philosophy*, ed. and trans. Lewis White Beck (Chicago: University of Chicago Press, 1949), 348.

Insofar as a secret—an intentional act of concealing knowledge from another person—limits another person's ability to make a fully informed decision, the secret is as morally contaminated as the lie.

Politically, secrecy inhibits the free communication between citizen-rulers that modern democracy requires. The most secretive regimes are frequently the most authoritarian, as secrecy is often an expedient strategy for consolidating power.[14] In extreme cases, a state's pervasive employment of secrecy makes for "systematically distorted communication"—not only between the state and its subjects but between the subjects themselves, as they become suspicious of each other and, hence, more isolated and unable to question state authority.[15]

If secrecy and public life are incompatible, then my project of articulating in theological terms a demand that Christians conceal their religious identities in American public life can go no further. My hope has been to show how Christians can fully participate in public life while maintaining the integrity of their religious identity if they keep that identity secret. To move forward, then, I need to show how Christians can be moral citizens even while they remain mum about the religious commitment that informs their moral, political, and economic activities.

Although Christians who conceal their religious identity might look no different from their non-Christian neighbors, in some cases performing the very same actions as the non-Christians, the ethic the Christians live out is undergirded by a rather different justification and a rather different notion of responsibility. And at the fringes of moral experience, secret Christians and secular persons do visibly different things. In the secular account, the account on which the public moral economy relies, such Christians sometimes do immoral things. One cost of discipleship may be that Christians have no recourse to justifying themselves in the face of the secular world's accusations.

Given the strong case against secrecy in the secular public realms of ethics and politics, the question becomes how far back to extend

14. Urban, "The Torment of Secrecy: Ethical and Epictemological Problems in the Study of Esoteric Traditions," *History of Religions* 37 (February 1998).

15. Jürgen Habermas, "On Hermeneutics' Claim to Universality," trans. Jerry Dibble, in *The Hermeneutics Reader,* ed. Kurt Mueller-Vollmer (New York: Continuum, 1992), 293–319.

the moral condemnation. Is it enough to say that secrecy itself is incompatible with modern public life, or should the sources of secrecy themselves be uprooted? Is the notion of interior selfhood at fault? Must the transcendent God who sanctions secret-keeping be cast aside?

These questions lie at the heart of Kierkegaard's *Fear and Trembling*, in which universalistic ethical norms and a particular religious duty to God are placed in dialectical opposition. In *Fear and Trembling*, secrecy poses a moral and political problem for Enlightenment thought that maps remarkably well onto the Enlightenment's verdict concerning the place of a revealed, historical, particularistic religion in public life. Despite casting its discussion in terms of a strict either/ or between secular ethics and revealed religion, *Fear and Trembling* in fact illuminates a way for Christians to have both God and ethics, even if the ethics that lies on the far side of Mount Moriah does not resemble Kantianism or Hegelianism. In this transformed version of ethics, secrecy is embedded in the very nature of the ethical task of taking responsibility for another person.

Abraham's Secret from Isaac

In *Fear and Trembling*, the ethical is an aspect of "the universal," the broad set of standards that regulates all of social life: not only morality, but language and cultural customs, too. In Hegelian terms, the universal is *Sittlichkeit*. These standards are presumably well-known to any member of a society, as they are acquired by upbringing. In a Kantian account, the standards are similarly knowable by any and all through the exercise of practical reason. The intellectual conflict in *Fear and Trembling* concerns the relation between the universal and religious faith. Is the universal the highest expression of human existence, such that religious life is a subset of social life, confined to the bounds of local custom or the reach of human reason? Or are there situations in which an individual can depart from the universal and be said to stand "above" it, justified by an "absolute" relation to God in faith? Abraham is the locus of Silentio's dialectical exploration of this conflict.

By the time God commands Abraham to sacrifice Isaac in Genesis 22, Abraham is already party to the specific and finally unsayable revelation that God will make him the father of many nations. In carrying out the command to sacrifice the vehicle of that prolific parentage, Abraham intentionally withholds knowledge of the sacrificial plan in the face of Isaac's straightforward questioning.

The Genesis 22 account is divisive for historical, theological, and philosophical reasons, as Christian theologians have seen it as prefiguring the sacrifice of Jesus Christ, some Jewish theologians see is as having fueled Christian supersessionism, and secular philosophers (most notably Immanuel Kant) see it as the paradigm for the amoral or immoral deference to a personal God engendered by both of these religious traditions.[16] The commentary in Kierkegaard's *Fear and Trembling* illustrates this very divisiveness in its dialectical approach to Abraham's moral and religious situation of having been commanded to violate his public duty (not to kill) and his familial duty (not to kill *his son*) in the service of his religious duty (to obey God). This commentary is exceptional not only for its extraordinary literary character, but also for the attention the pseudonymous author Johannes de Silentio gives to Abraham's secret from Isaac.

Fear and Trembling is famous for asking whether Abraham should be praised or blamed for his willingness to sacrifice Isaac. A second issue has received far less attention, even though it is the explicit question in the last of three "problemata" the pseudonymous author Johannes de Silentio raises in the second half of the book: "Was it ethically defensible for Abraham to conceal his undertaking from

16. Jon D. Levenson, *The Death and Resurrection of the Beloved Son: The Transformation of Child Sacrifice in Judaism and Christianity* (New Haven, CT: Yale University Press, 1993). Immanuel Kant, *Religion within the Limits of Reason Alone*, trans. Theodore M. Greene and Hoyt H. Hudson (New York: Harper Torchbooks, 1960), 81–82, 175; Kant, *The Conflict of the Faculties*, trans. Mary J. Gregor (Lincoln: University of Nebraska Press, 1992), 115 fn. See also Carol Lowery Delaney, *Abraham on Trial: The Social Legacy of Biblical Myth* (Princeton: Princeton University Press, 1998) and Edward Kessler, *Bound by the Bible: Jews, Christians and the Sacrifice of Isaac* (Cambridge: Cambridge University Press, 2004) for accounts of the reciprocal relationship between Jewish and Christian interpretations of Genesis 22. For a discussion of how ancient interpretations of Genesis 22 and Surah 37 subvert the modern dichotomy between Abrahamic-religions-as-peaceful and Abrahamic-religions-as-violent, see Yvonne Sherwood, "Binding–Unbinding: Divided Responses of Judaism, Christianity, and Islam to the 'Sacrifice' of Abraham's Beloved Son," *Journal of the American Academy of Religion* 72 (Dec. 2004): 821–61.

Sarah, from Eliezer, and from Isaac?"[17] If "the ethical" means the Enlightenment moral and political outlook that values the manifest and allows for no exceptions based on particular circumstance, this question must be answered no.

Abraham's concealment does, however, receive a yes from religion. In fact, Silentio's investigation portrays secrecy as essential to the religious; it would be impossible to separate concealment out from religion in order for religion to pass judgment on it. But this does not mean that Christianity or revealed religion in general is hopelessly unethical. Just as Abraham "gets Isaac back" (*FT 57*, cf. Heb. 11:19) by virtue of his faith in God's providence and power to bring about what to human eyes is impossible, Abraham also gets ethics back, though not in the form of Kantian universalism. The story of Abraham's obedience to God and consequent secret from Isaac as told by Johannes de Silentio reveals how the interiority underlying both historical monotheism and the capacity for secret-keeping further enables a transformation of the individual's duty to uphold universal moral laws into an absolute responsibility for a particular other.

Unlike the aesthetic stage in Kierkegaard's three-stage scheme, in which one's own whims are the sole motives for undertaking any course of action, and unlike the particularism characteristic of the religious sphere, the ethical makes the same demand on everyone to act on maxims of conduct that apply despite individual particularity and to work toward the common good, rather than toward merely individual ends. In the realm of the ethical, everyone is bound by the same rules of conduct regardless of particular circumstances or commitments, and when placed in the same situations, two people acting out their moral duties should behave in the same way.

In Problema III, Silentio equates the universality of the ethical with "the disclosed," and he finds that Abraham is, ethically considered, as guilty of secrecy as he is of (attempted) murder: "ethics passed judgment on him because he was silent [not answering to the best of his knowledge Isaac's direct question about the sacrificial victim] on account of his accidental particularity [i.e., his relationship to

---

17. Kierkegaard, *Fear and Trembling*, 82. All subsequent references to this work will be parenthetical, *FT* and page number.

176

God]. It was his human prescience that led him to remain silent. Ethics cannot forgive this" (*FT* 112).[18] Nevertheless, Silentio also concludes that Abraham is at the same time potentially justified in his actions from a religious perspective.

Silentio's initial explanation of Abraham's ethical condemnation amounts to saying that in public life, we cannot have people going around like Abraham does, claiming to have secret reasons for all manner of unethical undertakings:

> The ethical as such is the universal; as the universal it is in turn the disclosed. The single individual, qualified as immediate, sensate, and psychical, is the hidden. Thus his ethical task is to work himself out of his hiddenness and to become disclosed in the universal. Every time he desires to remain in the hidden, he trespasses and is immersed in spiritual trial from which he can emerge only by disclosing himself. (*FT* 82)

Throughout the three problemata, Silentio contrasts—as he does in this quotation—the ethical view of the human person with the religious view, the universal with the single individual. This simple equation leads us to conclude that, if the ethical is the disclosed, then the religious is characterized by hiddenness. Incidentally, the same is true of the aesthetic, a stage "lower" than the ethical. An aesthete might play with secrecy and disclosure simply to try to escape the boring straightforwardness that ethics demands. But the putative "higher" nature of the religious cannot prevent religious hiddenness from escaping the same condemnation aesthetic hiddenness receives from ethics. The ethical perspective does not allow one to "see" the difference between aesthetic and religious hiddenness—even though an "absolute dissimilarity" differentiates them (*FT* 85). The ethical only "sees" hiddenness, and judges it guilty of ignoring the "ethical task" to become disclosed. Insofar as Abraham does not do this, "ethics condemns him, saying, 'You must acknowledge the universal, and you acknowledge it specifically by speaking'" (*FT* 110).

In drawing these contrasts between the aesthetic and the religious, and between the ethical and the religious, Silentio is in effect under-

18. While Abraham never actually kills Isaac, Silentio refers to Abraham as a "murderer" a number of times. See *FT* 30, 55, 57, 66, 74.

taking Christianity's post-Enlightenment project of distinguishing itself from modern secular culture. Bourgeois culture does not need the historical faith of Abraham to undergird it. It needs only the polite presumption that all have faith (FT 7). This is just as well. Not only do all forms of hiddenness look the same, but there is also no way of knowing that something is hidden until it is revealed, so hiddenness looks externally the same as its opposite. But among faith's many paradoxes is that as soon as faith discloses itself, it enters the universal, the realm of ethics and public life, and thereby ceases to be faith any longer. Thus, trying to distinguish Christianity from the culture of public life makes faith into something public, which faith can never truly be. Taking the interiority of faith seriously means that "they who carry the treasure of faith are likely to disappoint" someone who goes looking for them, "for externally they have a striking resemblance to bourgeois philistinism, which infinite resignation, like faith, deeply disdains" (FT 38).

Bourgeois culture at its most banal reduces the person to a collection of outwardly visible political, social, and consumer identities. In the highest expression of bourgeois culture—the infinite resignation that characterizes the ethical hero—these identities are stripped away, and the person loses his or her particularity. The universality of the ethical requires a person always to consider himself or herself as only a "moral agent" or a "citizen," to abstract from all of the experience, self-interest, personal history, and communal memberships that would mark someone as an individual, and to act solely upon maxims accessible to any other rational agent.

By contrast, the religious requires acting based on things "hidden" from reason's public gaze. For John Caputo, Fear and Trembling asks above all "whether one admits a sphere of the interior secret, which is justified by the fact that the individual is higher than the universal; otherwise, Abraham is lost."[19] This "hiddenness" encompasses any sort of individuality, including individual historicity and personal commitments, knowledge, and revelations, none of which arise purely from reason. A rationalistic ethic "assumes no justified hiddenness"

19. Caputo, "Instants, Secrets, and Singularities; Dealing Death in Kierkegaard and Derida," in Kierkegaard and Post-Modernity, ed. Martin J. Matuůtík and Merold Westphal (Bloomington: Indiana University Press, 1995), 221.

(*FT* 82). Hiddenness could only be justified (if at all) through appeal to something outside of the rationalist's immanentist system. Hence, the question of secrecy's justifiability hinges on whether we think of "the divine" as an immanent or a transcendent reality (the issue in Problema II). If one accepts divine transcendence, as Abraham did in his faith, then there might be a justification for secrecy arising from the religious: a personal God who, though hidden, may without compulsion reveal his will to a human being, demanding that the human obey this will, even if obedience means that the human being must violate rational, universal ethical maxims.

Abraham's relation to a transcendent God is possible by virtue of his interiority, which is both the site of the unsayable secret and a site of agony. Silentio claims that keeping a secret is psychologically burdensome, inviting the kind of "spiritual trial" and uncertainty concerning conduct that Abraham experiences. The universal agent of the ethical will always know if his or her actions are justified; as "the disclosed," the ethical is supremely knowable, and thus, there can never be any doubt concerning the justifiability of one's actions. (Isn't Kant's categorical imperative meant to erase uncertainty about what maxim to follow?) By keeping the secret from his family, Abraham steps into a sphere in which he cannot make appeal to any source outside his own experience to determine the rightness of his actions. That is, if he is justified, he is justified only in secret. According to Silentio, someone who keeps silent in matters when he might ethically be called to speak "will add a little spiritual trial to his other agonies, for the universal will constantly torment him and say: You should have spoken. How are you going to be sure your resolution was not prompted by cryptic pride?" (*FT* 111). When someone becomes the single individual of the religious sphere, she leaves behind any recourse to universal techniques for testing moral maxims. Such a person keeps secrets only at her moral risk, and there is always a chance that her true motives are secret even to herself.

A Secret Sign of Responsibility

Most of us know from experience that keeping secrets is burdensome. We speak of secrets "weighing on" us, just as we speak of the "weight" of responsibility. The burden that Silentio names "spiritual trial" is a sign of someone's having taken a heavy responsibility for another person. Recall that Kant warned against lying because it overtakes another person's autonomy; in so doing it makes the liar responsible in the other person's place. Such a radical sense of responsibility has no place in a moral system that demands respect for others as moral lawgivers of equal stature as oneself.

But this is the level of responsibility demanded of Christians. As Kierkegaard reminds us in *Works of Love*, "love does not seek its own" by carefully surveying where one's own responsibility ends and others' begins. The quiet example of the Good Samaritan shows that Christian responsibility is open-ended; the Samaritan promises to pay for whatever services the wounded man may require (Luke 10:35). The Samaritan's responsibility is determined not in advance by an a priori moral law, not by the amount of money he gives the innkeeper at the moment he brings the victim to the inn, but by the victim himself, through any need that particular person might have in the future. If American Christians are to be more like the good Samaritan in their public lives and less like the priest and the Levite—who stood on appearances in taking no responsibility for the man who fell among thieves—then they, too, must see their role in public as primarily one of taking a radical responsibility for their neighbors, whether or not they have a legal obligation to care for them.

In making "responsibility" a keyword for Christians' stance in their public lives, I am breaking no new ground. Responsibility has become an almost uncontested positive concept in theology and other disciplines. It is so, perhaps, because it is so expansive. "Be responsible" is a nearly contentless ethical mantra; on its own, it rules out no specific actions and recommends none other than owning up to committing one's other deeds. This is part of the point, as my interpretation of the parable of the Good Samaritan shows; if a person's actions are determined by others' needs, then we shouldn't limit in advance what actions may need to be undertaken. But the expansiveness of the concept also means that much of the work of advocating responsibility, then, must be defining what kind of responsibility we are talking about.

Just as secrecy highlights how revealed religion and Enlightenment ethics diverge on selected normative issues, secrecy also reveals a rift between two different conceptions of individual responsibility. On one hand, responsibility as the duty to uphold universal moral laws has little room for secrecy, as all moral decisions occur in public, informed by objective knowledge accessible in principle to all. In such a conception of responsibility, the moral law (however its content is determined) dictates what actions to undertake and what ones to avoid. On the other hand, responsibility *for* someone else is radically individual; it cannot be communicated to another and typically does not give a public account of itself. In this conception of responsibility, moral content is supplied largely by the person for whom one is responsible, as the responsible agent must be attentive to the specific needs of the other person at a particular time. This latter sort of responsibility is closely allied with secrecy. As we will see, not only does responsibility make a person secretive, but secrecy makes that person responsible for something or someone.

This recognition is imported from the political and ethical thought of such Continental thinkers as Jacques Derrida and Emmanuel Levinas. To these rebellious heirs to Edmund Husserl's phenomenology, the project of building a universal philosophical system that could reduce any and all appearances to noetic categories is an intellectual cousin to totalitarian political projects that reduce human beings to one or another of their identities. Levinas's other-determined ethic of responsibility builds off of his contention that there is an essential core to the human that resists political and philosophical systems. To him, human sociality and morality depend not on free intersubjective communication, but on recognizing a "*secrecy* that interrupts the continuity of historical time" and inhibits any drive toward forcing the other to conform to a philosophical or political system.[20] Ethics stands above and regulates politics (though we should note that Levinas's "ethics" resembles to a great extent Kierkegaard's "religious" sphere). Politics serves ethics by

> render[ing] justice to that secrecy which for each is his life, a secrecy which does not hold to a closure which would isolate some rigorously private domain of closed interiority, but a secrecy which holds to the responsibility for the Other. This would be the responsibility which

20. Emmanuel Levinas, *Totality and Infinity: An Essay in Exteriority*, trans. Alphonso Lingis (Pittsburgh, PA: Duquesne University Press, 1969), 58.

181

is inaccessible in its ethical advent, from which one does not escape, and which, thus, is the principle of an absolute individuation.[21]

Though Levinas's use of the term "absolute individuation" will give pause to anyone suspicious of modern individualism, it must be measured against the assertion that inwardness is not "closed," but rather sends the person back out to the world of moral activity. What no one else can account for is that for which only the individual is accountable; what is secret to any investigation and nontransferable (i.e., incommunicable) to anyone else is the one's responsibility for another. Derrida, in an essay in *The Gift of Death* dealing with *Fear and Trembling*, argues that otherness *is* secrecy: if the other "were to speak to us all the time without any secrets, he wouldn't be the other, we would share a type of homogeneity."[22] Politics furthermore cannot account for the individual's unsayable decision, for which that individual is nonetheless wholly responsible. "By keeping the secret, Abraham betrays ethics" and enters a sphere of responsibility for the other.[23]

In *Fear and Trembling*'s Problema III, Silentio suggests that a religious existence requires, as the consequence of keeping the unsayable secret, that the individual take on a responsibility for another's autonomy. Both of the senses of responsibility that I mentioned earlier in this section appear in *Fear and Trembling*, corresponding to the two existence-spheres featured in Silentio's "dialectical lyric." In the ethical sphere, there is a responsibility to uphold one's universal moral duty. In the religious sphere, however, the one who chooses to keep a secret—especially a secret of great magnitude like Abraham's secret plan to kill Isaac—often takes a significant burden of responsibility for the other upon his or her shoulders. Silentio writes that if a tragic hero, who for Silentio represents the ethical, "remains silent [and thereby steps into the religious], he takes a responsibility upon himself as the single individual, inasmuch as he disregards any argument that may come from the outside" (*FT* 87), and that the knight

---

21. Levinas, *Ethics and Infinity*, trans. Richard A. Cohen (Pittsburgh, PA: Duquesne University Press, 1985), 81.

22. Jacques Derrida, *The Gift of Death*, trans. David Willis (Chicago: University of Chicago Press, 1995), 57.

23. Ibid., 59.

of faith like Abraham "remains silent on his own responsibility" (*FT* 111). Thus, by keeping his dilemma a secret, a Junius Brutus or Agamemnon would cease to be a tragic hero by stepping outside the scope of the ethical. Still, Silentio maintains that such an individual would retain some kind of responsibility, although his new responsibility would be a religious one, characterized by hiddenness and inwardness. By keeping silent, the would-be tragic hero removes himself from the public world of the ethical and political, and in so doing abdicates his responsibility to act in accordance with universal duty. We might imagine Abraham answering Isaac directly ("Son, there is no lamb. God and I intend for you to be the holocaust"), thereby fulfilling his responsibility to the universal while divesting himself of responsibility for Isaac's fate. In that case, Abraham would give Isaac the chance to control his own fate, either to free himself or to die willingly as an offering to God. Isaac would then take a measure of responsibility for himself, absolving his father of at least some of his culpability as a murderer.

The ethics of disclosure offers a spiritual safe house in which we know our duties, we know how to fulfill them, and we need not be burdened with inward spiritual trials. An individual can trade in open-ended, other-centered forms of responsibility for finite duties to perform exactly what the law requires. For Derrida, "This is ethics as 'irresponsibilization,' as an insoluble and paradoxical contradiction between responsibility *in general* [i.e., the duty to uphold the law of the ethical] and *absolute* responsibility."[24]

Problema III thus forces a decision between these two views of responsibility. In being responsible in the sense of always acting in accordance with universal duties, we gain security and certitude. In becoming responsible in the sense of becoming accountable *for* others, we risk serious culpability for the consequences. Still, Silentio thinks that there can be a great reward for this responsibility:

> Despite the rigorousness with which ethics demands disclosure, it cannot be denied that secrecy and silence make a man great simply because they are qualifications of inwardness. . . . The tragic hero, who is the favorite of ethics, is the purely human; him I can understand,

24. Ibid., 61.

and all his undertakings are out in the open. If I go further, I always run up against the paradox, the divine and the demonic, for silence is both. Silence is the demon's trap, and the more that is silenced, the more terrible the demon, but silence is also divinity's mutual understanding with the single individual. (*FT* 88)

This is Silentio's strongest assertion of the ambiguous place occupied by secrecy in human life, and encapsulates the conflict over secrecy that takes place between Enlightenment philosophy and revealed religion. *Inwardness* sits at the center of the conflict, separating Abraham from the tragic hero. The source of Abraham's greatness is that he, the religious man, by virtue of his unsayable relation to God, has an interior life that the hero of ethics lacks—or at least discounts. The tragic hero has a host of advisers with whom to debate courses of action; the knight of faith debates only within himself. And Silentio is careful to show that someone who wants to imitate Abraham should not try to murder his or her family members, but rather have faith (*FT* 31).

Of course, Abraham is not great from all perspectives.[25] By accepting the responsibility concomitant with keeping a secret, he accepts moral culpability. The secret he keeps from Isaac is powerfully destructive, even "demonic," inhibiting the drive to secure universal autonomy. But at the same time, if there is such a thing as a religious sphere, a possibility of particular revelation to concrete individuals, the Abraham story shows that secrecy is "divine" insofar as it is the mode of communication between a personal God and the concrete individual whom God chooses or calls.

In Silentio's account, then, Abraham's secret is religiously justified because the transcendent God, by entering into an exclusive relation with the single individual Abraham, exploits an interior space in him, with ambiguous results. The very interiority that enables Abraham to receive the secret from God also enables him to violate the maxims of the outward ethical sphere by keeping a secret from Isaac. If there is a moral to *Fear and Trembling*, then it is that having a God or an inward life (and for Silentio, there is little distinction), a shelter from the public sphere in which to keep secrets, is necessarily an invita-

25. Abraham shows little integrity when he is deceptive about Sarah's identity in Genesis 12:10–20, earning him great worldly rewards.

tion to sacrifice. It is an invitation to take on a secret responsibility, at the cost of ceding a spot in the bright light of universal morality. Believers, confronted with this fact, can only hope that God will mercifully provide a suitable lamb for their sacrifice.

Recovering the Ethical: The Secret Disciple's Love for the Neighbor

Abraham's religious life is a deeply pared-down version of the religious life of his remote descendants. Any law God has given Abraham is severely limited in scope, although God's promise to make a great nation of Abraham's descendants though Isaac is the ground for the Genesis 22 episode's religious intelligibility. Also, while Abraham and his household bear the mark of circumcision, there is nothing like the elaborate sacrificial system of Leviticus. Especially as Silentio interprets the story, Abraham's religious life is strictly between God and him. His public life, however, entails his interactions with Sarah, Isaac, Lot, and so forth. Despite the small number of elements in Abraham's religious life, his example remains instructive insofar as it shows that selfhood, secrecy, and transcendent, monotheistic religion are not easily separable, and that together they issue an ethic of radical responsibility for the other. This responsibility is the self's primary stance in public life, expressed in Christianity as neighbor love.

Abraham, as Silentio depicts him, is a model of secret faith in public life because he will not reveal the secret that grounds his religious life for the sake of his public life. To Bonhoeffer, too, Abraham is a model for Christian discipleship in the modern age. Abraham eschews all concern for public acclaim in the name of obeying God's will. Chapter 5 of *Discipleship*, "Discipleship and the Individual," is recognizably Kierkegaardian in theology and tone, as Bonhoeffer discusses how following Christ requires one to break with "immediate" relationships to family and nation and to become a "single individual" for whom all relationships are mediated through Christ.

Bonhoeffer recognizes, as Kierkegaard does, the danger of apotheosizing one's membership in the family or the family-writ-large of the nation (*D* 92). Without question, Bonhoeffer is here sensitive to the Nazis' inculcation of a nationalist, racialist mob mentality

185

among the German people. Yet by noting that Kierkegaard makes *exactly* the same argument for the Christian's need to become a single individual who stands above the "crowd" at a time of far less extreme political circumstances, we see that Bonhoeffer issues a call relevant to modernity itself—any circumstances in which Christians are tempted to make their lives as family members, citizens, or consumers into their primary means of relating to others.

In Bonhoeffer's account, two paths to becoming a single individual stand open to Christians: the visible path of breaking with immediate familial and national ties, and the secret path of silently obeying God's command while remaining tied to family and nation. In either case, the aim is to have Christ alone mediate one's relationships with others. If we translate these into proposals for Christians' stances in public life, then the two options for "looking only to the Lord" are either to break entirely with public life or to remain within it while bearing a secret commitment to Christ alone. Although both options exhibit the costliness of grace, the latter one is more difficult (D 98), because continuing to participate in the economy and the nation presents the constant temptation to put them before Christ. A potential third way—remaining in public life while openly claiming a commitment to Christ—is not brought up at all. This is the way of cheap grace.

Bonhoeffer sees Abraham as a model for both legitimate paths (D 98), as Abraham left his family and nation to answer God's initial call (as in Gen. 12:1–3 and 17:1–8), only to step onto the secret path of inward obedience when he answered God's second call to sacrifice Isaac.[26] Bonhoeffer writes that Abraham gets Isaac back, though "in a different way than before," because "Abraham had left everything

26. It is hard to imagine that Bonhoeffer could have written this chapter without consulting Kierkegaard's *Fear and Trembling*, in which Abraham is a test case for the possibility of faith. Many of the key concepts in that book—including the single individual, infinite resignation, the teleological suspension of the ethical—figure prominently in "Discipleship and the Individual." Furthermore, as I pointed out in chapter 3, *Fear and Trembling* is framed by a preface and an epilogue that anticipate Bonhoeffer's notion of costly grace: Silentio's lament that even religious ideas are for sale at such a deep discount that no one bothers to "make a bid" (FT 5), with the result that we may need "to jack up the price" of faith (FT 121).

Bonhoeffer even echoes the Kierkegaardian "stages" when he writes that Abraham "takes God at God's word and is prepared to obey. Against every natural immediacy, against every ethical immediacy, against every religious immediacy, he obeys God's word" (D 97).

and had followed Christ" (D 97). In recovering Isaac, Bonhoeffer's Abraham regains a community, as the Christian will in the church after making the break with family and nation to follow Christ alone (D 98–99). To Silentio, the knight of faith is thus "a new creation by virtue of the absurd," recovering himself and the entire finite world after making the movement of faith (FT 40). As Bonhoeffer retells it, in "bring[ing] his son to be sacrificed," Abraham "is prepared to make the secret break visible, for the sake of the mediator" (D 97). Making a secret break with family and national ties allows a Christian to continue having commerce with family and fellow citizens. But this break may one day have to become visible; as we saw in chapter 6, the Christian may publicly have to leave family and nation behind.

To be sure, Abraham is an imperfect example even of a hidden Christian discipleship today, for he has only the merest contemporaneous religious community and no community with which he can share his secret plan for Isaac. His community is in the future, "hidden, so to speak, in Isaac's loins" (FT 59). For Bonhoeffer, this shows how the Christian will only regain a community, in the church, after he or she has made a commitment to God.[27] The Christian also regains public life, too, though in a different way than before, as those the Christian encounters in public are transformed into "the neighbor."

If Abraham's faith is legitimate, then it expresses an "absolute duty to God." The duty to God relativizes all other duties, but it does not thereby *annul* them. Even in a book like *Fear and Trembling* that seems to paint the option between God and the ethical in exceedingly stark terms, there is a recognition of a transformed version of ethics on the far side of the God-relation. In Silentio's words, after making the commitment that characterizes the knight of faith, "the ethical receives a completely different expression, a paradoxical expression, such as, for example, that love to God may bring the knight of faith

27. For Cyril, the shift to becoming a Christian entails far less loneliness. Baptismal candidates already have an incipient Christian community, united in principle by their common lack of knowledge about the sacraments. For reasons that I will provide in the next chapter, a Christian today who had Abraham's faith would have "transversal" relationships with others within the church to help make sense of that faith's demands or of any purported mystical experience.

to give his love to the neighbor—an expression opposite to which, ethically speaking, is duty" (*FT* 70), because ethics commands only duties to others and does not suppose that such duties draw someone into relation with a personal God. The paradox is that by loving God absolutely, a person comes to love the neighbor.

Loving the neighbor is the Christian's first duty in public life. Considerations for promoting the common good are important, but they are derivable from this first duty. A neighbor, moreover, is an entirely public person. Saying that someone is a "neighbor" removes the particularity of any other relationship I have with that person (spouse, cousin, client, enemy)[28] as much as treating each other person as an end in himself or herself would. "Neighbor," then, is a distinctively Christian substitute for the Kantian moral or rational agent (or vice versa). It is a universal category. Anyone could, in principle, recognize the same duty to love a particular woman as neighbor, even if she is someone's wife, just as in a Kantian account, any and all would have to recognize her as a moral legislator. Thus even in apparently violating a universal norm of public life by keeping their religious identity secret, Christians retain a form of universality by virtue of the unsayable faith that grounds that very identity. Their vision of universality is different from the secular vision, however, reflecting as it does the distinctiveness of the identity they keep hidden.

Conclusion

Abraham may seem like a poor example of taking responsibility for or caring for the other, insofar as he is willing to put Isaac to death. Except in the lingo of film and television Mafiosi, in which "taking care of" someone means murdering that person, caring and willingness to kill are utterly at odds. Thus the story only makes sense if we consider Isaac to be not only Abraham's son, but the entirety of finite and public existence, encompassing all of Abraham's worldly commitments: to family, nation, friends, and (if he had them) employer and coworkers. And Abraham, caught between two apparently

---

28. It does not, however, need to remove the person's particularity. Indeed, someone loving the neighbor must attend to the neighbor's particular needs in a way that takes the neighbor's particular capacities into account.

conflicting demands and left to negotiate them within his interiority, is a paradigmatic modern monotheist. He is called to something higher than public life, but he still must fulfill its obligations.

In this light, we can see the Abraham story as a lesson about the risks of bothering to be a disciple at all, about the necessarily hidden nature of discipleship, and about the rewards that such discipleship holds in store. Indeed, Abraham recovers not only ethics by virtue of the new possibility of responsibility for the neighbor, but he recovers the whole of finite existence as well. The finite becomes for the knight of faith "a new creation" (*FT* 40) as he takes as much or more joy in the finite—eating, working, socializing—as an aesthete does. If the Christian takes Abraham as a model for reconciling religious identity and public life, he or she need not entirely shun the goods of the world. It is not a rejection of worldliness, but a way of dealing with the world in such a way as to keep the universal in its proper place—below the absolute realm of religious commitment.

One of the many paradoxes surrounding the Abrahamic discipleship advocated by Kierkegaard and Bonhoeffer is that after renouncing the universal, and with it, human society, the individual gets society back "in a different way than before" (*D* 97). The Christian individual gets the church, a body that may not include the individual's family, but one made available to the Christian only by virtue of the individual's willingness to sacrifice. In that respect, although Christian disciples do get a form of society back, the grace mediated by the church is necessarily costly.

8

The Church as a Community of Hidden Disciples

Abraham walked up Mt. Moriah with Isaac, but in his religiosity he was alone, as God's covenant and command were given only to Abraham. The unsayable secret of his faith meant that Abraham could not, in Silentio's account, be understood by any other human being. He is, partly by virtue of his secret, completely isolated, a "single individual" absolutely devoted to God and only relatively devoted to any other person.

His devotion to God is admirable, but his isolation seems to raise problems for a modern accounting of Christian life. How can Abraham possibly be the model for Christian discipleship that Kierkegaard and Bonhoeffer insist he is? Where is the community of the church? Where is the historical tradition of sacraments and doctrine? Where is the mission to evangelize or otherwise engage the world? If Christian selfhood demands secrecy, then it seems to demand an individualism so extreme as to rule out so much else that is distinctively Christian. Indeed, an argument supporting the concealment of Christian identity in public life can appear to be an *argumentum reductio ad absurdum*, proving in fact that Christian identity properly should be displayed in public life.

It's true that the Kierkegaardian version of the Abraham story is not the full story of Christian life. It's also true that selfhood does not exhaust what it is to be a Christian person. Selves are, of course, always in relation to others, and Christian selves are additionally in relation to others in the church. The severance of social ties brought about by faith in God, discussed in the last chapter, is not the whole story. In fact, a purely individualistic Christianity would be an aberration, a denial of Christ's having attracted a community of disciples and handed his ministry on to the church.

In this chapter I will show how the secrecy I have been advocating is compatible with a Christian's membership in a body like the church, which seems to require open discourse about Christian identity. I have already touched on this issue in chapter 6, where I explained the *Arkandisziplin*'s requirement that Christians confess their identity to each other in secret. I will explore this issue further in this chapter. I will also address Christian evangelism. The undeniably public nature of Christians' mission to evangelize the world poses a major challenge to my view. Much of contemporary theology presupposes that the Christian's mission to witness the faith to the world trumps any considerations to take Christian identity out of public circulation. Indeed, any thought that Christian identity could be concealed in public life is quickly dismissed if it is considered at all, the clear instructions of Matthew 6 notwithstanding.[1] My answer to the question of how Christians can evangelize while keeping the signs of Christian identity secret will stretch over this chapter and the next one. If we consider evangelism to be a subset of neighbor love, then the hidden agency incumbent on all practitioners of Christian neighbor love is incumbent upon missionaries as well. Even the work of bringing new Christians into the fold, then, is most authentically done secretly, to avoid the ostentatious status-seeking that is always a temptation in American public life. Accepting this answer requires acknowledging that the church is a sociological entity as well as a theological one. This fact is, of course, not inherently bad—the church is and must be a living institution in the world—but the social nature of the church is the source of certain dangers to the church's integrity and to the Christian identity upon which it is founded. Its

---

1. As, for instance, in Charles Mathewes, *A Theology of Public Life* (Cambridge: Cambridge University Press, 2007), 25.

members can reinscribe the extra-ecclesial society within the church, seeing one's fellow congregants as contacts, as part of a network, as a potential market. If the church is to be a community of Abrahamic discipleship, then its members must leave the extra-ecclesial society behind in order to gain a new society entirely. Concealing Christian identity in public life and seeing membership in small, local churches as normative best guarantee this view of the church.

Secrecy and Tradition

To be a member of the church is to share a Christian identity not only with one's contemporaries but also with a long tradition of Christians in the past. Because Christians have nothing that they have not received, and because they are to be humble stewards of the mysteries they have inherited (1 Cor. 4:1–7), the church's responsibility today is partly to hand Christian identity on to worthy candidates.

In sifting out the worthy from the unworthy, Christians are trying to preserve the integrity of the tradition and the distinctiveness and decisiveness of Christian identity. Such judgments are not final; the "unworthy" are only the *not-yet* worthy, whom the church hopes one day to embrace. But these judgments are meant to care for the tradition, in a sense parallel to Christians' love, or care, for the neighbor. Stewardship of the Christian tradition is a form of caring perhaps best thought of as *curating*, which is linked conceptually to caring through the words' common Latin root, *cura*.

Museum curators are gatekeepers. They do not grant access to the museum's entire collection to any and all.[2] While select works will go up for public display, many, many more remain behind closed doors because they are fragile or because they are not crowd-pleasers. The curator will grant access to these works to people like collectors or scholars, who can demonstrate genuine interest in and appreciation for them. No doubt, because curators love the collections they are charged with, and because people tend to want others to love what

2. This was not always so. In the natural history museums of the nineteenth century, museums typically put all of their specimens on display in a taxonomic order useful to specialists but daunting for laypersons. See Catherine Paul, "'Discovery, not Salvage': Marianne Moore's Curatorial Method," *Studies in the Literary Imagination* 32 (1999): 95.

they love, many curators wish more people would view the hidden gems of the collections. But they do not as a consequence call the public into the storerooms that house these items. Museums sort the collection and their constituencies into groups, and attempt to match segments of the collection to the groups who will best profit from them. Through outreach programs, museums bring people into the life of the museum and encourage them to develop the kind of interest in art or science or history that ordinarily grants people access to the full collection. Christians likewise have two separate constituencies for their tradition, and they present aspects of the tradition differently to other Christians than they would to non- or not-yet-Christians. Judicious sorting of Christian thought and practices, and of persons who have access to different aspects of Christian thought and practices, is essential to both preserving and passing on the tradition.

Caring for a tradition, a collection, or an institution requires that judgments be made that follow the logic of secrecy, the first step of which must be to sort people and cultural objects into categories. In this way and in others, the social dynamics of traditions are analogous to those of secret-keeping and secret-telling.[3] Most obviously, both activities feature a receiving and a handing-on. Unless I discovered the content of my secret on my own, I must have found it out from someone else. If I learn a trade secret when I attain a higher position within a company, I may later need to pass that secret along to another person who attains that position. In addition, like a tradition, secrecy is particularistic, intentionally excluding some people. Traditions typically exist in parallel, however, so that no one is excluded from traditions altogether. If I am in on one tradition of secrecy, I will surely be excluded from others. In principle, however, all persons ultimately *could* know many sorts of secrets, including trade secrets. There is nothing inherent to a trade secret that would prevent some persons from knowing it; rather, the holders of the secret might deem certain people not (or not yet) ready to receive the secret knowledge. In this respect, the analogy between secrecy

3. Of course, not every secret establishes social relations or implicates the secret-keeper in a tradition—for example, my secret that I trampled my neighbor's flower bed. For the most part, however, such secrets are irrelevant to issues of Christian identity.

and the tradition of receiving and passing along Christian identity is especially striking: a secret divides all of humanity into those who have it and those who do not, but those who do not could also be seen as not *yet* having the secret. The tradition of Christian identity is similarly open-ended: in principle, any and all could become Christians, just as any and all could know the Coca-Cola secret formula (even though the legal costs to the person leaking that secret would be astronomical). This is unlike, say, a family or national tradition, which could never include all people.

But because a candidate for being incorporated into a tradition or told a secret must be deemed worthy to receive, and therefore, traditions and secrets are generally not handed on to all comers, both traditions and secrets are inherently conservative. Insiders are concerned with protecting the integrity of what they have received.[4] Indeed, traditions and secrets are similarly susceptible to betrayal if someone (a traitor; in Latin, *traditor*) seeks personal gain by handing a secret or a privilege of the tradition over to someone who would otherwise be deemed not yet worthy of receiving it.

These analogies allowed Cyril of Jerusalem to treat the creed and the sacraments like secrets, warning potential traitors to "'hold fast to the traditions' (2 Thess. 2:15) which will now be given to you; and engrave them 'on the tablet of your heart' (Prov. 7:3)," and, after they have been baptized, to "Preserve these traditions inviolate and keep yourselves free from offence" (*MC* 5.23). Cyril's constant reminders to the candidates about what they still did not know about the sacraments and Christian life contributed to the candidates' liminal status. By setting the baptismal candidates apart from the rest of the church community, Cyril attempted to inculcate mutual care among these candidates, providing them with a miniature Christian community even before they became members of the church, not unlike how basic training bonds military recruits to each other before they fully enter the hierarchical structure of the armed forces. Cyril even had a "leave no man behind" policy for the candidates: "If one of

4. To Tom Beaudoin, this integrity is a fantasy. He argues that traditions are inherently unstable and subject to change to suit the interests of the holders of the tradition. The Christian tradition, then, could never have been conserved; it has always been being given away. See his *Witness to Dispossession: The Vocation of a Postmodern Theologian* (Maryknoll, NY: Orbis, 2008).

you is missing, go to look for him. . . . If one of you had a brother, wouldn't you look for what was good for him" (*P* 13)? Becoming Christian in fourth-century Jerusalem, then, involved learning simultaneously that one had a responsibility to care for one's fellow Christians and that one had a responsibility to care for the tradition itself. Keeping the church's distinctive sacramental practices secret from these not-yet Christians contributed to communicating both types of responsibility.

Cyril's example also shows that handing on Christian identity involved both liturgical rites and neighbor love. Only the clergy may hand on the sacraments of initiation that fully make and mark a Christian. The laity, however, help maintain the tradition and incorporate new members into it by loving their neighbors, both in the church and in public. Christian love has always had an evangelistic purpose, even unintentionally so, as we see in Tertullian's familiar claim about the pagans who were so astonished by Christians' love that they sought to convert to Christianity themselves.[5] In Tertullian's time, Christendom was unimaginable; some of us in America may live in its last remnant. Thus the one amendment I wish to make to Tertullian's model of evangelizing through loving one another is to say that in contemporary America, where everyone knows what Christianity is, and where being very publicly Christian can still be of great benefit in many sectors of public life, Christians ought simply to love unselfconsciously, allowing the "pagans" to find out on their own if the people they saw loving each other were Christians.

Hidden Neighbor Love as Initiation into the "Secret of Faith"

A Christian's primary activity in public life is neighbor love. In asserting this, I am denying the primacy of justice, the hallmark of Reinhold Niebuhr's highly influential theology of public life. One of Niebuhr's complaints against advocating love as the main principle guiding Christians' public life is that because one can only perform

5. Tertullian, *Apology* 39, in *The Ante-Nicene Fathers*, vol. 3, ed. Alexander Roberts and James Donaldson, rev. A. Cleveland Coxe (New York: Christian Literature Publishing Company, 1885; reprint, Peabody, MA: Hendrickson, 1994), 46 (page references are to reprint edition).

works of love for some people, agape quickly degenerates into love only for the people one is already inclined to love. In this respect, insisting on neighbor love cannot by itself root out the sinful self-love that impedes any work, either of love or justice. Thus Niebuhr advises Christians to avoid the "simple Christian moralism [that only] counsels men to be unselfish" and recommends the "profounder Christian faith" that will establish "systems of justice which will save society and [Christians] themselves from their own selfishness."[6] But these systems are not enough on their own, either: conceptions of justice can be crafted to serve the interests of the conceptions' framers, and selective application of justice can be just as self-serving as selective love can be. Furthermore, limiting love with justice is not the sole means available for trying to save Christian love from self-interest. A requirement to conceal the identity of the Christian performing a work of love would also be a safeguard (on the scale of individual interactions, at least) against the very selfishness Niebuhr sees as the reason for the primacy of justice.

This paradox—that the neighbor love that characterizes Christians' public lives must be done secretly—seems to render the Christian public activity of evangelism impossible. As then-Cardinal Ratzinger writes concerning evangelism, it is a form of neighbor love: "real love of neighbor . . . desires to give him the deepest thing man needs, namely, knowledge and truth."[7] But how can this knowledge be given, and the gospel be spread, secretly?

To answer this, we first need to view spreading the gospel as an act not of broadcasting it, but of handing it on. The dynamic of receiving and handing on the gospel (and, in so doing, receiving and handing on Christian identity) shares characteristics with receiving and passing on secrets, as I argued above. Handing on the gospel is itself an act of neighbor love, but it need not be done through direct teaching. It can also be accomplished indirectly through other acts of neighbor love. Loving the neighbor builds up the loved one's rela-

---

6. Reinhold Niebuhr, "Justice and Love," in *Love and Justice: Selections from the Shorter Writings of Reinhold Niebuhr*, ed. D. B. Robertson (Philadelphia: Westminster John Knox, 1957), 28.

7. Joseph Cardinal Ratzinger [Pope Benedict XVI], *The Nature and Mission of Theology: Essays to Orient Theology in Today's Debates*, trans. Adrian Walker (San Francisco: Ignatius, 1995), 27.

tion to God, who is the source of all love. In this sense, we can see neighbor love as a quasi-sacramental initiation into the relation to God that Kierkegaard calls the "secret of faith."

Recall from chapter 4 that for Kierkegaard, "the greatest benefi-cence" was to help another person to stand by himself or herself. The linchpin of this beneficence is the need for the benefactor to conceal his or her aid in helping the other person. When this happens, the beneficiary receives the gift of self-mastery in part because he or she cannot see anyone else who might be his or her master. This absence of a proximate human giver can now prompt the individual to look to God—the unseen source of love—as the agent of his or her self-mastery. From the very beginning of Kierkegaard's treatment of the greatest beneficence, he asserts that love, "giving of oneself," is ultimately directed toward "helping the other person to seek God" (WL 264). This is the absolute pinnacle of Christian love: "*To love God is to love oneself truly; to help another person to love God is to love another person; to be helped by another person to love God is to be loved*" (WL 107, italics in original). Because someone can love only by virtue of having "the secret of faith," the relationship to God, and because love's aim is to give someone else a God-relationship (without thereby losing one's own), the work of love in granting the greatest beneficence is an act of leading another person into a new way of life—an initiation into the secret of faith.[8]

Loving another person accomplishes this initiation indirectly. As Kierkegaard points out, every person already has an incipient God-relationship, simply by virtue of being "created . . . in [God's] image, so that [the person] might be like him, might become perfect as he is perfect" (WL 264). As the italicized quotation in the previ-ous paragraph indicates, Kierkegaard sees the God-relationship of faith as roughly equivalent to the capacity for love. The initiation into the secret of faith can be accomplished, then, by focusing on the person's incipient capacity to love. As this improves, so will the God-relation (and vice versa). Neighbor love does not put love into another person, but rather "builds up" the beloved by presuppos-

8. Kierkegaard in *Works of Love* only mentions initiation three times by my count; on two occasions, the initiation is said to be an initiation into a secret (WL 240, 284). One other time, it is simply an initiation into "knowledge" (WL 228).

ing that love already exists in the beloved, and then "draw[ing] it out" of that person.[9] Because the ground for a God-relationship has been given to everyone, initiating another into that relationship is mainly a matter of providing the occasion for the other to enter the relationship, while God himself, through granting the *imago dei*, provides the necessary condition. So, having accomplished that task, the worker of love

> declares: Now this individual is standing by himself—through my help. But there is no self-satisfaction in the last phrase, because the loving one has understood that essentially every human being indeed stands by himself—through God's help—and that the loving one's self-annihilation is really only in order not to hinder the other person's God-relationship, so that all the loving one's help infinitely vanishes in the God-relationship. (*WL* 278)

The one who loves, then, is hidden because he or she disappears into the hiddenness of God. The lover gives by taking himself or herself away, communicating the God-relation indirectly. There is no deceit in concealing oneself in performing this sort of work. In fact, it is much more honest to forestall any credit being given to the loving individual, insofar as God granted this benefactor the faith that enabled him or her to love, granted the beneficiary an incipient God-relation that could be built up, and is the ultimate source and object of all human love. In *Works of Love*, neighbor love circulates in a way that could be seen as an attribute of grace. In this respect, the initiation brought about by neighbor love can readily cooperate with and reinforce a sacramental initiation into the church. In helping another person to love God, the individual participates in God's love, both imitating it and enabling the one who is loved to receive it. As Kierkegaard writes, this person "is completely and wholly transformed into simply being an active power in the hands of God. This is why his activity cannot be visible" (*WL* 279).

To be sure, it requires tremendous confidence in love to think that unseen works of love can bring another person around to adopting the Christian faith. Because so much confidence is required, "the first and last thing to say about" love is the command, "Believe in

9. Kierkegaard, *Papirer* VIII² B 50:3 *n.d.*, 1847, in *WL* 448.

199

love!" (*WL* 16). Relying on more visible means of drawing people of the world into the tradition of Christian faith betrays a lack of confidence in love. Given that I am relying here on a profoundly paradoxical thinker, the counterintuitive nature of my claim that handing on Christian identity could be accomplished secretly should not be surprising.

In fact, my claim here runs against the grain of contemporary theology of mission. To the missionary and missiologist Lesslie Newbigin, among the worst things the church can do with the gospel is to "keep it wrapped up or buried in the ground" out of fear of the risks posed by its exposure to the world. In his opinion, the "treasure" entrusted to the church need not necessarily be "preserved inviolate and without the change of a comma." The church should not make the mistake of thinking that this treasure is even its own; the treasure is Christ's, though it is held by the church for now, in order for it to accomplish his purposes.[10] But the question of orthodoxy in contemporary America is not simply a matter of commas (although theologians certainly know how much can hinge on a single iota); it is a matter of the danger posed by using the gospel to serve self-interested worldly ends. Affirming that the gospel is Christ's—and the church's only as something held in trust—does not entirely skirt around this problem. It is simply too easy to project one's own purposes onto Christ for Christians to be optimistic about their ability always to be faithful stewards.

The church does have a responsibility to carry out the genuine work of Christ in the world—and that work includes spreading the gospel. But the church in the United States of America must acknowledge, perhaps more so than the church elsewhere must, that a Christian faith can come at the cost of worldly flourishing. Indeed, Christians should expect this.

This is not meant as a plea to shut down all Christian missions. This book's argument is addressed to Christianity in a highly developed country in which the material rewards of public life are enormous and in which Christianity has for a long time circulated as the unofficial religion of that public life. Although the latter is

10. Lesslie Newbigin, *The Open Secret: An Introduction to the Theology of Mission*, rev. ed. (Grand Rapids: William B. Eerdmans, 1995), 189.

no longer universally true of America, there are huge sectors of American society where it still is, such that it is still very much worth it to flaunt Christian identity even in nationwide political or marketing campaigns. Few other places in the world share these characteristics. Thus I cannot say whether my argument applies to other countries being actively missionized now. My guess is that it does not. Nevertheless, to many American Christians, America is prime mission territory, and the gospel is rightly to be spread in all facets of life; to give it maximum exposure. It is here that that conflict between preserving the tradition and passing it on while participating in public life is especially acute.

A Distorted Witness: American Evangelical Elites' Ecclesiology

This basic tension in Christian evangelism means that because the tradition is not shared by the general public, making it fully available to the public can cheapen it. Likewise, publicizing one's care for the neighbor threatens to undermine the gratuitous character of that care, causing it to lose what distinguishes it from the contractual and reciprocal duties characteristic of worldly existence. No major religious group has been more visible in American public life in recent decades than evangelical Christians. Their prominence is apparent both at the popular level, where they participate in mass movements like the Promise Keepers and consume the output of a number of explicitly Christian mass media outlets, and at the elite level, where evangelicals have attained positions of great political and economic power. At both levels, evangelicals tend to believe that witnessing to the gospel, in part by making their religious identity highly visible, is a major element in being a Christian at all. For these reasons, they are a good example of how insisting on a broadly public religious identity for its members can contribute to the distortion of a Christian group's self-understanding.

One reason that evangelicals have made it into and thrived in the upper reaches of American public life is that they act as a network, relying on each other's influence to draw fellow evangelicals into influential positions. A sociological study published in 2007 by D. Michael Lindsay shows how this has happened; in doing so, Lindsay has perhaps unintentionally shown what compromises on matters of doctrine—especially ecclesiology—this increased public prominence has required. Although his aim is in general not to criticize his subjects,[11] Lindsay delineates the social and theological ingredients to American evangelical elites' recipe for using their Christian identities to advance their public lives. His narrative is one in which committed Christians have managed to forge a happy marriage for themselves between Christianity and the values of their professional fields, accomplishing both their religious and their career goals. In so doing, they have effected small but significant changes in the American workplace and in the academy, the media, and politics, making these arenas friendlier to religion in general and to Christian morality and discourse in particular.

A suspicious reading of this population's outlook—which is necessary because of the strong human tendency toward self-interested self-deception—discovers a different narrative. That is, the real change resulting from evangelicals' increasing presence among the American elite has been in their readiness to adapt their views of the church and of Christian doctrine to the paradigms of power in American culture. The main ingredients to these elites' style of evangelicalism all contribute to Christianity being for them an expedient for advancing their own personal standing in their political, work, or business lives. The theology implicit in this activity severely distorts orthodox ecclesiology and dulls the distinction between the church and American culture.

11. Lindsay, *Faith in the Halls of Power* (New York: Oxford University Press, 2007). Lindsay's method may indeed make it impossible for him to criticize the phenomenon he describes. Lindsay's data about the network of American evangelical elites come primarily from interviews he conducted with an astounding 360 elites, including two former presidents of the United States. To gain access to these people, Lindsay asked his interviewees to name other prominent evangelicals whose faith was important to their secular work, and then Lindsay contacted those people, often with the help of the person who had mentioned the prospective interviewee's name. This way, Lindsay bypassed "the usual impediments of secretarial gatekeepers or organizational barriers" (248). Inasmuch as he attained the direct personal access to powerful people that membership in the network grants, Lindsay in effect became a part of the very network he was studying.

No one can ever merely glide along a network, at least not for very long; because people *are* the network, any attempt to exploit the network makes one a part of the network. Lindsay lacks a fulcrum outside of what he's studying and against which he can leverage criticism.

To these elites, the church is a network. Lindsay notes with some dismay that evangelical elites often are only loosely affiliated with a particular church. He interviewed "a senior White House official [who] calls a church in St. Louis his 'home church,' despite the fact that he has never lived there." This official visits the church a few times a year, meeting up with "a Hollywood producer friend, a Nashville country singer, and several other leading evangelicals."[12] Considering the diversity and number of churches in the Washington, D.C., metro area, it seems unlikely that this official's spiritual needs could be adequately met only at this church halfway across the country. The official's reason for going to this church could not be that he needs to be with the people around whom he grew up. It also seems unlikely that he wants to connect with the lower members of the body of Christ, as the salt of the earth can be found anywhere. It seems likely, rather, that he wants primarily to connect with his powerful non-Washington friends, the ones who could keep him in work after the administration he works for is out of office.

Many evangelicals at all levels of social status hope to transform American culture, bringing it more in line with what they see as Christian principles. But the methods preferred by the "cosmopolitan evangelicals" Lindsay studied show that their concern is very likely also to advance their own careers. For instance, evangelical elites prefer to establish and encourage professional internship programs for young Christians rather than participate in the mass rallies and prayer services favored by "populist evangelicals." While it is true that placing evangelicals in positions of power "could have more lasting results"[13] than a stadium prayer service could, it is also true that internship programs do a lot to help elites find good future employees and thereby strengthen their companies. These programs are no doubt very attractive as well to young people, in light of the boost it can give their own careers.

It is thus convenient that evangelical elites' preferred methods for changing America coincide so neatly with methods for accruing power and profit. Participating in an internship program for young Christian professionals and praying at a stadium rally are both ways

12. Ibid., 222.
13. Ibid., 220.

of displaying one's Christian identity in public life: at work and in the broad realm of public discourse. These ways are not equivalent, however. Taking part in a mass rally will probably not further an individual's career. At the stadium, the point is to be part of the crowd, to demonstrate that the society or government must reckon with the raw popular force of the movement in question. The point is to be unrecognizable as a specific person at all. Participating will probably not accrue substantial benefits to one's work life, for one ceases to be an individual who *could* benefit. Indeed, the social impact of a stadium prayer service would not be diminished in the least if all the attendees wore masks.

Elite evangelicals furthermore bind their faith and their careers with what Lindsay terms, without any apparent appreciation for the term's irony, "elastic orthodoxy." To realize their vision for American society, evangelicals need to collaborate with nonevangelicals and non-Christians. And to collaborate with these persons, evangelicals may need to assuage others' fears that evangelicals are narrow-mindedly insistent upon their own theological positions and intolerant towards others'. Moreover, any collaboration on the issues evangelicals see as important will require some kind of compromise on both sides. Evangelicals may need to show that a Christian position can embrace principles that appear to be opposed to Christianity. Thus an "elastic orthodoxy" is perceived to provide room for evangelicals and their collaborators to come to some common theological or moral ground.[14] The strong teleological focus here—concerns for orthodoxy need not get in the way of attaining social goals—meshes well with the concern for results and the bottom line that American elites, evangelical or otherwise, display in their public lives.

Elasticity in adherence to doctrine is, of course, not the mark of a religious group seeking to shore up its religious identity's distinctiveness. This notion of orthodoxy is especially problematic for evangelicals, whose self-identification over and against liberal Protestants has often included criticism of the mainline denominations for capitulating doctrinally to social and cultural forces.

Cosmopolitan evangelicals' use of the church as a network and their highly accommodating view of doctrine signal the loss of their

14. Ibid., 230.

distinctive religious identity. They can use the church as a network only because they have allowed their public lives to determine their approach to their church lives. For many of the elites Lindsay studies, the church seems to serve some of the same functions as a country club or alumni association would, and the evangelical elites' taste for publicly prominent churches often far from their homes (if they go to a single church regularly at all[15]) suggests that a church's spirituality or the need for commitment to a local community are not deciding factors for them as they look for a church to join. The spiritual content churches provide may be seen as a homogeneous good—like aluminum or oil, it's the same no matter where it comes from—whereas the social goods churches offer are heterogeneous, differentiated by location.[16] This view is not inherently bad ecclesiologically; the fact that the sacraments confer grace *ex opere operato* means that Roman Catholics can go to any mass anywhere in the world and receive the same spiritual benefit. But the traditional factor that determines where Catholics go to mass—residency within the parish's territory—binds the parishioners to a local community, including everyone who lives in that community, no matter their social status.[17] It forces people to recognize that the body of Christ is a given reality, that its members are selected not by human beings but by God. The problem comes in when the networking opportunities churches offer become major criteria for deciding which church to attend. There is no Christian theological basis for making such criteria determinative in such a decision. Rather, to the extent that someone employs them in selecting a church to join, the church at large is being used to advance that person's public life.

Most of the elites Lindsay interviewed became evangelicals only as adults, and many did so in college.[18] Lindsay sees this as evidence of their true, chosen commitment to Christianity, but again, there could be another side to the story. Young adults studying at elite col-

---

15. See Ibid., 222.

16. Thanks to the economists Valerie Kepner and Margarita Rose for calling this distinction to my attention.

17. Territorial location is nevertheless problematic, as it traditionally reinscribed ethnicity and today may reinscribe social class. Furthermore, American Catholics are now willing to "church-shop," driving long distances to attend a church that suits their tastes.

18. Lindsay, *Faith in the Halls of Power*, 220.

leges and universities are learning how to be American elites. They are beginning to form the networks that will sustain their careers for decades. The on-campus religious programs that help spur and sustain evangelical faith among college students are often sponsored by organizations that actively encourage professional networking as well.[19] Does the network exist to encourage the sustenance of faith, or vice versa?

The distorted view of the church as a professional network is itself a fruit of the elastic orthodoxy that points to a loss of distinctiveness in evangelical elites' religious identities. When orthodoxy expands in order to accommodate an individual's professional aims, it inevitably conforms more closely to the creed of American public life. Lindsay asserts that the elites he spoke with have generally maintained a set of inelastic "core principles,"[20] though he does not specify what those principles are. It is clear, however, that some Christian principles are not being retained by cosmopolitan evangelicals. Most of the business leaders Lindsay interviewed have few qualms about living large and making the extravagant purchases the popular mind associates with CEOs: multiple homes, private jets, yachts. They "tend to bracket off their faith from decisions about purchases. Instead they focus on faith's implications for production," giving their wealth a measure of "balance" through philanthropy.[21] In this respect, the gospel's message is to them little different from that of management advice books. Whether a Christian ought to exploit every advantage he or she can (including having a marketable religious identity) seems unquestioned by many evangelical business elites. Lindsay's remark, "Evangelical leaders dream big and aspire to financial success, even though some Christian teachings express a preference for the meek and humble," understates by a wide margin the radical reorganization of society and the economy that Jesus proclaims. It requires a highly tendentious reading of the gospels to come to the conclusion reached by a Wal-Mart executive Lindsay interviewed: "I don't see that Christ was a patsy. He was ambitious."[22]

19. Ibid., 91–92.
20. Ibid., 226.
21. Ibid., 192–93.
22. Ibid., 170.

These corruptions could not exist without the insistence on the highly public Christian identity that underwrites evangelical elites' professional networks. These elites easily identify each other, and they believe that the public example of their lives and their success will draw more people to the faith.[23] While they recognize that overt expressions of their religious identity are not appropriate in all contexts, they can signal that identity through less-conspicuous means, including "double-coded" language that seems unremarkable to nonevangelicals but that other evangelicals will interpret as a sign that the speaker shares the listener's religious identity.[24] The high visibility of this identity is the *conditio sine qua non* for the cosmopolitan evangelical network, which itself is the vehicle for the elites' defective ecclesiology and, ironically, for the eroding distinctiveness of their religious identity. If secrecy concerning Christian identity were normative instead, these corruptions likely would not occur. If evangelical elites could no longer count on being able to identify each other in public life as Christians, then the networks would not form in the first place, and there would be little temptation to exploit the sociological character of the church for individual professional gain.

I should note that evangelicalism is hardly the only sector of the Christian church in America that is susceptible to overidentifying with American culture and making American political, economic, and social creeds into de facto doctrines. Indeed, virtually every religious group in America has capitulated in one way or another to American ways of thought and life.[25] But evangelicals are the most recent large group to mount the American public stage, so they represent a timely case for study. As they have gained so much from their religious identity lately, they rightly deserve attention now.

Reticence about Christian identity in American politics is exactly what the evangelical theologian Charles Marsh advocates as a mea-

23. Ibid., 216.
24. Ibid., 211. On double-coding, specifically in the speeches of George W. Bush, see Bruce Lincoln, *Holy Terrors: Thinking about Religion after September 11* (Chicago: University of Chicago Press, 2003), 30–32, and Hugh B. Urban, *The Secrets of the Kingdom: Religion and Concealment in the Bush Administration* (Lanham, MD: Rowman and Littlefield, 2007), 32, 46–49.
25. Alan Wolfe, *The Transformation of American Religion: How We Actually Live Our Faith* (New York: Free Press, 2003).

sure against the distortions of the gospel that he thinks have enabled Christians to support a war-mongering and plutocratic public agenda recently. And of course, Cyril, Kierkegaard, and Bonhoeffer in different ways advocated concealing Christian identity as measures against Christians' abusing that identity in the public crises of their times. Granted, Cyril himself seems to have been an ambitious politician, seeking to advance Jerusalem's standing within the universal church and the empire, but the evidence of the seriousness with which he handled matters of doctrine is very strong. He consistently quarreled with Arians and held enough confidence in the integrity of the creed as to place its teaching authority even above that of himself and his brother bishops. No "elastic orthodoxy" there.

The Church as a Community of Hidden Discipleship

This chapter and the previous one together present a picture of Christian selfhood within the church in which secrecy or its cognates contribute to nearly every element. That secrecy is an element in selfhood, moral responsibility, and the preservation and extension of Christian identity in church tradition implies that a call for secrecy about Christian identity is far from being a betrayal of Christian conceptions of the individual and his or her place within the church. That the church is a visible entity does not necessary entail every individual Christian being visible as a Christian at all times. As I have been arguing, a Christian, considered as an individual, is a disciple, committed to following Christ and living a life of holiness that is nourished by participating in the life of the church. Responding to the call to holiness entails living differently from nondisciples. And as the negative example of cosmopolitan evangelicals helps to indicate, ensuring the distinctiveness of discipleship in contexts like that of contemporary America demands that Christians of social privilege conceal their religious identity in public life.

In this case, we may consider the church to be a community of hidden disciples.[26] In so describing the church, I am modifying the

26. This is not meant to be an exhaustive account of Christian ecclesiology. It does, however, express an important aspect of what the church must be, if an individual Christian is a disciple. All models of the church must be corrected by complementary models.

model of the church as community of disciples proposed by Avery Dulles. This model, a version of the model of the church as mystical communion, emphasizes the church's and the individual Christian's relation to Christ. This ecclesial model also recognizes that Christians are active in the world but held to standards beyond worldly ones. To Dulles, lay people are to be "leaven" in the world. Transforming the world is no easy task; it requires the lay person to be "a committed disciple,"[27] secular, yet acknowledging the distinction between worldliness and Christianity. Adding secrecy about Christian identity to this version of discipleship does no violence to it. The breadth of the community-of-disciples model makes it appealing both ecumenically and with respect to a range of other ecclesiologies, "build[ing] bridges" between other visions of the church.[28]

The ecumenicity of this model can be seen in its clear affinities with the ecumenical collection of Christian authors I discussed in Part One. In the hidden Abrahamic discipleship of Kierkegaard and Bonhoeffer, a person of faith recovers family and community in the church after first severing their natural social ties. Dulles stresses that discipleship must not be thought of individualistically, giving the same priority to the Christian community that Cyril did:

> Discipleship always depends upon a prior call or vocation from Christ, a demanding call that brings with it the grace needed for its own acceptance. The Church mediates the call of Christ and makes available the word of God and the sacraments, without which discipleship would scarcely be possible. Thus the community of disciples is in some sense prior to its own members.[29]

This is true no matter which path one takes to membership in the church. Persons who are baptized as infants today are incorporated into its communal life even before they can understand what having a Christian identity entails. In Cyril's church, something similar is true of adults, because the sacraments and theology are kept hidden from the catechumens and candidates until they have already been

---

27. Avery Cardinal Dulles, SJ, *Models of the Church*, expanded ed. (New York: Image, 2002), 205.
28. Ibid., 198.
29. Ibid., 217.

incorporated into the community, interacting with catechists, with baptized Christians in the outer court of the church building, and with each other.

The church grew initially because its members presented a pagan world with an attractive alternative: "Seeing the mutual love and support of the Christians, and the high moral standards they observed, the pagans sought entrance into the Church."[30] In contemporary America, there can be no question of whether people have heard of Christianity. Indeed, American Christians perhaps need to attract people to the church in spite of what people already assume they know about Christianity.

A life of discipleship is a life of neighbor love, the distinctive way of interacting in the world that nondisciples do not exhibit.[31] Christians' love today, if it truly is expansive, will inevitably and without Christians' conscious deliberation catch others up into some form of communal life. A person so involved in that communal life may indeed, by virtue of that life, already be on the way to becoming Christian without even knowing it. When the time is right, these persons may inquire about the theological identity of that community. They may begin to recognize their attraction to the community as the call of Christ to discipleship.

Debating Discipleship within the Church Walls

The tasks of maintaining the boundaries around Christian identity and inviting non-Christians into the community of disciples require the community to deliberate about what constitutes genuine discipleship. Church authorities, pastors, laity, and theologians all take part in this debate, determining what the gospel demands of Christians, both across history and in particular historical moments. These debates take many forms, from informal conversations, to meetings of church boards and parish councils, to discussions in academic journals, to large cross-denominational meetings of church leaders. The ground for Christian identity—Christian faith—is assumed in these debates. Contributing to them therefore implies that the

30. Ibid., 213.
31. For Kierkegaard, "paganism" lacks the category of "the neighbor" (WL 44).

contributor is a Christian; there is no concealing that identity to the other participants in the debate or to anyone listening to the debates. Still, debate about the content of the tradition or about the demands of contemporary discipleship is done completely for the sake of Christians themselves. They alone have the experiential knowledge (including experience of the sacraments) necessary to make sense of discipleship. Non-Christians involved in such discussions could take the wrong lesson from the discussion, as Cyril feared might happen to baptismal candidates if they were taught Christian doctrine too early, harming themselves and the Christian tradition alike.

Add to this consideration the need in some circumstances to preserve Christian identity from being exploited for gain in individuals' public lives, and we come to the rationale for Bonhoeffer's *Arkandisziplin*. Bonhoeffer's concept carries the complementary requirements of concealing Christian identity in public and confessing Christian faith only in secret. If the notion of confession can expand to include debate about doctrinal and moral issues, church discipline and church authority, then *all* discussion among Christians about specifically Christian matters must occur behind closed doors, out of the world's sight.[32]

In an era of easy access to portable and rapid communications media and devices, this may well prove difficult to put into practice. Unless churches want to search their congregants at the door and force them to hand over their cell phones, there is no real way to guarantee that the liturgy or an internal church debate will not become part of extra-ecclesial public life. But the difficulty of implementing this proposal to its fullest possible extent does not mean that nothing should be attempted. The first steps will necessarily be small and will take the form of small internal debates like those I have been discussing. Pastors will need to preach on the difference

---

32. To Kathryn Tanner, a major task of the Christian "community of argument" is precisely what genuine discipleship entails. Indeed, on her account, being in search of a Christian identity *is* Christian identity. Kathryn Tanner, *Theories of Culture: A New Agenda for Theology* (Minneapolis: Fortress, 1997), 123, 155. Tanner's position is important to the issue of the relation between Christian identity and the cultures in which the church finds itself, but its nuance makes it difficult to treat briefly. In some respects, our positions are close, though mine differs from hers largely in the confidence I have that Christians can in many cases—for example, regarding whether the church should serve as a network of business contacts—articulate clear distinctions between Christian and cultural practices.

between publicity and mission. Churches will need to rethink whether producing and selling DVDs of their pastors' greatest sermons is not capitulating to the omnipresence of communications and entertainment media in American public life. Theologians will have to give more attention to their audiences and their purposes in publishing their research, ensuring that it is genuinely done for the benefit of the church. Reconsidering these issues is meant principally to hold public posturing about Christian identity at bay at a time when far vaster publics than anyone could imagine even a few years ago are available to American Christians.

But does attempting to contain Christian debate within the church walls simultaneously render the church insular and thereby vulnerable to ideology and self-enclosed groupthink? The church has made much use in its history of ideas and modes of thought it imported from the outside, from Greek philosophy to modern notions of gender. Outsiders can present any sociological entity with standards against which a group can be judged, as an independent board does for an institution. But here is a point where the theological nature of the church makes it unlike secular social forms. Although the church can profit from imported perspectives, it cannot simply adopt them uncritically. Seeking the criticism of the world can be seen as an attempt to become righteous *coram hominibus*, and in that regard it is no different from seeking to profit in public life from one's religious identity. A church that became, say, thoroughly democratic in its governance or thoroughly postmodern in its theology might rise in the esteem of some of the worldly, but in doing so, it might also lose its identity. If the church no longer makes its surrounding culture "odd," to use Kathryn Tanner's term, then it has lost a large part of its purpose.[33]

The remedy for a church of hidden disciples' insularity is transcendence. If transcendence means simply crossing boundaries, then admitting outside criticism of the church is a form of it, albeit a weak one, as only a social boundary is being crossed. The transcendence that should matter most to Christians is the transcendence of the human effected by divine grace and revelation. Although the church cannot accept worldly criticism uninvited and uncritically, neither can it simply rest assured in its righteousness through a blind traditionalism that

33. Ibid., 133.

ignores the fact that the church is a living organism animated by the Holy Spirit, who remains free.[34] Thus Christians must be ever attentive to divine grace. Here again, Abraham is a model disciple. The greatness of his faith is best exhibited not by his willingness to obey God's command to sacrifice Isaac but by his continued openness to hearing God's voice, which he then obeyed a second time, fulfilling his hope that he would be able to keep Isaac. Although Abraham "disregards any argument that may come from the outside" (FT 87), he does not close off the avenue of criticism from God's transcendence.

Within the church, however, the operation of grace still needs to be understood and interpreted collectively, and so openness to divine transcendence alone may not be enough to prevent the church from closing in on itself in a self-destructive way. Bonhoeffer's *Arkandisziplin* itself has been criticized for leaving open "the possibility of ideological misappropriation of divine revelation on the part of the exponents of the discipline of the secret; his ecclesiology lacked a strategy of 'suspicion.'"[35] In other words, maintaining secrecy about intramural deliberations concerning Christian discipleship must not be allowed to devolve into the deliberators claiming that they have a monopoly on grace. The purpose of this secrecy is partly to prevent Christian identity from being misappropriated in public, but employing secrecy poses the danger of establishing an ideological cabal within the church. Thus there must be an immanent critical apparatus that takes account of sinful self-deception and uproots its influence.

One such apparatus is to see some features of the tradition as unrevisable standards to which future doctrines and practices that develop would have to conform. These standards themselves would have to be protected to maintain their distinctiveness and integrity. Neighbor love is one such pillar of the tradition. And as I have argued, safeguards can help ensure that the one who performs works of love in secret remains, in one sense, self-critical. Kierkegaard's "dash," which requires the individual to be extremely circumspect in hiding his or her agency from the beneficiary of "the greatest beneficence," accomplishes this. Hiding oneself "in a dash," then, can

34. Ibid., 137.
35. Kenneth Surin, "*Contemptus Mundi* and the Disenchanted World: Bonhoeffer's 'Discipline of the Secret' and Adorno's 'Strategy of Hibernation,'" *Journal of the American Academy of Religion* 53 (1985): 403.

be thought of as a strategy of self-suspicion that aims at refusing the reciprocity characteristic of modern social interactions. Identifying and protecting similar pillars of the tradition—the sacraments, for example—similarly guard against the ideological or self-satisfied manipulation of divine revelation.

A second apparatus arises from the way that debate occurs within the confines of the church. Although Christians all share a single religious identity, they are not monolithically of one mind. Debate about discipleship will feature disagreement even without the presence of non-Christians' contribution to the debate. These differences can, however, be put to productive use. The "this-worldly" transcendence of "transversality," as put forward by the philosopher Calvin Schrag, may provide a means of balancing the needs for human selves, in all their differences, to come to nonhegemonic univocity in certain contexts. To understand this idea, imagine a transverse wave, like a light wave or a radio wave, composed of multiple overlapping elements that nonetheless propagate in the same direction. Transversality implies that multiple perspectives are in play, though seeking a point of unity among themselves; in this regard it is well-suited to the needs of contemporary American Christians. The unity that transversality attains is not imposed from above or outside, but emerges from within, the product of differentiation within the whole and the recognition of the contingency of the different identities that individuals bring to the discussion. As the different members of the whole interact and acknowledge a need for unity, they will in time come to "convergence without coincidence, conjuncture without concordance, overlapping without assimilation, and union without absorption."[36] Transversality is furthermore "a dynamic and open-textured process of unifying that allows for plurality and difference and neither seeks the metaphysical comforts of stable beginnings and universal telic principles nor displays an epistemological enchantment with zero-point epistemic foundations."[37]

Applied to the model of the church as a community of hidden disciples, all of whom have different histories and nonreligious identities

36. Calvin O. Schrag, *The Self After Postmodernity* (New Haven, CT: Yale University Press, 1997), 128.
37. Ibid., 129–30.

that help to inform their contribution to any debate about discipleship, this notion of transversality would describe a process of coming to gradual and provisional consensus about what unites the group itself. In that respect, the intramural debate within the church is analogous to the internal debate among various identities that occurs within the individual human self. Those identities open the self up to the world outside it, and unless the self is going to be reduced to one of the individual's identities, these identities need to be balanced and negotiated within the person. If the debate within the church is itself a tradition stretching across centuries, then there is no opportunity to set every possible participant on the same metaphysical foundation. And with no teleological picture of discipleship already in mind, the discussants can remain suspicious of any ideological appropriations of the debate.

Conclusion

Though discipleship and witness often are seen as equivalent terms, the latter term, unlike the former, implies a necessary visibility. Indeed, discipleship, as the distinctively Christian way of being in the world, is in many ways enhanced and protected by its being carried out invisibly. Christian identity must be revealed at some point, to bring new members into the church, to sustain Christian identity in worship, and to debate that identity's meaning. But these activities are best done in secret: out of the public eye and in the context of activities in which the removal of Christian identity would render the activities incoherent. In other words, these activities should be, to the fullest extent possible, revealed only to other members of the Christian "public," in Alan Wolfe's sense of the term. Otherwise, it is simply too easy to make the general public one's audience (or to turn the church into the general public), in a brazen display of piety that brings glory to oneself rather than to Christ.[38]

I mentioned in the introduction that this book begins from a stance of suspicion born out of the recognition that human beings are self-interested and self-deceptive, inclined to corrupt the best in

38. The analysis of contemporary ecclesiology in Nicholas M. Healy, *Church, World, and the Christian Life: Practical-Prophetic Ecclesiology* (Cambridge: Cambridge University Press, 2001) places much importance on this need to give glory only to Christ.

the service of their worst desires for worldly power and prestige. The fact that self-interest compounds when sinful individuals come together in an institution of any kind means that the church itself needs suspicious critique aimed at it.[39] But the unique status of the church as a theological institution means that the apparatuses that other institutions rely on to evaluate themselves will ultimately be inadequate. Christians need transcendence to go beyond even the world itself. Limiting intramural debate about internal church matters to Christians themselves cuts the church off only from the weak transcendence offered by outside perspectives.

To Schrag, the Kierkegaardian neighbor-love that gives without the expectation or possibility of return "most poignantly tells the story of the profile of the self in transcendence"[40] insofar as this kind of love "transcend[s] religion as a sphere of immanence, a culture-sphere alongside the culture-spheres of science, morality, and art."[41] The immanentist view of Christianity is expressed in America today partly by the reduction of the church to a purely sociological entity that can be exploited to advance an individual Christian's public life. The immanentist view is what I have been arguing against in this chapter. A strong sense of transcendence enables the church as a community of hidden disciples to be critical of itself and the world, and in doing so, to stubbornly sever ties with many worldly and anti-Christian ideas and practices, in the name of maintaining the distinctiveness of the church's identity. Simultaneously, however, as Hans Urs von Balthasar writes, by reaching out to the world through the promiscuous neighbor love of her members, "in the dark, [the church] remains in communion" with what is condemned, "just as Christ himself can make a judgment about the sinner only because he has, from within, experienced, known and borne away the sinner's darkness."[42] Indeed, the disciples' own sinful "darkness" demands that their love be performed "in the dark." Yet by that love, the disciples manage to enlarge the church, drawing more and more into that hidden life.

---

39. See Reinhold Niebuhr, *Moral Man and Immoral Society: A Study in Ethics and Politics* (Louisville, KY: Westminster John Knox Press, 2001).

40. Schrag, *Self after Postmodernity*, 141.

41. Ibid., 144-45.

42. Hans Urs von Balthasar, *Razing the Bastions: On the Church in This Age*, trans. Brian McNeil, C.R.V. (San Francisco: Ignatius Press, 1993), 88.

9

Secret Faith's Fulfillment
of the Church's Mission in America

An Engagement with Hauerwas

In chapter 5, I noted the ease with which Stanley Hauerwas claimed Dietrich Bonhoeffer as an ally in his theological project. To Hauerwas, Bonhoeffer's resistance to Nazism was grounded in a theology, consistently articulated "from the beginning to the end of his life,"[1] that demanded a highly visible, explicitly Christian witness to the world. As I have shown, this view of Bonhoeffer is inaccurate. Bonhoeffer's idea of the *Arkandisziplin*, developed piecemeal over more than a decade and in various theological genres (lectures, a book, letters), does give importance to confessing the faith; Bonhoeffer seeks to confine particularistic confessional statements, however, to liturgical settings. Except for the most extreme cases, Christians are to keep their religious identity secret in their public lives of work, politics, and the economy, allowing their "witness" to shine forth unselfconsciously as wordless deeds.

1. Stanley Hauerwas, *Performing the Faith: Bonhoeffer and the Practice of Nonviolence* (Grand Rapids: Brazos, 2004), 55.

Granted, theologians seem able to find virtually anything they want to find in Bonhoeffer; perhaps most often they find themselves.[2] Hauerwas claims that reading Bonhoeffer's *Discipleship* (i.e., the book that does the most to argue for the hiddenness of Christian identity in the modern era) was a kind of *preparatio evangelium* for him, opening him up to receiving John Howard Yoder's *Politics of Jesus*,[3] which set him on the theological course he has traversed ever since. This may be true, but it is very hard to see how someone can trace Hauerwas's current position on the public nature of Christian identity back to *Discipleship* in any way other than the book being an accidental occasion for Hauerwas to come to conclusions other than those Bonhoeffer draws. It is telling that Hauerwas has nothing to say, in his book-length commentary on Matthew's gospel, about Jesus' admonishments to his disciples that they conceal their pious actions.[4] Bonhoeffer devotes a full chapter to it in *Discipleship*.

There would be little use in making a detailed analysis of Hauerwas's misreading of Bonhoeffer. This misreading nonetheless provides a point of entry into the way Hauerwas's theological outlook gives undue privilege to the public visibility of Christian identity. The main question I want to answer in this chapter is why concealing Christian identity seems to have no place in Hauerwas's theology of Christian witness in contemporary America.

Understanding Hauerwas's position here will go a long way toward understanding North American theologians' general prejudice in favor of making Christian identity as visible as possible in public life. Although not all who advocate a visible Christian identity do so for the same reasons as Hauerwas,[5] Hauerwas's position is undeniably influential. To Jeffrey Stout, Hauerwas is not only "surely the most prophetic and influential theologian now working in the

2. Haynes, *The Bonhoeffer Phenomenon: Portraits of a Protestant Saint* (Minneapolis: Augsburg Fortress, 2004).

3. Hauerwas, *Performing the Faith*, 35.

4. Stanley Hauerwas, *Matthew* (Grand Rapids: Brazos, 2006).

5. See, e.g., Charles Mathewes, *A Theology of Public Life* (Cambridge: Cambridge University Press, 2007); Ronald M. Thiemann, *Religion in Public Life: A Dilemma for Democracy* (Washington, DC: Georgetown University Press, 1996); Richard John Neuhaus, *The Naked Public Square: Religion and Democracy in America*, 2nd ed. (Grand Rapids: Eerdmans, 1986).

United States," but also the one who "has done more to inflame Christian resentment of secular culture" than any other.[6] Anyone writing on Christian identity in American public life today either has to deal with Hauerwas or explain why he or she is not dealing with him. Hauerwas's thought is especially relevant to this book, as certain elements in Hauerwas's position bring his close to mine, even though his conclusion and mine differ considerably. Indeed, I will argue in this chapter that the important Hauerwasian goal of ensuring that Christians in America have a distinctive identity over and against American public life would be attained more readily if theologians traded some Hauerwasian theological elements for ones that I have been advocating.

A theology of Christian identity in American public life cannot easily be separated off from the rest of Hauerwas's thought, simply because his entire theological project for the last three decades has aimed to preserve and assert that identity in this particular context. Broadly stated, the central theme in Hauerwas's theological account of Christianity in contemporary America is the need for a distinctive Christian witness in this context. The two words *distinctiveness* and *witness* encompass nearly every other theological concept and category significant to Hauerwas's project. Thus, for instance, his emphasis on the peculiarly Christian narrative as formative of the Christian community serves to ensure distinctiveness, and his account of Christian virtue ethics is meant to promote the visibility of that community's witness. Hauerwas furthermore considers only the contemporary American historical context; therefore, what he considers an appropriate witness here and now, as well as what Christianity needs to distinguish itself against, are shaped by that context.

In his concern for maintaining the distinctiveness of Christianity in contemporary America, Hauerwas is an ally of my project in this book. To Hauerwas, the way American public life makes use of Christianity deeply distorts Christian faith and identity. In his view, religion in contemporary America "may be a source of strength in personal crisis and/or an aid in interpersonal relations. Accordingly,

---

6. Jeffrey Stout, *Democracy and Tradition* (Princeton: Princeton University Press, 2003), 140.

the church has become but one among many voluntary associations of like-minded people from similar economic strata."[7] As I showed in chapter 8, the church in America is often all too ready to accept this definition of itself and thereby ignore its primary status as a community of Christ's disciples.

Yet the kind of witness Hauerwas calls for ultimately is inadequate to maintain the distinctiveness of Christian identity while attempting to transform the world. In fact, there is a deep tension between the distinctiveness Hauerwas attributes to Christianity and the public nature of Christians' witness to the world. It is akin to the tension any secret-keeper faces: the secret is useless unless it is told, but telling it dissipates the distinctiveness that gives it its power. Managing this tension means telling the secret only with great care, ensuring that the recipient realizes the weight of the secret, and encouraging the recipient to keep and pass on the secret as judiciously as it was given to him or her. Too often, Hauerwas does not adequately maintain this tension. Too often, he gives too much weight to the need for a visible witness at the cost of the invisible aspects of Christianity, aspects that truly distinguish it from the post-Enlightenment, secular, public realms of the economy and the political sphere. So while the parameters that Hauerwas establishes for Christian witness in American public life exclude a proposal like mine, many of these parameters are shaky. As I will show, the exclusion of particularistic religious language from public life cannot always be equated with liberalism, visibility is not a normative ecclesiological category, and truthfulness about oneself does not necessarily demand laying every aspect of one's identity out in the open. In fact, under certain conditions, it can be more truthful to hold aspects of one's identity back from public view. In spite of my agreement with Hauerwas on the need for Christians to be concerned about preserving their religious identity's distinctiveness, I argue in this chapter that that concern should lead Christians away from the strident insistence on the public nature of Christian witness found in Hauerwas's writings.

7. Hauerwas, *The Peaceable Kingdom: A Primer of Christian Ethics* (Notre Dame, IN: University of Notre Dame Press, 1983), 12.

Hauerwas on Christian Identity in American Public Life

Hauerwas's promotion of a visible witness to the Christian faith stems from his straightforward and unapologetic conviction that the Christian story is true. Christians cannot but share this conviction, which implies a concomitant responsibility to make that truth more widely known by handing it on to others. Thus "the necessity of witness is at the heart of the Christian life. [Christian] convictions cannot be learned except as they are attested to and exemplified by" Christians.[8]

Exemplification is the key element here that leads Hauerwas to advocate a visible Christian identity in America. To Hauerwas, the specific form Christians' witness must take is for the church to be an alternative "peaceable" society, making visible to the world its own (the world's) violence, even to the point of suffering violence itself without retaliation. Performing this task adequately is more than enough for the church to do in its ministry. As Stout characterizes Hauerwas's position, "Being the church . . . is a matter of maintaining a pacifist community of virtue in the midst of a violent world, thus providing a foretaste of the peaceable kingdom in which God reigns absolutely and eternally."[9] If the world—or rather, the worldly—are drawn to the church's visible life and its preaching of the story of God, Israel, and Jesus, then that will surely be to the good. But this is only a corollary to the church's primary task, which "is not to *make* the world the kingdom, but to be faithful to the kingdom by showing to the world what it means to be a community of peace."[10] This does not mean that the church is obsessively self-concerned about its own purity and the individual salvation of its members. Rather, the church's life is done for the sake of the world; without that life, the world will be stuck with its violent ways. Saying that the church is simply "to be the church," Hauerwas writes, is meant as a "reminder that the church is in the world to serve the world."[11] The world is in desperate need of the truth that Christians can give it by exemplifying a peaceable life

8. Hauerwas, *The Peaceable Kingdom*, 14–15.
9. Stout, *Democracy and Tradition*, 146.
10. Hauerwas, *The Peaceable Kingdom*, 103.
11. Hauerwas, *Performing the Faith*, 231.

together; "Without such a witness we only abandon the world to the violence derived from the lies that devour our lives."[12]

Hauerwas's frequent claim that "the first task of the church is not to make the world more just but to make the world the world"[13] must be understood in light of his equally oft-made claim that the church does not have a social ethic, but rather *is* a social ethic. That is, the church's teaching about how to live collectively is in no way separable from its concrete life in the visible realm of history. It tells its members and the world how to live by showing them, living in the way a redeemed people should. Thus "the church gives no gift to the worlds in which it finds itself more politically important than the formation of a people constituted by the virtues necessary to endure the struggle to hear and speak truthfully to one another."[14] Although Christians do not primarily speak to the world, their actions toward each other must be visible to the world, in order to indict the world of being violent, and their speech to each other must be audible to the world. Their hope must be to show the world that their society is better than the world's version of society and that the narrative that informs Christian society is a better one than the world's narrative. As Hauerwas puts it, "Faithfully enacting the Christian story, then, is effectively to 'out-narrate' the world by situating the world's 'givens' within a more determinative, peaceable, and hence more encompassing, narrative."[15] Despite the note of competition between church and world that Hauerwas strikes in this statement, the aim of out-narrating the world is to give it an objectively better narrative, one that would liberate it from its self-destructive violence. To do this, the church clearly must maintain its distinctiveness with respect to the world, so that it has something to teach the world. Losing that distinctiveness compromises the church's mission: its "service is rendered less than it should be when the church is no longer able to maintain the politics of Jesus."[16]

12. Hauerwas, *The Peaceable Kingdom*, 15.

13. Hauerwas, *Performing the Faith*, 56. Elsewhere, Hauerwas phrases it like this: "the first social task of the church is to help the world know that it is the world. For without the church, the world has no means to know that it is the world." Hauerwas, "The Gesture of a Truthful Story," *Theology Today* 42 (1985): 182.

14. Hauerwas, *Performing the Faith*, 15.

15. Ibid., 92.

16. Ibid., 231.

The visibility demanded by the church's mission to the world fits felicitously with Hauerwas's virtue ethics. On the Aristotelian account of the good life that Hauerwas favors, moral goodness is not simply a matter of reasoning rightly. Rather, one needs to train oneself in performing the right actions in the way that a virtuous person performs them. Hence one needs to see those actions performed so that one can imitate them, and one needs additionally to be taught the right way to perform the actions. Thus, virtuous individuals arise out of virtuous communities and indeed, simply by being virtuous, testify to the virtue of their communities. To a large extent, virtue is its own pedagogy. Virtue ethics is thus entirely unintelligible unless visible, bodily actions that exhibit virtues are privileged. Hauerwas's commitment to virtue ethics has naturally led him to describe Christian life as a performance.[17]

Christian virtues and the church's distinctiveness over and against the world come together in the lives of virtuous Christian individuals. The attractiveness of their witness ultimately leads one to the virtuous communities from which they arose. The contrast between their lives and the way of the world also focuses Christians' task in the world. Because the church and the world "desperately need" to continue "arguments" with each other, "Christians and non-Christians alike should despair when it becomes difficult to distinguish the church from the world. Of course, for Christians, despair is a vice that robs us of our ability to see what is before our eyes—that is, lives with names like John Howard Yoder, John Paul II, and Dorothy Day."[18]

The three individual Christians mentioned in the last paragraph are often held up by Hauerwas as exemplars of Christian virtue in large part because they share a commitment to embodying peaceable-

---

17. James Fodor and Stanley Hauerwas, "Performing Faith: The Peaceable Rhetoric of God's Church," in *Performing the Faith*, 75–109. Hauerwas's recent emphasis on performance places him in the intellectual company of literary critics like Eve Kosofsky Sedgwick and Judith Butler. The association is telling, as we shall soon see. Sedgwick sees the inner/outer distinction as a weapon in the fight to promote heteronormativity, while Hauerwas sees it as a weapon in the fight to promote Constantinianism. See Sedgwick, *Epistemology of the Closet* (Berkeley: University of California Press, 1990) and Butler, *Giving an Account of Oneself* (New York: Fordham University Press, 2005).

18. Hauerwas, *With the Grain of the Universe: The Church's Witness and Natural Theology* (Grand Rapids: Brazos, 2001), 240.

ness and pacifism. The greatest threat to Christian distinctiveness is what Hauerwas, following Yoder, calls Constantinianism,[19] the church's alliance with the state—and the state's inherent violence. But if Constantinianism is the perennial threat to the church's distinctiveness with respect to the world, then liberalism is a threat peculiar to modernity and prevalent in the contemporary United States. Liberalism prevents the person (and, *a fortiori*, the church) from presenting a peculiar narrative, a truthful witness, to the world because it presumes to disembed the individual from all communities and then give the individual an opportunity to choose any interest groups he or she wishes to join.

Hauerwas is concerned that liberalism's infiltration into the church means that Christianity is no longer seen as needing to be true, for it is purely "functional" as a civil religion. The main function of Christianity on such an account is to give religious justifications for secular social projects intended to promote justice. Such conceptions of justice are not peculiarly Christian and are instead derived from Enlightenment principles, and so Christians' participation in secular social justice projects implicates the church in an ultimately violent and hegemonic liberalism.[20] Hence Hauerwas maintains that the church must be indifferent to "political change and justice" and "progressive forces."[21] Getting all Americans, Christians and otherwise, to accept the agenda of the "progressive forces" requires public discussion and propaganda, worded in maximally universal ways. To Hauerwas, this eviscerates Christianity, as "all our more particularistic beliefs must be socially defined as 'private' and thus admitting of no social role."[22] Christians would then become unable to speak "[w]ithout apology" in

19. For the pacifist Hauerwas, the association with the state's militarism and violence poses the greatest danger to the church's integrity when it allies itself with the state. The term "Constantinianism" is intended to draw attention to this violence. Christians who are not pacifists may still find much wrong with the church–public life synthesis. "Christendom" is meant to represent this synthesis without necessarily giving the state's use of violence primary importance.

20. Hauerwas, "Creation, Contingency, and Truthful Nonviolence: A Milbankian Reflection," in *Wilderness Wanderings: Probing Twentieth-Century Theology and Philosophy* (Boulder, CO: Westview Press, 1997), 188–98. See especially 190.

21. Hauerwas, "The Gesture of a Truthful Story," 185.

22. Hauerwas, *The Peaceable Kingdom*, 13.

unambiguous Christian terms and hold the truth of the crucified Christ up to American society.[23]

Liberalism furthermore cooperates with a Constantinian internalization of Christian faith; "speaking of faith principally in subjective terms . . . cuts off Christianity and effectively quarantines it within the narrow, inner realm of the private."[24] Thus the entire inner/outer distinction, integral to an account of concealing Christian identity in public life, is, through its association with liberalism, a party to the forces that erase the distinction between the church and the world. This distinction, absent from virtue accounts of personal character, fosters several illusions. Two of these illusions—that one is ultimately in charge of one's body, and that one can "step back" from one's work and detach one's "real" self from concrete actions—compromise personal wholeness in the name of liberal notions of autonomy.[25]

Hauerwas's opposition to liberal doctrines seems equally to be opposition to my argument in this book. If one of liberalism's vices is its demand that particularistic Christian claims not be made in public, then a theological call for Christians to conceal their particularistic religious identity in public life is guilty of the same vice under a different name. This is not so, however, as I will show a little later in the chapter. For now, we need to judge the validity of Hauerwas's account of the visibility of the church in light of its mission to the world.

The Real Church, Visible and Invisible

Hauerwas's insistence that the church's witness must be a visible alternative to the world leads him to enunciate sharp criticism of positions he perceives as advocating an invisible Christian church. Surely, it stands to reason that if the church cannot be seen, then it cannot be seen by the world, and it therefore cannot present the world with an alternative way of being.

23. Hauerwas, *A Better Hope: Resources for a Church Confronting Capitalism, Democracy, and Postmodernity* (Grand Rapids: Brazos, 2000), 11.

24. Fodor and Hauerwas, in Hauerwas, *Performing the Faith*, 76.

25. Hauerwas, *Sanctify Them in the Truth: Holiness Exemplified* (Nashville, TN: Abingdon, 1998), 80–81, and *Performing the Faith*, 225. As Hauerwas notes in *Performing the Faith*, he once advocated such a "stepping back," but has since repudiated it.

Still, Hauerwas reaches for an ecclesiologically richer explanation than this, claiming that there can be only one "real" church—the visible, physical, historical community that performs particular bodily practices.[26] In his words, "I have no use for distinctions between visible and invisible church. The church can be no less real than he who was crucified. The church cannot be an ideal that is never quite realized. Rather, the church must be as real as the nation we confront if we are to be capable of challenging its imperial pretension."[27] Hauerwas cites Yoder in claiming that the theological assumption that the invisible church is the true church is a consequence of Constantinianism, causing Christians to believe that "the distinctive character of Christian life is now primarily identified with inwardness since everyone by definition is already Christian."[28] The visibility of the church that Hauerwas advocates is rooted in the visibility of the crucifixion, and it flourishes in the ordinary life practices of "the concrete church with parking lots and potluck dinners."[29]

A presumption against the invisibility of the church sits at the heart of Hauerwas's discussion of Bonhoeffer—and provides much of the basis for Hauerwas's misapprehension of Bonhoeffer. He does not see the problem inherent in saying that Bonhoeffer's "stress on the necessity of visibility led him to write a book like *Discipleship*."[30] To Hauerwas, Bonhoeffer's life demonstrates the truth of the church's visibility. A church "trapped by its invisibility and unwilling to risk itself on behalf of the world" is incapable of "provid[ing] an alternative" to the death-dealing of what Bonhoeffer called the "world come of age."[31] Elsewhere in *Performing the Faith*, including the

26. In light of Hauerwas's assertions of the "reality" of the church as he describes it, it is ironic that he has been sharply criticized for espousing too idealistic a picture of the church. See Stout, *Democracy and Tradition*, 160–61, and Theo Hobson, "Against Hauerwas," *New Blackfriars* 88 (2007): 300–12.

27. Hauerwas, "On Being a Church Capable of Addressing a World at War: A Pacifist Response to the United Methodist Bishops' Pastoral *In Defense of Creation*," in *The Hauerwas Reader*, ed. John Berkman and Michael Cartwright (Durham and London: Duke University Press, 2001), 430.

28. Hauerwas, "A Christian Critique of Christian America," in *The Hauerwas Reader*, 475. Cf. John Howard Yoder, *The Priestly Kingdom: Social Ethics as Gospel* (Notre Dame, IN: University of Notre Dame Press, 1984), 136.

29. Hauerwas, *The Peaceable Kingdom*, 107.

30. Hauerwas, *Performing the Faith*, 44.

31. Ibid., 54.

chapters on Bonhoeffer, Hauerwas criticizes H. Richard Niebuhr for advocating the "invisibility of the church."[32]

If Hauerwas is warning Christians against seeing the church as a purely metaphysical shelter against the messy ambiguities of history, then he is right to see Bonhoeffer as an ally. Such a "metaphysical" conception of the church is exactly what Bonhoeffer criticizes in proposing a "religionless Christianity." But Hauerwas's claims here are not tempered by Bonhoeffer's counterbalancing emphasis on the hiddenness of discipleship. Consequently, his account is one-sided and ultimately mischaracterizes the complete reality of the church.

To Hauerwas, visibility is so essential to the church's mission to the world that visibility has become a normative category. In fact, he goes so far as to say that "There is no ideal church, no invisible church."[33] Anyone placing *any* emphasis on the invisible church, then, is simply wrong about an undeniable reality. Hence Hauerwas sees Bonhoeffer edging toward dangerous territory in his "account of the mandates" that God gives to different spheres of life, which "can invite the distinction between the private and the public, which results in Christian obedience becoming invisible."[34] Here Hauerwas implies that the real problem with liberalism is that the public/private distinction it assumes ultimately invites Christians to think that there can be such a thing as an invisible witness.

When this normative view of visibility is added to Hauerwas's contention that the world must actually see Christians doing distinctively Christian things and to Hauerwas's suspicion of any "liberal" move to keep particularistic Christian language and action out of the public sphere, it forms what seems to be a strong case against Christians intentionally concealing their religious identity in public life. Any who did so would ultimately be operating under a false ecclesiology tempting them to think that an interior relation to God is the sum total of Christian life.

Of course, it is not. Even Kierkegaard, who advocated Christian inwardness more vigorously than virtually any other Christian thinker, recognizes that Christian faith is inseparable from Christian love,

32. Ibid., 16, fn.
33. Hauerwas, *The Peaceable Kingdom*, 107.
34. Hauerwas, *Performing the Faith*, 51.

which itself must bear visible fruit. Kierkegaard's example shows that asserting the inwardness of faith as a necessary condition for all other aspects of Christian life in no way reduces Christian life to inwardness, any more than driving a car legally can be reduced to having adequate eyesight.

Hauerwas's real error lies in his treating visibility and invisibility as normative categories for the Christian church. They are not. They rather describe different senses of the church's single reality. It is both a historical reality and a theological one, and unavoidably so. That the church is visible means that it cannot be a refuge from history or social life. In insisting on the church's visibility, Hauerwas hopes to establish this much. But what makes the church distinctive with respect to the world is, paradoxically, invisible. The invisible aspect of the church is what makes it, in Hans Küng's words, "not an ordinary people or group, but a chosen people; . . . not an ordinary body, but a mystical body." Yet precisely because what is truly decisive is invisible, the church can appear to some on the outside as "a religious organization among many other organizations, institutions and societies, something to be furthered, combated or tolerantly ignored, something to be taken seriously or not so seriously."[35] As Kierkegaard's authorship indicates, the principal question facing Christianity in modernity is whether there is a life beyond and invisible to *Sittlichkeit*. If the visible is all there is, Abraham is not a disciple but a murderer. By denying the possibility of the invisible church, Hauerwas cedes to the world the major point of contention between it and the church.

A Roman Catholic understanding of the church as a sacrament illustrates how difficult it can be to maintain the strict equation of "visible" with "real" that underlies Hauerwas's use of visibility as a normative term. If the church is considered to be a visible sign of the invisible reality of God's grace active in history for the sake of the whole world, then we cannot say that the church's reality is exhausted by its visibility. Sacraments necessarily participate in a reality that is both visible and invisible. Absent the invisible reality, sacraments become rituals like any other. If the church itself is a sacrament, then the invisibility of the grace it conveys means that

35. Hans Küng, *The Church*, trans. Ray and Rosaleen Ockenden (New York: Sheed and Ward, 1967), 37.

the church can no more avoid being in some sense invisible than it can avoid having a visible corporate life.

A model of the church as sacrament in fact lends justification for keeping the distinctively Christian activity of the church's members out of public view. As Avery Dulles explains, "a sacrament is a sign chiefly to those who actively participate in it, and is fully discernible only through a kind of connaturality given by grace."[36] To see the church as the church—that is, as a historical and theological reality—is itself a gift of grace. Receiving that grace enables one to participate in the life of the church, and through participating in it, understand what constitutes its full reality. A justification that Cyril of Jerusalem employed in completely concealing the sacraments from the unbaptized—that they would be harmed by seeing what they lacked the grace to understand—thus can apply to the entire life of the church insofar as the church is a sacrament.

I do not mean to argue that the invisibility of the church and secrecy about Christian identity are equivalent. They are, however, compatible, as the ecclesiological point reinforces the prudential judgment about individual Christians' stances in the public life that is inevitable in modernity. At the same time, a proper understanding of the church's visibility in no way diminishes the plausibility of such secrecy. If modernity has made the mistake of making the invisibility of the church normative, then the way to correct the mistake is not to push back with an equal force in the direction of visibility. Doing so only repeats the fundamental error of ignoring the full reality of the church, in its visible and invisible aspects. Ironically, asserting the church's visibility at the expense of its invisibility disables the theological ground for the very distinctiveness of the church that Hauerwas, in promoting visibility, is trying to preserve.

Truthfulness and Visible Christian Identity

As I mentioned earlier in this chapter, the visibility that Hauerwas advocates for Christians' witness derives from the truthfulness of Christianity. To Hauerwas, the truth is a lamp that belongs on a lamp

36. Avery Cardinal Dulles, SJ, *Models of the Church*, expanded ed. (New York: Image, 2002), 125.

stand and not under a bushel basket. Christians must be uncompromising in their commitment to the truth, as "God has given us" a task "to be a people capable of speaking truthfully to ourselves, to our brothers and sisters in Christ, and to the world"[37]—hence the tremendous "political significance of the Christian refusal to lie."[38] In that case, it is worth investigating whether calling for Christians to be less than fully forthcoming about their Christian identity is asking them to lie and, in doing so, to forfeit this important task.

Hauerwas's conception of the truth is part and parcel of his critique of liberalism. To Hauerwas, liberalism puts a placid social order atop the list of goods. Hence liberal regimes value tolerance more than truth. They will accept lies if the lies contribute to peaceful coexistence among persons. Christians, on the other hand, though they aim to be peaceable, must put the truth and not the functional value of the gospel first; for truth is the source of a peaceableness that is not identical to a lack of social unrest. Commitment to anything less than the truth, which is necessarily God's truth, is an abandonment of the gospel.

Hauerwas sees Bonhoeffer as an ally on this point, describing Bonhoeffer as "a relentless critic of any way of life that substituted agreeableness for truthfulness."[39] To be sure, the liberal attempt to keep religious acts and discussion out of public life can be seen as an attempt to sacrifice truthfulness (honesty about one's true convictions, identity, and reasons for taking a course of action in public) for agreeableness (not upsetting those who do not share those strongly held convictions). My project in this book therefore seems to share these liberal aims. Does this mean that Bonhoeffer cannot be used to support a call for Christians to voluntarily conceal their religious identity in public life? Does it furthermore mean that this call cannot even be seriously entertained by Christians committed to the truth?

No. Although advocates for liberalism might welcome the upshot of my proposal, I have been arguing for it on particularistic religious grounds that strict forms of liberalism would not admit in public.

37. Hauerwas, *Performing the Faith*, 72.
38. Ibid., 57.
39. Ibid.

Furthermore, the good of a calm and orderly public life has not been brought out in support of this proposal. Christians need to conceal their identity in public life not so that American public life will be less divisive, but so that Christianity can maintain the very distinctiveness that Hauerwas fears is threatened by liberalism's encroachment on the church. This shows that there is a third option between liberalism and Hauerwas's version of Christian witness. It is the option actually favored by Bonhoeffer.

We can see this in the political meaning of Bonhoeffer's view of truth, which does not support Hauerwas's position as well as Hauerwas thinks it does. Hauerwas acknowledges with Bonhoeffer that truth-telling is not only a matter of speech but of having the right relation to reality. Living or speaking truthfully means acting in accordance with this God-defined reality.[40] At times, this reality will conflict with the false reality claimed by the world, and so what may appear untrue to the world may nevertheless be fully in accord with God's reality.

Taking Hauerwas and Bonhoeffer seriously on this point means that Christians are not necessarily compromising the truth when they conceal their religious identity in public. Where truthfulness is concerned, context matters.[41] The entire thrust of Bonhoeffer's essay, "What is Meant by 'Telling the Truth,'" on which Hauerwas relies to support his position, is to show that truth is not the "formal" correspondence between thought and speech, or between speech and the empirical facts of the world. Rather, the different relationships humans have demand different kinds of speech and standards of truthfulness. Thus, truthfulness in business dealings and truthfulness in family life are not equivalent. Still, Bonhoeffer does not intend here to advocate a complete relativism. He recognizes the Word of God as the truth, and consequently he affirms that God's lordship over all reality must govern Christians' attempts to speak truthfully in all contexts. The fact that reality is God's imposes certain limits on human speech, "and the assigned purpose of our

40. Ibid., 64.
41. Hauerwas recognizes this to some extent, though much of his essay, "Bonhoeffer on Truth and Politics" (55–72 in *Performing the Faith*), is meant to argue against context-dependent situation ethics. To Hauerwas, Bonhoeffer is an ally in the fight against Christian defenses of lying.

silence is to signify" those limits.[42] As Bonhoeffer writes in a letter to Bethge, the desire for total, undifferentiating "exposure is cynical" (*LPP* 158). It fails to acknowledge that not everything should be exposed at all times or to everyone. An SS officer, for example, has already so distorted reality that "lying" to him about the hiding place of one's Jewish neighbors is more truthful—because it does more to return the historical situation to a truthful reality—than straightforwardly telling him their location would do. The "lie" in this case is not complicit in the genuine lie the SS officer makes of reality. Bonhoeffer does not explicitly mention the church as a social context in the essay, but we can infer from his comments about the difference between family and political life that the standards for truthful speech in ecclesial life will at least not be identical to those that obtain in public life.

And in fact, given Bonhoeffer's and Hauerwas's suspicion of the public life of their historical contexts, it is safe to infer that both would consider that some speech acts that would count as lies in church would be praised as truthful in the world. Christians' task is always to witness to the truth, to reality as God establishes it. The "reality" in American public life, though a far cry from that of the Third Reich, would have to be seen by both Hauerwas and Bonhoeffer as a distortion: it sees nothing but advantage and status and capital. Christian identity in this context is often taken to be a personal asset ripe for exploitation, no different from a good head for numbers or an Ivy League diploma. This is a lie. A Christian who refuses to allow his or her or another person's Christian identity to be so exploited does more to live in accordance with and even to help re-establish the truth of Christian identity and of faith than does the "cynic" who thinks that honesty demands the exposure of everything hidden, no matter the cost to what had been concealed. Exposure is cynical because it recognizes no difference between God's truth and humanity's many lies that are nonetheless the basis for our societies.

Being truthful about oneself and about the gravity of one's commitments may therefore require holding some things back from others. A Kantian absolutist about truth-telling would, as I argued in

---

42. Bonhoeffer, "What is Meant by 'Telling the Truth'?" in *Ethics*, ed. Eberhard Bethge, trans. Neville Horton Smith (New York: Macmillan, 1964), 332.

chapter 7, see this as a violation of the "universal" standards of ethics that should obtain in public life. That a Christian may have to violate those standards in order to live in accordance with the higher truth of the gospel should not be surprising. Especially to Hauerwas.

Living truthfully is certainly difficult by any thinker's account, as the temptations to lie are many and the immediate benefits of lying to others are often so great. This is equally true of lies people tell themselves. A commitment to the truth therefore also demands the uprooting of self-deception through a range of individual and communal practices. For Christians, self-deception invites the worst sort of identification with the world: "Violence results from our attempting to live our lives without recognizing our falsehoods" and "self-deceptive" narratives.[43]

Hence Hauerwas, in an essay written in 1974 with David Burrell, sees a need for a communal commitment to truthful narratives—in the case of Christianity, the narrative of redemption from sin through the death and resurrection of Christ—that in their telling constantly challenge individuals' strong tendency toward self-deception. After all, as Hauerwas and Burrell note, self-deception is an effective social lubricant.[44] Its effectiveness in small matters causes it to bleed into larger ones in our public and religious lives. It protects "the particular identity we have achieved"—pillar of society, good Christian lady or gentleman—seemingly without having to come to grips with the inherent conflict between being a Christian and holding any kind of status in public life.[45] To ensure that this gap is acknowledged, Christians need to employ strategies (or narrative "skills") of self-suspicion: paradigmatically, the "hard and painful discipline" of recognizing and confessing sin.[46]

Christians learn to confess sin from each other; indeed, the linguistic practice of confessing sins is surely a major part of the Christian narrative. Hauerwas goes so far as to say that "nothing is more important for the world than for Christians to learn to confess our

43. Hauerwas, *The Peaceable Kingdom*, 94.
44. Hauerwas and Burrell, "Self-Deception and Autobiography," in *The Hauerwas Reader*, 206.
45. Ibid., 207.
46. Ibid., 220.

sins."[47] The reason for this seems to be that a violent world desperately needs to recognize its sinfulness, confess its sins, and ask for forgiveness, and the only ones who could teach the world this are Christians themselves. But it is worth asking if, in a culture where prominent public officials and entertainers stage professionally expedient confessions all the time, the world could even recognize confession as confession of *sin*.

Hauerwas's stress on the public visibility of Christian activity implies that the world must be able to see that activity, and the world must be able to see it so that the world can, one hopes, understand and accept it. But this overestimates the intelligibility that activity yields to outsiders. In Roman Catholic Christianity, the sacramental character of confession and reconciliation signals their unlikeness from analogous worldly practices. And yet, the difference is not immediately obvious to those lacking the grace to see it. The Lutheran Bonhoeffer also aimed to preserve the exclusivity and secrecy of Christian confessional practices. Bonhoeffer writes to Bethge, shortly after referring to the aforementioned essay on truth, that "What is secret may be revealed only in confession, i.e., in the presence of God" (*LPP* 159). Whether Bonhoeffer means the confession of sins or the confession of faith is unclear. In either case, though, the truth—even Christian truth, told in distinctively Christian language—demands "showing respect for secrecy, intimacy, and concealment" (*LPP* 159). Some such truths can only be told in the context of a believing and worshipping community, gathered explicitly in God's name.

Hauerwas thus undermines his aim of protecting the distinctiveness of Christian identity through making the church's goods as publicly visible as possible, just as he does in failing to recognize the inherent invisibility of the church. If the confession of sin is truly a distinctively Christian act, arising out of the distinctively Christian narrative, both requiring grace to be accomplished and conveying grace to the Christian, then it is not clear that such an act is finally intelligible to the worldly anyway. Cyril of Jerusalem and Dietrich Bonhoeffer may well have agreed with Hauerwas's assertion that

47. Hauerwas, *Performing the Faith*, 25.

the sacraments "are our most important social witness."[48] The fact that the sacraments are not fully intelligible to a world that has not been incorporated into the church's narrative means that this kind of witness is rightly done out of the world's sight. Nourished by the sacraments, Christians can go into the world, loving their neighbors with quiet abandon.

This does not entail giving up attempting to convert the world, but it does require seeing this task in a new light. To explain how the worldly can become Christian, we should substitute the circularity of joining the church's sacramental life for the circularity of learning Christian virtues.[49] Someone learning the virtues must begin at some arbitrary point, making a discontinuous movement from a vicious habit to a virtuous one. The move from being unbaptized to being baptized is similarly discontinuous, and the shift is only really intelligible after the fact. The desire for baptism, then, must be built up in the person in the absence of his or her knowledge of what is in store for him or her. That desire cannot be built up through the grace of the sacraments; it must be built up in advance through being loved by the community of the baptized.

Conclusion: The Church as Leaven to the World

A sacramental approach to the church's stance with respect to the world gives the lie to the simple dichotomy between genuine Christianity and liberalism that Hauerwas sometimes presents. Actions like the sacraments, taking place within the walls of the church, defy the public/private dichotomy without refuting it. They have relevance to the public sphere, and they are performed in a way that other people in the church can see, but they have a different character from actions like voting, working for pay, and buying and selling. They are the activities of a different sort of "public." The context in which they are conducted—a community's relation to God—is so particular that outsiders would not be able to make sense of the

48. Hauerwas, *The Peaceable Kingdom*, 108.
49. On the circularity of learning the virtues, see Hauerwas, *A Community of Character: Toward a Constructive Christian Social Ethic* (Notre Dame, IN: University of Notre Dame Press, 1981), 138–39.

sacramental actions taking place within it. Given that the church has very good reasons for concealing its otherwise visible life from the broader American public realm, then its mission cannot be primarily to exist as an alternative society recognizable to the world as different from it.

Even if that were the church's mission, it is not clear that the concrete, historical church is capable of fulfilling it. Hauerwas has been accused of being overly idealistic about the church's holiness.[50] For Hauerwas's account of the church to be coherent—a church whose service to the world is constituted by a particular visible form of communal life—the church here and now must actually be genuinely virtuous. But as Stout points out, "The actual church does not look very much like a community of virtue, when judged by pacifist standards." Thus the actual church cannot truthfully claim to be virtuous. At the same time, the church cannot simply own up to its sinfulness either, for then it loses its claim on being an alternative to the sinful world. So, whether the church presents itself as virtuous or vicious, "it is in danger of collapsing into something it purports to criticize."[51] A church with members who concealed in public that they were part of the church would not encounter this problem, as such a church would make no public claims to holiness.

Hauerwas's idealism is admirable, but it is misplaced. In trying to avoid making sin normative for the church, Hauerwas posits the existence of a visibly holy church just because the church *must* be visibly holy if it is to carry out the mission he gives it. It would be better to place confidence in God's grace, active in an imperfect community of disciples in part by strengthening them in their works of neighbor love. The holiness of a mystical communion like this consists "primarily [in] the lived holiness of an interior communion with God, pouring over into communion with one's fellow men," its "dynamic catholicity" that "of a love reaching out to all and excluding none."[52]

A church whose members cannot be seen as members of the church in their public lives, as they blend in with the rest of society, but

---

50. See Stout, *Democracy and Tradition*, 160–61, and Hobson, "Against Hauerwas."
51. Stout, *Democracy and Tradition*, 161.
52. Dulles, *Models of the Church*, 122.

whose work nonetheless makes a palpable difference in the world, is a church working like leaven in the dough (Matt. 13:33, Luke 13:20–21). As Marianne Sawicki has shown, this was one way that the earliest Christian communities managed to resist succumbing to and even to subvert the values of the Roman Empire. This church "does not 'gather' for social visibility; it scatters for invisibility and maximum disruption of other targeted institutions."[53] Communities like the Q community did not show themselves as alternatives to the empire. Rather, "[t]he people of the paleochurch found [the Kingdom of God] by working stealthily, on a small scale, and in the symbolic idiom of their own world."[54] The Christian church should do the same in America today. It does have a distinctive narrative forming its identity, as did the early church, but it only need tell the narrative explicitly to its own members until such a time as the world is prepared (by grace) to understand.

The Christian church in America is not an ideal church; it is certainly guilty of many sins. The fact that it is being called to holiness means that the church as a whole and its individual members must seek the grace to be forgiven and to leave those sins behind. A particularly dangerous sin for the church in America is individual Christians' use of the visibility of the church to serve their interests in public life. This sin can be combated through taking the prudential course of concealing Christian identity in the public life characteristic of contemporary America. This therapy may not be necessary forever. If successful, it will transform Christians and non-Christians alike, as they will be freed from the illusion that being Christian is meant to bring material rewards to American Christians. The church stands to benefit greatly from this therapy. Though it is not meant to benefit American public life, it may have that result, too.

---

53. Marianne Sawicki, "Salt and Leaven: Resistances to Empire in the Street-Smart Paleochurch," in *The Church as Counterculture*, ed. Michael L. Budde and Robert W. Brimlow (Albany: State University of New York Press, 2000), 71.

54. Ibid., 79.

Epilogue

The Challenge of Ambiguous Religious Identity in Wise Blood *and* The Moviegoer

If American Christians were to conceal their religious identity in public life as I suggest, their behavior might be puzzling to some. Without question, it would be difficult to conceal their Christian identity entirely: they might let a word loaded with Christian significance slip out, they would perform the "extraordinary" acts of holiness and forgiveness enumerated in Matthew 5, and someone following them on a Sunday morning would see them walk into churches.

What should Americans, Christian or not, do about persons who display religious behavior, even ambiguously? Events near the end of two novels from the middle of the last century, Flannery O'Connor's *Wise Blood* and Walker Percy's *The Moviegoer*, intimate what it is like to suspect that someone you encounter in public life might be a Christian, but to be unable to determine if that person truly is. It would surely be tempting to demand that the person explain himself or herself and say, definitively, if he or she is Christian or not. It would be frustrating not to get an answer to that demand. This frustration, though, is born of a toxic cynicism about the purpose of having and exhibiting a Christian identity. In order to save American Christianity from Christendom, the assumption that Christian identity is *for* any worldly purpose is finally what needs to disappear.

239

Near the end of *Wise Blood*, Hazel Motes, the street-corner evangelist of the Church Without Christ ("where the blind don't see and the lame don't walk and what's dead stays that way"[1]), runs his car over his double, the "Prophet" Solace Layfield, killing him. Soon after, Haze loses his car and blinds himself with quicklime. He begins to eat less and to spend his days walking—not just in the streets, but around his rented room, apparently without purpose. To his landlady, Haze's new habits make him like "one of them monks . . . he might as well be in a monkery" (*WB* 218). His self-mortification is "not natural. . . . [I]t's something that people have quit doing—like boiling in oil or being a saint or walling up cats. . . . There's no reason for it" (*WB* 224).

The air of mystery around Haze's actions frustrates his landlady, Mrs. Flood, who "didn't like the thought that something was being put over her head. She liked the clear light of day. She liked to see things" (*WB* 218). She assumes that, like a monk who is no doubt up to something in his "monkery," Haze is keeping a secret from her, and she can no more tolerate the secret than she can his strange behavior. Still, she is drawn to him. Her suspicion of Haze is matched by her opportunism, as she wants the small fortune she assumes he must have, since he never spends his money on anything.

In fact, Hazel is keeping secrets. After Mrs. Flood discovers evidence of Haze's self-mortification while she is cleaning his room—the insoles of his shoes are covered with sharp stones—she wonders, "Who's he doing this for? . . . What's he getting out of doing it? Every now and then she would have an intimation of something hidden near her but out of her reach" (*WB* 222). Hazel falls ill, and while ministering to him, Mrs. Flood sees that he has been wearing barbed wire around his torso, concealing it under his shirt. She presses him for an explanation, and the reasons Hazel only grudgingly gives for the stones and the barbed wire—"to pay" and "I'm not clean"—make no sense to her. He seems to invest the terms with moral meaning, though for her they are literal, as her responses to his reasons show: "What have you got to show that you're paying for?" (*WB* 222) and "You ought to get you a washwoman" (*WB* 224).

1. Flannery O'Connor, *Wise Blood* (New York: Farrar, Strauss and Giroux, 1962), 105. Subsequent references to this work will be parenthetical, *WB* and page number.

The semantic distance between Hazel and Mrs. Flood might be attributable to a conversion that has taken place in him. According to Kierkegaard, a religious and a nonreligious person "say the same things: yet there is an infinite difference, since the latter has no intimation of the secret of the metaphorical words." The landlady "is using the same words, but not in their metaphorical sense. There is a world of difference between" her and Hazel, but this difference is only noticeable to "the person who has ears to hear" (WL 209–210). What might identify Haze as a Christian is a secret to the rest of the world.

O'Connor states in a brief note introducing the second edition of *Wise Blood* that whereas many contemporary readers will see Haze's "integrity" in his attempt to run away from Jesus Christ, O'Connor herself believes that his "integrity lies in his not being able to do so" (WB 5). A reader who took O'Connor's commentary here at face value would have to say that Haze has some form of incipient faith. O'Connor seems to want her readers to see her character as a genuine penitent who has (perhaps unconsciously) recognized how far short of the glory of God he falls, and who thus is open to receiving grace. His self-mortification, done in secret, certainly grants him no benefit in material goods or status. In renouncing self-love, he may have, contrary to his stated scorn for Christianity, taken the first necessary step toward loving his neighbor as Jesus demands.

But O'Connor's interpretation notwithstanding, we cannot be sure that Haze has any faith whatsoever. It would be presumptuous to say definitively that he does. Haze kept a secret from his landlady, but even after that secret is found out, Mrs. Flood still senses that he is hiding something deeper. Haze finally dies, and as Mrs. Flood contemplates Haze's dead body, "She felt as if she were blocked at the entrance of something" (WB 232). O'Connor wanted the reader to think that that something was genuine Christian faith—and indeed, it is compelling to think that the landlady is like a catechumen drawn toward Hazel by his secrecy but debarred from the deeper mystery within him—but there is no good reason within the novel itself to think that Hazel's faith, if he has any at all, has progressed beyond his attempt to "satisfy" Jesus as a child, by paying for his sins by walking a mile with stones in his shoes (WB 63–64). The reader has no way of determining the truth about Hazel. By the end of the novel, the narrator has lost all access to his mind. While we are told the contents of Mrs. Flood's thoughts in the final chapters, we only ever read about Haze's actions. His hermeneutical intransigence rebukes the reader's curiosity about him as well as it does Mrs. Flood's. In this respect, Haze serves as a good model for Christians in public life who face direct questions about their religious identity; rather than flat-out lie, they can speak in riddles, confuse, frustrate, rebuke. The belief that Christian identity is meant to serve American public life is the real lie, and those who perpetuate it need to realize its falsehood. O'Connor places the reader in Mrs. Flood's position, and so as we inquire about whether Haze is really a Christian, the question is turned back on us as investigators: Why do we want to know? Who are we doing it for? What are we getting out of it?

We stand in a similar situation near the end of *The Moviegoer*. The narrator in Percy's novel, the young ironist Binx Bolling, has just made perhaps the first real commitment of his life, agreeing to be married to his cousin Kate. Binx and Kate can hardly believe what they are getting themselves into as they sit in her parked car on Ash Wednesday, watching people go into and out of a Roman Catholic church.

One person in particular catches Binx's attention in the rear-view mirror: "a Negro gets out [of his car] and goes up to the church. He is more respectable than respectable." The man sees that Binx is watching him and "plucks a handkerchief out of his rear pocket with a flurry of his coat tail and blows his nose in a magic placative gesture (you see, I have been here before: it is a routine matter)."[2] A few minutes pass, and

The Negro has already come outside. His forehead is an ambiguous sienna color and pied: it is impossible to be sure that he received ashes. When he gets in his Mercury, he does not leave immediately but sits looking down at something on the seat beside him. A sample case? An insurance manual? I watch him closely in the rear-view mirror. It is impossible to say why he is here. Is it part and parcel of the complex business of coming up in the world? Or is it because he believes that God himself is present here at the corner of Elysian Fields and Bons Enfants? Or is he here for both reasons: through some dim dazzling

2. Walker Percy, *The Moviegoer* (New York: Vintage, 1998), 233.

trick of grace, coming for the one and receiving the other as God's own importunate bonus?

It is impossible to say.[3]

Binx very much wants to make several assumptions about what he cannot see. His restricted, inverted view of the man in his Mercury does not allow him to see what the man is looking at in the passenger seat. It may very well be a sample case or an insurance manual. But it hardly need be. Binx also wants to draw a direct link between whatever artifacts of public life the man is studying and the ashes that, presumably, the man went into the church to receive. Ash Wednesday is after all a perfect opportunity to display Christian identity without seeming to want to display it. If receiving ashes, perhaps to be seen by Catholics with or for whom this man works, is "part and parcel of the complex business of coming up in the world," then the man is doing a poor job of ensuring that the right people notice him—the ashes, if he has in fact received ashes, disappear into his complexion. The sign of the man's faith, if he has faith, is hidden.

The endings to both of these novels say more about the people observing the ambiguous disciples than they do about Haze and the black man themselves. In fact, Binx knows nothing at all about the man he's watching. As he realizes in the end, Binx can only project expectations onto him, including the expectation that Christian identity is meant primarily to serve one's public life. Binx is right— "it is impossible to say" if either the black man or Hazel Motes has genuine faith. Faith is an unsayable secret within the self. Our impatience with its unsayability is what prompts our desire to find signs of faith in others and in ourselves: ashes on a forehead, Christian speech, economic prosperity, snake handling. But these signs do not necessarily tell us any more than that the person wants to exploit the Durkheimian synthesis between religion and public life. In public life, we have no choice but to evaluate people by the visible actions they perform. The same is not true in Christianity, where the ultimate judge sees in secret.

The reflected image of the man in the car behind him causes Binx to reflect on the "post-Durkheimian"[4] possibility that receiving ashes

---

3. Ibid., 234–35.
4. Charles Taylor, *A Secular Age* (Cambridge, MA: Belknap Press, 2007), 486–92.

serves a nonsocial end. To the extent that Binx even considers that the man he watches might believe "that God himself is present" in the liturgy, Binx is much further on the way to shedding his cynicism than is Mrs. Flood. Like her, we in public life might very much like to have access to the secret world of another person's self, but we never can have it, and we must resist the temptation to act as if we do. And those who have faith must resist the temptation to treat it as sayable—and therefore saleable.

The expectation that religious identity be visible is abetted by a second expectation that religious identity be worth something in a person's public life. In most of this book I have been arguing against the former expectation. Indeed, I have been arguing that we should begin to expect that Christian identity not be publicly visible. The gospel reading for a Catholic Ash Wednesday service thwarts the expectation of visibility: Jesus calls on his listeners to conceal their piety and to maintain public decorum when they fast, washing their faces, keeping their clothes tidy, anointing their heads as they ordinarily would (Matt. 6:16–18). Yet the expectation that faith will yield cultural capital via religious identity is the more pernicious one; this expectation is the one that truly distorts the point of having Christian faith. Without this expectation, the visibility of Christian identity in American public life would not pose a problem to the integrity and distinctiveness of the faith.

The possibility that Haze and the black man in the Mercury are Christians and do not make their religious identity public is simply frustrating to the curious. But the possibility that they are Christians and *do not care to use their religious identity as a means of getting ahead in the world* is downright shocking. It goes against one of the longest-standing American traditions. This tradition's longevity should not be mistaken for immortality, however. Killing it will require cutting off what nourishes it: the assumption that Christian identity is only real if it is publicly displayed.

Index

245